TALKING

RICHARD
HERRING

A CELEBRATION OF
MAN AND HIS MANHOOD

EBURY
PRESS

First published in Great Britain in 2003

10 9 8 7 6 5 4 3 2 1

First published by
Ebury Press
Random House, 20 Vauxhall Bridge Road, London SW1V 2SA

Random House Australia (Pty) Limited
20 Alfred Street, Milsons Point, Sydney, New South Wales 2061, Australia

Random House New Zealand Limited
18 Poland Road, Glenfield, Auckland 10, New Zealand

Random House South Africa (Pty) Limited
Endulini, 5A Jubilee Road, Parktown 2193, South Africa

The Random House Group Limited Reg. No. 954009

www.randomhouse.co.uk

A CIP catalogue record for this book is available from the British Library.

Designed by seagulls

ISBN 0091894417

Papers used by Ebury Press are natural, recyclable products made from wood grown in sustainable forests.

Printed and bound in Great Britain

photo credits

Akg-Images/Erich Lessing: pp.55, 220, Akg-Images: p.68; Archaeological Museum, Naples, Italy: p. 65; The Art Archive/Egyptian Museum, Turin/Dagli Orti: p.150, The Art Archive/Bibliotheque des Arts Decoratifs, Paris/Dagli Orti: p.252; David by Michelangelo Buonarroti, Accademia, Florence/Bridgeman Art Library: p.92, Women Riding Phallus's, from The Tower of Love by Reunier/Bridgeman Art Library: p.176; www.CartoonStock.com: pp.88, 130, 246; © Bettmann/CORBIS: p.138, © Dimaggio/Kalish/CORBIS: p.141, © James W. Porter/CORBIS: p.280; Francesca Radcliffe/Dalgleish Images: pp.62 & 74; Mary Evans Picture Library: pp.122l, 124, 162; David L.Gollaher, California Healthcare Institute: p.106; R.Wayne Griffiths, NORM Organisation, USA: p.109; Courtesy Universal International/Ronald Grant Archive: p.211; "Photos from NOCIRC Collection": pp.102 & 104; Matthew Fearn/PA Photos: p.158; Sam Barcroft/Rex Features: p.2, Stewart Cook/Rex: p.5, Sim/Rex: p.43, Sipa/Rex: pp.163 & 214l & r, Nils Jorgensen/Rex: pp.180, 273, Mark Campbell/Rex: p.231, Tony Kyriacou/Rex: p.235, Sutton-Hibbert/Rex: p.275; Stanley B. Burns MD, and The Burns Archive, N.Y/Science Photo Library: p.45, John Walsh/SPL: p.78, Sam Ogden/SPL: p.228; Staatliche Museen zu Berlin – Antikensammlung: p.117; Venereology, Volume 8, no 2, May 1995, published by Venereology Publishing Inc. University of New South Wales, Australia: pp.222 & 223; Wellcome Library, London: pp. 71 & 122r.Authors own photos pages 21, 97, 184-188, 190-191, 195.

Picture Research by Sandie Huskinson-Rolfe of PHOTOSEEKERS

For Stephanie and Paddy.

Remember, not all dicks are attached to dicks.

The author in a herring-piece
(which is of course an upside-down cod-piece).

PRECOCK

i was sitting in a public toilet the other day.

On the door of the cubicle in front of me was some graffiti. In six-inch-high letters, someone had written the words,

Suck My Cock!

What a pathetic, stupid, childish, ignorant thing to write.

There's no name, no phone number, no address. Nothing. How was I meant to get in touch with him? What a waste of my valuable time. Three hours I waited in that cubicle. Not a dickie bird. Not a sausage.

It did remind me, however, of a better graffito that I noticed a few years previously, also in a public convenience. Someone had written on the wall,

I am twelve inches, do you want me?

Underneath which someone else had written,

THAT DEPENDS ON HOW BIG YOUR COCK IS!

The second person there had misunderstood the first writer, possibly deliberately, and was imagining that his correspondent was just a foot tall. A ridiculous misunderstanding. How could he have reached so high up the wall? Possibly he carried a small stepladder with him everywhere he went. Though you'd have to ask yourself, 'How big a stepladder could a twelve-inch-high person actually carry and would it increase their reach to any more than two feet at the very most?' All things considered I would still say the 'foot-high-man hypothesis' was unlikely.

But, you know, in their own way, both the men who took the trouble to write 'Suck My Cock' and 'I am twelve inches, do you want me?' were both celebrating their masculinity. Letting the world (or rather, in this case, other men who needed to do a shit, or possibly a wee, if they were one of those blokes who is too shy to do it next to other men and has to go into the cubicle, or people who were wanking, or having sex with other men, or possibly, with courageous and shameless women), letting all those other cock-users and cock-suckers and cock-lovers know, that they too have a cock. A cock that they would be proud to have sucked, a cock that they are delighted to proclaim – and possibly exaggerate – the dimensions of. Providing it's on the wall of a toilet cubicle and no one knows who they are.

Because isn't that the problem with men? The only place we will really try to get to grips with our penis – maybe that's the wrong choice of words (I could do jokes like that all through this book, but I'm really going to try not to) – the only place we will express ourselves about our penis is anonymously. On the wall of a toilet.

The one place where all the functions of the penis are explored, and people also do shits as well.

Isn't it time for men to celebrate their porridge guns outside the murky confines of the water closet? Shouldn't we be getting them out in public, proud and unrestrained? Can't we rid ourselves of the shame and the sniggering, the

COCKQUOTE

'The comedian from hell always thinks he can entertain us,
With everything we didn't want to know about his penis.'

from 'Everything You Didn't Want to Know About My Penis' by Momus

smear campaigns and the stigma (and the smegma), and honour this little thing that, at its best, gives us all so much pleasure.

This book aims to do just that.

Ironically, of course, most of you will choose to keep it next to your lavatory.

Who says size isn't important?

INTRODUCTION

So, let's just make one thing very clear from the start,

I am not obsessed with cocks.

I know that I have written a book called *Talking Cock*, which takes cocks as its principal subject, and within which I clearly display my vast and detailed knowledge of cocks, cock history, cock anatomy and other cock-related issues, and wherein I have already, at this early stage, equalled the world record for 'the book containing the most uses of the word "cock"' (there, beaten it! *I'm a record-breaker!* Take that, *The Macmillan Encyclopaedia of Domestic Fowl*), but I am not obsessed with cocks.

I know that writers are often advised 'write what you know', but that wasn't what happened here. I didn't think, 'Hmmmm, I'd really like to write a book, but what on earth could it be about? Well, I suppose I should write from experience. In which case, it'll have to be about cocks. Men's big cocks.'

That didn't happen, because I am not obsessed with cocks.

I know that I said that thing in the preface about waiting in the toilet for the 'Suck My Cock' man, but that was just a joke. It didn't really happen. Honestly. I have never sucked a cock, nor have I had any serious desire to ever do so. The idea of me having some kind of manhood mania, fuckstick fixation or penile preoccupation is palpable poppycock ... I mean, palpable poppyrot.

I AM NOT OBSESSED WITH COCKS.

So you are probably asking yourself, 'How did such an avowedly, self-proclaimed non-cock obsessed man come to write a book exclusively about cocks (the very antithesis of his interest), when his masculinity and heterosexuality are clearly beyond any kind of doubt and men's big, erect cocks obviously hold no allure for him whatsoever?'

And I would say to you, 'What an excellent question. I couldn't have put it better myself.'

My Knob Odyssey began in October 2001. I was performing my one-man show, *Christ on a Bike,* at the Arts Theatre in London's West End. I was sharing the stage with the worldwide smash *The Vagina Monologues* (or as the comedian Jenny Eclair more amusingly calls it, 'Twat Chat'). The Vag girls were on first and I would sit in my dressing room each night listening to the show on the theatre intercom. You can't imagine what a delight it was for me to hear the 360-capacity audience laughing themselves stupid and shouting out 'Cunt!' in unison, when asked to do so by Miriam Margolyes. It was made especially pleasurable for me, because I knew I was about to go on to perform to the 20 people who had bothered to turn up to see me, who occasionally also shouted out 'Cunt!', but in less orchestrated circumstances and rarely in unison.

After I had finished my show, I would usually head to the bar where sometimes ten per cent of my audience were waiting to greet me. Practically every

A load of celebrity cunts - it's OK, that's what they want you to call them. It's positive. They've reclaimed the word.

night, one (or both) of them would buy me a beer and say, 'That was quite good. Shame there weren't a few more in.'

I'd say, 'Well, you know, the whole September 11th thing has affected West End audiences really badly.'

They'd remark, 'That's weird, 'cos there were thousands of people coming out of *The Vagina Monologues*.'

I'd correct them, maybe a little abruptly, 'There weren't thousands, there were 360. There are only 360 seats in the theatre. And of course they're going to get loads of people in if they put *vagina* in the title. I'd have 360 people in my audience if I called my show "Vagina on a Bike", or "Tits on a Pogo-stick" but I wouldn't do that. I've got some artistic integrity.'

I was trying to get them to back off, but many of them failed to pick up on the subtlety of my hint, and would blather on, saying, 'Hey! Have you ever thought about doing a male version of *The Vagina Monologues*? You could call it *The Penis Monologues* or maybe *Cock Tales*!!'

I'd laugh a bit too much, slightly too close to their faces, and then sarcastically slur, 'No, I've never thought about doing that. What an amazingly original and unpredictable idea. Oh, if only I could be as clever and inventive as you.' Then, in case they hadn't understood that I was being sarcastic I would add, 'I am being sarcastic.'

That usually cleared up any confusion over the sarcasm issue.

'Why don't you just call me a cretin to my face?' I would continue. 'Of course I've thought about doing that. I thought about it the exact second I first heard about *The Vagina Monologues* and then immediately discounted it as the most pathetic and hackneyed idea that has ever been imagined. Men don't need a show about penises and they don't want a show about penises. Any male answer to *The Vagina Monologues* would be stupidly macho and competitive and misogynist. So there's no way I'm going to do it, all right? Now get out of my sight, you idiots, you make me sick.'

Then as the people were leaving I'd shout, 'Thanks for the beer. Do tell your friends about my show.'

For some reason, they chose not to.

After three weeks of drunkenly antagonising the few people who liked me, I began to wonder if I was making a mistake. I have to admit that, despite my artistic integrity, I had started imagining what it would be like to perform to a packed audience and not lose hundreds of pounds a night. I imagined that it would feel really nice and that instead of shouting at people who were trying to be civil to me, I'd probably say something like, 'Oh you are a sweetie, thanks for being there for me! Do tell your friends' … and this time they would. Allowing me to spend the money I made on luxury items for my home.

However, more important than that was the realisation that the Vag show had been going for six or seven years and despite the obvious obviousness of doing a cock version as well as the commercial potential of such an enterprise, no one had ever actually done it.

Why was that?

It struck me that it was probably because *The Vagina Monologues* is about celebration and no one could argue that the penis was worth celebrating. The best thing anyone could say about the penis was that it was funny. Which is why, while women were rejoicing in and venerating their vaginas at the Arts Theatre, on a stage not far away some Australians were twisting their genitals into the shape of hamburgers in the show *Puppetry of the Penis*. There was clearly a disparity here.

Surely there was more to the penis than its ability to do a vague and distasteful impression of the Eiffel Tower, but if there was I was having trouble thinking what it might be. If not portrayed as a comic appendage, the penis was seen as a dangerous weapon. As a man I was so used to the concept that 'all men are potential rapists' that I would scarcely think to challenge the idea. Similarly I took it as read that on the rare occasions when women did actually consent to sex that men were selfish and incompetent lovers.

Were these stereotypes fair? If not, why did men seem to accept them without question? Was the penis really only a battering ram or a jester's pole? Wasn't there more to it than that? Wasn't it time for the twisting to stop and the schlong celebration to begin? Wasn't it time for a Vagina Monologues with balls?

I decided to give it a go. I booked a slot at the Edinburgh Fringe the following year and got to work. There was no turning back.

Immediately I wanted to turn back.

Puppetry of the Penis ruins the romance of the Paris skyline forever.

COCKQUOTE

'A man who is ashamed to show or name the penis is wrong. Instead of being anxious to hide it, a man ought to display it . . . With honour.'

Leonardo Da Vinci

I shall be calling him as a witness in my forthcoming trial

It had struck me why no one had done this before. The success of *The Vagina Monologues* was due to the fact that it got women talking about their genitalia in a way that they never really had before. In an early article in *Scotland on Sunday* about my project, Barbara Littlewood, a lecturer in sociology at Glasgow University, questioned the necessity of a cock show, saying that before *The Vagina Monologues*, 'the vagina was ... a source of shame and embarrassment. The show broke a firm taboo'.

Dammit, she was right.

Men didn't need any similar encouragement to talk about their penises. Men constantly talk about their penises. They won't shut up about them. Not only was my show redundant, no one was going to pay to see what they could witness for free on any street corner (or toilet wall) in the world. And let's face it, it's hardly a fresh comedic subject. Most male comedians have at least 20 minutes on the subject. Some talk about practically nothing else (both on and off stage).

Then I asked myself, 'What do men actually say about their love rockets?' and I had to conclude that, despite men's constant prick schtick, we actually say very, very little. And of that very, very little, only a minute proportion of our comments are in any way serious.

Ninety-nine per cent of the conversations involved men bragging about how massive theirs is:

'I make King Dong look like Wee Willie Winkie.'

Or how tiny everyone else's is:

'He's got a cock like an anorexic anchovy ... in size and also smell.'

Or possibly somewhat fanciful renditions of sexual scenarios:

'So there I was watching the football, with a beer in my hand and her on her knees, in front of me, when blow me ... and she did ... her twin sister walks in and decides to join in.'

(Doubtless some of that story is true. I believe it up to, and possibly including, the bit about the beer.)

Can you imagine a man discussing the subject seriously?

'Fellas, can we all just stop singing rugby songs for a moment. I want to talk to you about my ongoing struggle with erectile dysfunction.'

It would make him a laughing stock. Moreover, it would make him a laughing stock, who obviously had a tiny cock.

The more I thought about it the more I realised that men only discuss their placenta pokers in humorous tones (for example by referring to them as placenta pokers), because, just like pre-*Twat Chat* women, they are embarrassed and ashamed of the inadequacies of their genitalia. We're embarrassed and ashamed, aren't we, fellas? We're embarrassed and ashamed and we're ashamed and embarrassed to admit it, even to ourselves. We can't admit that we feel anxious about the size or shape of our genitalia, worried about our sexual performance or concerned that we might not be able to get an erection. Because being a man is all about having a cock the size of a baby's arm, which can get erect at the drop of a hat. When I was a teenager, that wasn't a problem. If someone dropped a hat – BANG – I'd be erect, instantaneously. Sometimes just a hat on its own would be enough, perhaps precariously perched on the edge of a table. It could drop any second. The anticipation was half the fun. Occasionally hats didn't even have to be involved. That's how easy it was. Now I'm 36 and I need hundreds of hats. Each more depraved and disgusting than the last.[1]

If I was honest I knew there were several cock-related worries that I had secretly harboured my entire adult life. Things I had never discussed, ironically, for fear of looking like a knob. If you read on, I might even tell you what they were!

Barbara Littlewood was wrong. Men *did* need this project. As long as it wasn't too worthy. As long as it was funny, so they could still laugh along and

---

1. *Those hats have to be dropped from increasingly high heights. I'm sending Sherpas up Mount Everest with the hats, they're chucking them off. Even then I'm only getting a semi.*

confirm their masculinity. If I got it right they would be laughing and thinking, 'Thank Christ, I'm not alone!'[2]

So, would it be a show exclusively for men? To begin with I thought so.

It was very important to me that *Talking Cock* would not merely be a parody of *The Vagina Monologues*. Although I would never deny that the *Minge Whinge* was the inspiration for my idea, I wanted to avoid falling into the trap of trying to compete. I didn't want to try to claim that these days men are more oppressed than women (it's clearly not true) or to claim that the penis is better than vagina. Mainly because, if I'm honest with you, I *prefer* the vagina. I think it's great. I would go as far as to say that the vagina is my all-time, third favourite bodily orifice.

Top three, girls. Not bad. Keep trying.

I had assumed, however, that because *Muff Guff* was written from a female perspective, then my show should be constructed from exclusively male voices.

What changed my mind was actually going to SEE *The Vagina Monologues*.

I took a lady friend with me, on a first date. I have to warn you, guys, that this was a mistake. As we sat, reading the programme, waiting for the show to start, I was struck with a weird feeling of unease and isolation. I looked around the audience. *I was the only man there!*

Surely that was impossible. The place was pretty full. I checked again. The row behind me, all women. In front, all women. I peered over the balcony and was hit by the shrill sound of female voices. Wait! Four rows in front of me, a couple snogging. Thank God! No! Dammit! Both women!

Hold on, what do I mean 'Dammit!'? It's two women snogging. All my dreams have come true. But, no, in these panicked circumstances there was no time for eroticism.[3] At this moment, all I wanted was to see another man, to

---

2. *In fact last night, when I was doing a gig, a scary-looking, tattooed bloke came back into the auditorium on the pretext of looking for his girlfriend's cigarettes. He came up to the stage and said, 'Thanks for that bit on the snapping the banjo string. That happened to me. Hurt like buggery. Thought I was the only one.' He was palpably relieved. You know, having a man telling me about his unpleasant penile injuries makes all this worthwhile. Oh and by the way, he couldn't find the cigarettes. Weird that.*

3. *And they didn't exactly look like the lesbians in any of the videos that I have seen.*

hold him in my arms and realise that I wasn't alone. And there he was. Seat N23. Another sweating, fidgeting man. I caught his glance, saw the terror in his eyes. We were both clearly thinking, 'Women, women everywhere. We'd better have a drink.' But as we rose to go to the bar, the lights went down and the show began. We had missed our chance. We were trapped. It was Room 101 and our lives would never be the same again.

OK, it wasn't quite that bad and the piece was pretty funny in places, though it was clearly funnier for women. They were all shrieking like that one old lady who is always in the studio audience of *Are You Being Served?* and who thinks that the word 'Pussy' is the most outrageous thing she's ever heard. Very much like that, thinking about it. Except this time there was no doubt that the women on stage were referring solely to their sexual organs. And they call that progress.

As the evening progressed I was wondering when to make my move with my date. But every time I tried to put my arm around her, or hold her hand, there seemed to be a declaration on stage about how evil and predatory men are. I was feeling guilty and paranoid, like I personally had done something to embarrass myself. Usually I have to wait until the morning after the date before that happens.

The show seemed to treat the vagina in isolation and gave the impression that vaginal penetration was a bad thing. No wonder no blokes were there. You only spend 40 quid at the theatre in the belief that looking classy will guarantee you some action. The rude title of the piece could only add to those beliefs. But this show would only make your girlfriend hot in the head, which is the last place you want heat on a date. The only positive story about a male in the production is about a man who likes looking at his girlfriend's vagina. For hours on end.

Pervert!

There was nothing about men and women putting their genitals together for mutual pleasure. Joking aside, I thought this was a bit weird.

The fact is that genitals do not exist to be treated in isolation. Genitals are made for sharing. Like Quality Street chocolates. Especially as I always seem to end up with the unpleasant-tasting green ones.

At the end of the show, my date turned to me and said that she had decided to become a lesbian. That was a first. Normally women have to sleep with me before making that lifestyle choice. I searched around the auditorium for the one other bloke, but when I found him he had crudely hacked off his own penis in shame and was calling himself Rebecca.

Surely there had to be a better, less divisive way.

I decided that *Talking Cock* should be aimed at men *and* women. Highlighting the positive, as well as the ridiculous and disgusting. Because the penis is of significance to everyone … except for lesbians and nuns. But that's OK, because lesbians and nuns are of particular significance to the penis (especially lesbian nuns, funnily enough). The important point is that even lesbian nuns wouldn't be here, if it wasn't for a penis.[4]

We all owe our existence, in part, to a penis and most of us get some kind of enjoyment out of it, if only in dildo form. *Talking Cock* would try to use the penis to bring us together, not as a wedge to drive us apart.

Not unless that's what you're both into.

So with my audience demographic neatly set out as everyone, I had to decide what questions needed to be answered. Here were some that struck me immediately.

- **Is size important? And if not, why are there no two-inch, pencil-thin vibrators?**

- **Do men think with their dicks? Do we truly have two brains in our body and only enough blood to operate one at a time? Or do we, in fact, have no brain and an excess of blood, just looking for something to do?**

- **How can men cope when getting harder is getting harder? When we're 18, we're probably pointing at the ceiling. By the time we're in our mid-30s, after a little effort and a few dropped hats, we're pointing at the picture of our gran on the mantelpiece … Or so some of my friends have told me.**

---

4. *So* suck on that, *you lesbian nuns. Not so clever now, are you?*

- Are all men really lazy, arrogant, sexually self-serving, responsibility-shirking, promiscuous adolescents? Or are some of us actually not all that lazy?

As a comedian (who is also a man) I was interested to find out why John Wayne Bobbitt being dismembered and having his penis thrown out of a car window is universally regarded as a *humorous* event? By men as well as women:

- Did you hear that Lorena Bobbitt is going into weather forecasting? She's predicting four to six inches on the ground by morning ...

- MAN: What's this? (*He tosses imaginary object between his hands.*) John Wayne Bobbitt playing with himself.

- Apparently Lorena Bobbitt is now dating a golfer? It's nothing serious. She's just working on her slice.

Ha ha ha. How amusing. If a man did anything remotely similar to a woman, (whatever she had done to *deserve* it) he would quite rightly be condemned as evil. If a woman had disfigured a man's face by, say, cutting off his nose, it would be seen as an atrocity. So why is it funny when a penis is attacked?

Why don't men complain?

Despite my early reservations it seemed there were many valid reasons to continue.

My next stumbling block was how I was going to get men to discuss their retractable doughnut holders. My original plan was to follow (or as some might term it, copy) the example of Eve Ensler (author of *Muff Guff*) and interview men face-to-face. Unfortunately, I could envisage getting a lot of responses of the King Dong variety. As a man it also filled me with dread having to discuss these issues with other men.

Would men even want to discuss the subject? Or have anything to say?

Men may be accused of thinking with their dicks, but they rarely think *about* them. Because to many men even thinking about your own penis is unmasculine or 'gay'. (Note my exuberant and slightly suspicious defence of my sexuality at the beginning of this introduction.)

One way round this, I thought, might be to set up an Internet questionnaire. I didn't really expect to gather all that much material from such a study. I thought it might provide me with a few good gags, maybe some statistics. I had no idea if anyone would even take part. In fact, I nearly didn't bother. And there were occasions, reading some of the responses, that I wished I hadn't.

However, in May 2002, I set up a website www.talkingcock.co.uk (which can also be located at www.richardherring.com/talkingcock/) with two anonymous questionnaires all about the spam javelin (one for men, one for women).

Of course there was a definite danger that people wouldn't take my quest seriously. So I prefaced the questions with a plea:

YOU ARE ABOUT TO TAKE
THE TALKING COCK QUESTIONNAIRE

Although it may be tempting to put in 'hilarious' joke answers to these questions I would really appreciate it if you would refrain from doing so. My intention with this show is to finally give an honest response to what men (and women) think about penises.

I actually think that despite the importance of his penis to every man, men rarely talk about it (or even think about it) honestly. Believe me I can imagine all the amusing answers you could put to these questions, and yes, they are great, so I'd be really pleased not to see any of them here.

Don't be afraid to be serious. Although this is a comedy show outwardly, I want it to have a serious intent. So think before you answer. Consider. Surprise yourself.

I am not intending to mock anyone. I will use the information you give me sensitively (unless the way you tell your stories is clearly with a sense of humour).

If there are any questions you do not wish to (or can't) answer, then please leave them. Any answers I use will be completely anonymous.

I then sat down and wrote down every possible question I could think of. Some of them were statistical:

 PENIS LENGTH – ERECT (IN INCHES)?

Some were designed to find out how much the penis meant to its owner:

 WOULD YOU RATHER LOSE YOUR PENIS OR ONE OF YOUR LEGS?

Some concentrated on positive feelings:

 DO YOU LOVE YOUR PENIS?

Others were more concerned with the negative:

 HAS THE SIZE OR SHAPE OF YOUR PENIS EVER CAUSED YOU ANXIETY OR EMBARRASSMENT?

Some were deeply personal:

 HOW MANY TIMES A WEEK DO YOU MASTURBATE?

Others were sexually graphic:

 HAVE YOU EVER PUT ANYTHING DOWN THE END OF YOUR PENIS?

Some were based on my own personal experience:

 DO YOU HAVE TROUBLE URINATING IN THE COMPANY OF OTHER MEN?

Others were more philosophical:

 HOW DO YOU FEEL AS A MAN?

And some were just silly:

 IF YOUR PENIS COULD SPEAK, WHAT WOULD IT SAY IN TWO WORDS?[5]

To be honest, I don't know why I asked some of the questions, but those were the ones with the most surprising results. For example, I asked men:

 HAVE YOU EVER TRIED TO SUCK YOUR OWN COCK?

Yes: 3,120 (70.86%)   **No:** 1,283 (29.14%)   **Total:** 4,403

Amazingly, over 70 per cent admitted that they had! It's so close to being 69 per cent which would have been so much more ironic, when you think about it.

I then asked:

 COULD YOU DO IT?

Yes: 772 (19.16%)   **No:** 3,258 (80.84%)   **Total:** 4,030[6]

---

5. *This is also a question I nicked from* The Vagina Monologues. *But it was my original idea to ask it about penises instead of vaginas. So it isn't plagiarism.*

6. *It has just struck me that I was one of the people who answered yes to this question. I made the attempt when I was around about 13, and being a bit more limber in those days I found I could get the end of my penis into my mouth. So although earlier in this chapter I claimed that I had never sucked a cock and didn't wish to, you can now all see me for the cock-sucking liar that I truly am.*

Almost one in five men say they have managed it. Those fellas never go out. Finally I wondered:

DID YOU SPIT OR SWALLOW?

Spit: 666 (40.46%)   **Swallow:** 980 (59.54%)   **Total:** 1,646

It's around about 50/50 on the spit or swallow your own semen issue.

I think that's saying something if you're not prepared to swallow your *own* semen. It's a bit much expecting someone else to do it for you. I don't understand what your problem is, you spitting fellas. You've already sucked your own cock! But to swallow your own semen, oh no, that would be *strange*, wouldn't it?

It should be noted here that although only 772 men confessed to being able to suck their own penis, 1,646 men answered the question about whether they spat or swallowed their own semen. I don't know what question the additional 874 men thought they were answering. Possibly they were thinking that I was asking whether they would spit or swallow their own semen, if they got the chance. Possibly they were saying that they would spit or swallow another man's semen if they got the chance. I don't think the final percentage answer will be affected too much, but it maybe gives you some indication of how drunk some of my subjects may have been (both when filling in the questionnaire and when they tried to fellate themselves).

So I had the questionnaire up on the World Wide Web, but how could I let the world of cock-users know that it was out there?

I sent out an e-mail about the site to friends and fans and asked them to forward it to anyone who they thought might be interested (probably not their grans, unless they were open-minded enough to answer the question 'Do you enjoy anal sex?').

The site was immediately a massive hit. A thousand people responded within the first 24 hours. Less than a week later, I was a news story, making page five of *The Independent* newspaper, which falsely claimed the survey has 69 questions. (There are actually 68 for men and 26 for women – see how the press will lie to us if it makes a good story. Shame on you, Cahal Milmo. That can't be your real name, surely?)

The site was mentioned on many Internet news groups as well as in newspapers all over the world, which explains the sudden surge in responses from China a couple of months in. Although most of the responses have come from people in the UK, the countries of Ireland, the USA, Canada, Australia, New Zealand and Europe are all well represented. Other countries with a few respondents include Brazil, Kuwait, Mexico, Pakistan, Egypt, Botswana, Singapore, Japan, Serbia, Croatia, Samoa, Jamaica, Trinidad and Macedonia. One man described himself as Polish/Irish/Cherokee. That's quite a combination. I won't give any of his answers here, as I'm guessing people might be able to work out who he is! Another man, when asked his nationality, replied, 'Not your business,' though he did then go on to tell me the length and girth of his penis and all about his erectile dysfunction. It's interesting what people consider to be other people's business!

Ages range from 11 to 89 with an average of around 30.

All sexualities have been represented, though unsurprisingly, not all that many lesbians have filled in a questionnaire about penises (but 22 have, God bless them, along with a further 370 women who define themselves as bi-sexual).

By the time of going to press (with the questionnaire having been on line for almost exactly a year), it has been completed by 5,214 men and 2,267 women.[7] The survey is still running, so please do go and fill it in. I will be constantly refining the statistics and responses I use in my live show. The more, the merrier!

I have to say that I was astounded and delighted by this massive response, and the variety of backgrounds of the respondents. However, I am aware that it is still far from being a scientifically accurate survey.

First, people can of course lie. I can't be 100 per cent sure, but from reading the responses I would say that the vast majority of people have taken the questionnaire in the spirit it was intended and answered honestly (occasionally with devastating honesty). I am able to deactivate the occasional 'joke' responses (for example, I chose not to believe the man who said his erect penis was four

---

7. The respondents to each question vary, partly because some people have chosen not to answer every question and partly because about a week or so into the project I added some further questions when I realised that the survey failed to cover a few important areas. During the lengthy men's questionnaire, a lot of people got bored and stopped before they could finish it!

miles long). Secondly, it is only open to people with access to computers, which is bound to skew the demographic. Thirdly, people have to choose to take part and certain types of people are going to be inclined or disinclined to do so. Finally, it is a subject which men notoriously exaggerate and lie about (to themselves as well as to others), which, as you'll see, may be the reason for the surprisingly high average for erect penis size!

For all these reasons we should not take the statistics as gospel.[8] However, I do feel that they demonstrate definite trends and thus should not be discounted. The individual responses to questions are also fascinating, revealing and again, I would argue, brutally honest. It is reassuring to see the same answers occurring over and over again. It is partly for this reason that I have decided to make this a book which concentrates more on common experience, rather than on the extremities of the penile world that are commonly covered in sensational TV documentaries.

With thousands of lengthy questionnaires to read and dozens more arriving every day I soon realised that I had far too much material for a one-hour stage show. Especially as the Internet survey was only meant to play a small role in the project. In the preview shows I did in tiny rooms above pubs in London, I was finding that I had hours and hours of material already, and I had only scratched the surface of the penis. I had to drop entire subjects in order to cover others properly. It was very frustrating.

At the same time media interest was heightening. I started getting emails from countries all over the world, asking whether the script of my show could be translated and performed by local actors. And there wasn't even a completed script in English at this point. I began to suspect I had a hit on my hands.[9] It became clear that the subject was bigger than the show. I realised that I could only do the dagger of desire justice by writing a book. Read on to find out whether I succeeded in finding a publisher.

Although the main aim of the project was to make people laugh, I was also keen to make it as factual and well researched as possible. Initially, I bought as

---

8. *Having read the Gospels, and noted all the impossible and contradictory things that happen in them, I would also advise against taking anything in them as gospel either.*
9. *So far deals have been struck with theatre groups in Germany, Portugal, Norway, Denmark, Finland, Italy, Israel, India, Iceland, Switzerland and the USA.*

IF YOUR PENIS WERE TO GET DRESSED, WHAT WOULD IT WEAR?

- A beret and striped shirt. With onions.
- Something slimming, it's quite fat.
- A nice Paisley dress.
- A sombrero with a hole in the top.
- A willing mouth.
- A Puritan hat.
- Jeans and a T-shirt.

Approaching 50 per cent of men went for something similarly casual.

- It would probably like to get dressed up in Huggy Bear pimp gear, but I wouldn't let it leave the house like that.
- On current form, a monk's habit.
- Prada.
- Nothing. It is not interested in material goods or making a fashion statement. It just wants to have sex with girls.
- It would be a velveteen-coated aesthete.
- Kickass jeans, awesome hoodie and an Afro.
- A Napoleon costume.
- Earmuffs.
- Chinese Kung Fu clothes.
- A condom.
- Strawberry jam.
- Complete Celtic kit.

Quite a few men chose the colours of their local team.

- You don't dress something already beautiful.

The most eloquent answer of the 33 per cent of men who said 'nothing'.

- A Darth Vader outfit.
- A wet suit?
- Dyed red pubes (spiked) and a T-shirt emblazoned with a cutting political remark.
- A comedy arrow through its head.
- It would disguise itself as an ice cream.
- A Dracula cloak and an Indiana Jones hat.
- Reins.
- Earth tones. It's a redhead.
- The sort of crap that Jonathon Ross wears every day of the week.
- A droog outfit from *Clockwork Orange* complete with cane and false eyelashes.
- Evening suit, top hat, monocle. If possible, it would smoke.
- Not a crown of thorns.
- A Fonzie-style leather jacket.
- A GI Joe uniform.
- A fireman's helmet.
- Shabby clothes that make it look like a tramp.
- Catherine Zeta Jones.

But my favourite answer, which probably sums it up for about 5 per cent of the participants:

- Do other men have serious answers to this question? It seems absurd to me.

many books on the subject as I could. I went to www.amazon.com and typed in the word 'penis' and received a couple of recommendations. When I put one in my virtual trolley, a page came up suggesting other books about penises that I might like to purchase. This was very helpful to me, but I did wonder who else would really be trying to buy every cock book that had ever been written. I bought about 15 books, but only for research purposes, whatever the person who mailed them out to me may have thought. I suspect that I might now be on some list in a government computer somewhere.

A few of the tomes that arrived over the next few weeks were extremely useful (and there's a bibliography at the back for anyone who wants to research this subject further), but others were either too 'comedy' or full of strange religious teachings. I realised I would need to research in more depth and so joined the prestigious British Library.

I have caused a fair amount of mirth there as I collect my special interest books, and it has been most amusing to me to be sitting in those hallowed chambers reading about cocks, when the person next to me is researching Anglo–Papal relations in the 12th century. It is both wrong and wonderfully right at the same time.

With all the important decisions made I was ready to begin my cock-tastic voyage in earnest. It really was an Odyssey. I thought it would be over in months, but it seems destined to take over years of my life. The penis has become like a Siren, determined to draw everything it saw on to its rocks; it has become like a Cyclops, trapping me in its lair and looking at me with its terrifying single eye, and I expect it has become like some of the other characters from the Odyssey as well, but I can't remember any of them.

Within a few weeks I would be experiencing cock fatigue, and for the first time in my life this was a purely psychological disorder. I was spending every day thinking about cocks, looking at pictures of cocks, talking to men about their cocks. It was driving me insane. I was beginning to wish I was writing a show about really big tits instead.

Just re-asserting my masculinity once more there. Just to make it crystal clear that I am not obsessed with cocks. At least I wasn't when all this began …

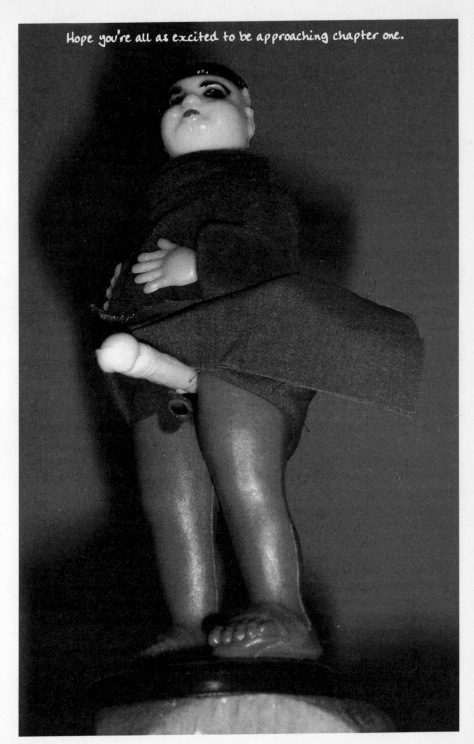

Hope you're all as excited to be approaching chapter one.

COCKFACT

According to a survey carried out by Gordon Gallup and his colleagues at the State University of New York in 2002, semen makes women happy. Working on the theory that semen contains the mood-improving hormones testosterone and oestrogen, they did psychological tests on nearly 300 female students They found that the women whose partners never wore condoms were the happiest, followed by women whose partners sometimes used condoms. The women whose partners always used condoms were the least happy. Gallup said that the findings might also apply to women who engage in unprotected oral and anal sex, but added that further research was required. But I'm going to take a chance and save them some work and say that the findings definitely apply to them too. Especially from anal sex.

1

NEVERMINDTHEBOLLOCKS ... HERE'STHESEXPISTOL!

So what is this thing?

It's a source of shame and pride; it can inspire laughter and fear; it's a symbol of power, yet it's incredibly fragile and weak; it can be a pound of flesh or an ounce of winkles; it can be used to express both love and hate; it can create life, it can condemn us to death.

And it can do wees as well.

How can one tiny and ridiculous, wrinkly flap of skin and spongy tissue be all these things?

I hope this book will explain some of the reasons for these contradictions and reveal the amazing truth about the Honourable Member for Fuckinghamshire. But to achieve penile veracity is more difficult than it was for King Dong to achieve an erection

King Dong - if he climbed the Empire State Building his cock would still be touching the pavement.

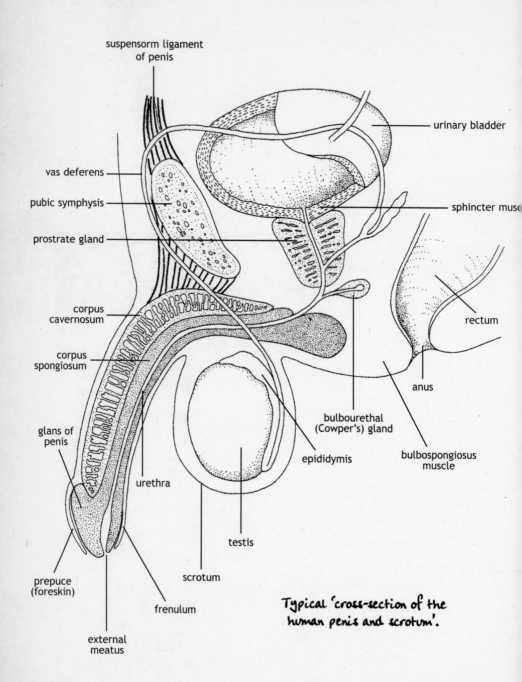

suspensorm ligament
of penis

urinary bladder

vas deferens

pubic symphysis

sphincter musc

prostrate gland

corpus
cavernosum

corpus
spongiosum

rectum

anus

glans of
penis

bulbourethal
(Cowper's) gland

bulbospongiosus
muscle

urethra

epididymis

prepuce
(foreskin)

testis

frenulum

scrotum

external
meatus

Typical 'cross-section of the
human penis and scrotum'.

without fainting.[1] Because this is a subject that, throughout all human history, has been shrouded in myth, exaggeration, conjecture, confusion and downright phallusy (do you see what I did there?) It's lies, damned lies and statistics that generally have a couple of inches added on to them.

I will expose the manhood falsehoods. Because this must be a story with cock, but no bull. Unless the bull has a cock. In which case he's in.

Surely on a basic anatomical level there is no doubt what the penis is. I think most of us are familiar with diagrams like the one opposite.

Undoubtedly, on looking at this picture, many of you are instantly transported back to a very specific day in a very specific classroom. I think you might even be able to remember the exact seat you were sitting in when you first saw it. Are you beginning to recall the heightened tension and sense of confused excitement in the room, the blood rushing to your cheeks in prickly embarrassment, the childish snickering, the teacher saying, 'That's right. Get it out of your system. Can we try and be grown-up about this?'

For me that teacher was Mr Walker, and you know the image of that day is so vivid, that I can now recognise, in hindsight, the then unperceived discomfort that he was feeling. How his speech sometimes faltered, how his voice even raised a tone or two in pitch, how irritating he was finding the stifled laughter. (Sorry for laughing, Mr Walker, but as you can see, it's 25 years later and I still haven't got it out of my system. Though I probably will have done by the time I've finished this book.) I see now that he didn't want to teach the anatomy of the penis to another class of ten-year-olds any more than we wanted to learn. It was less sex education than an education in the study of embarrassment.

Because next to none of us will remember anything more than the sensations we felt on that day. Do you recall where the *corpus spongiosum* is, or what

---

1. *King Dong was a porn star in the Seventies with a penis of jaw-aching proportions – purportedly around about 18 inches in length. In the 1970s a story spread around the school playgrounds of the UK which stated that it took so much blood to make this legendary cock tumescent that whenever King Dong got an erection he would pass out. Subsequent adult investigation has revealed that King Dong's penis was a prosthetic. So ironically even that penile fact is a lie.*

it does? Can you tell me the function of the bulbourethral gland or which lucky man it is alternatively named after?[2] Could you put your finger on the external meatus? (No, it's not what it sounds like. Get your finger off that!)

Of course not, because this pitiful line drawing gives us no real sense of what the penis is, or what it does, what pleasure it can bring, nor how miraculous is the process by which it becomes erect. The textbook anatomy is antiseptic and cold. The only possible emotional response to such a cross-section is to imagine how painful it would be if your genitals were similarly sliced open.

And the scientific and Latin names for the various bits and knobs further distances us from the reality. The *corpus cavernosum*, the pubic symphysis, the bulbospongiosus muscle. Oh please! There is no poetry in this name, no beauty and certainly no inkling of what wonders these constructions can achieve. It is unsurprising that we all forgot these terms the very second we first heard them.

The only name with any spunk (quite literally in this case) is the *vas deferens,* which is the tube that carries sperm from the testis (crap name) to the urethra (sixth most popular girl's name of the 1950s).[3]

Vas deferens! It's got a good ring about it, hasn't it? It sounds important and manly and faintly mysterious. And they've wasted it on a cum conduit. That should have been the name for the whole thing. Not penis. 'Do you want to see my VAS DEFERENS?' Women would go giddy at the mere mention of the words.

I've always thought it would make a great stage-name for an actor. Especially one who appears in action-movies. Imagine that gravelly-voiced trailer man saying something like 'Final Absolution starring Vas Deferens'.[4] If you are an actor and fancy a new moniker, please, I beg you, call yourself Vas Deferens. I, for one, will come to see all your films.

---

2. *It's English surgeon, William Cowper, if you're interested. In 1702 he first described the yellowish pea-sized glands which are located near the base of the prostrate gland and which produce a thick seminal liquid that you would probably know better as pre-cum. And as a thank you for describing that fluid-producing gland, it was then named after him. And that is all his life is remembered for.*

3. *Thanks largely to the fame of Urethra Franklin.*

4. *And yet ironically by using Vas Deferens as a family name, it becomes the ideal pseudonym for a Merchant-Ivory style actor –* 'A Month in the Country *starring Peter Vas Deferens.'*

COCKFACT

Davro's Constant states that at any party decorated with balloons, someone will arrange three appropriately shaped balloons into an approximation of male genitalia.

It is through using such uninspiring diagrams and confusing terminology that the scientific community has disarmed the purple-headed love missile. They've clipped the angel's wings and then made a beeline for his foreskin. Not content with unweaving the rainbow, they've also had a go at untangling all the little tubules in your testicles as well. Just as the medieval Church refused to allow the Bible to be translated so they could limit its access to ordinary people, scientists are trying to keep the mystery of the tallywhacker to themselves.

It's time to give the cock back to the people. We need a Martin Luther, who will nail his protests to the laboratory doors (just his protests mind – nailing your privates to a piece of wood is illegal in this great country of ours, even if you do it quite willingly, as that unusual group of fellas found out to their cost a few years back). And like Cock Protestants (Cockestants?) we must strive to translate penile terminology into a living language that can be understood by the masses.

I am not afraid to be that Martin Luther. Better, I will be a Vas Deferens, breaking through the glass dome of the evil scientists' undersea base and spearing them through their skulls with their own pathetic, plastic anatomical models of the penis, before monotonously proclaiming, 'Nice to meet you, dickheads!'

It is my hope and dream that one day, in the not too distant future, the old school terminology will fall into disuse and my new classification will be taught in schools. If you are a teacher please feel free to photocopy any relevant sections of the book and use it in your lessons. If you are a student, refute the old system and use my words to label that diagram in exams.[5] If you mark examinations for

---

5. *The first few thousand of you may fail, but eventually the system will change, and though you personally will be unqualified and working in a fast-food restaurant you will have made a difference to the world. Which should be reward enough in itself.*

On the website questionnaire, I asked men:

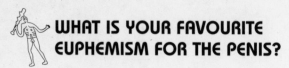

WHAT IS YOUR FAVOURITE EUPHEMISM FOR THE PENIS?

These are some of the more imaginative answers:

- Purple headed bedroom python.
- The veiny love-tree.
- The bald-headed, one-eyed monk.
- Policeman.
- Morning flagpole.
- The happy lantern.
- Billy Joel.
- Wazzler.
- Pink, bendy belly banana.
- Moisture-seeking love dart.
- Unknown soldier.
- Badger.
- It's a ferret carrying two shopping bags.
- Purple-bristled womb broom.
- Blue-veined Havana.
- Chopper! (It's so Seventies.)
- Spurt Reynolds.
- My grandmother used to refer to it as 'your little Liquorice Allsort'.
- The herring (not kidding!)

So it seems that, as Richard and Dick are other popular euphemisms, my name turns out to be Penis Penis!

- Love tusk.

- Jack the Dripper.

- The raw prawn.

- Abdullah the tent maker.

- The limbless Chihuahua.

- Cunt spear.

That's just unpleasant.

- Captain Pickard.

And as with all these questions there is the odd dissenting voice:

- Euphemisms are childish and idiotic.

I have to say that after months of study on this subject I tend to agree with this last fellow. It soon stops being amusing. For me the funniest thing about the answers to this question was how many people didn't know what 'euphemism' meant! I got some interesting comments and misspellings along the lines of 'What's an epharism?', but best of all were the blokes who clearly had some alternative definition of the word. So my favourite answer to the question '*What's your favourite euphemism for the penis?*' is:

- Having a chick swallow it all the way down.

You realise that in that case, euphemism itself has become a euphemism. How cool is that?

a living, please do not deduct points for any candidate who uses these new terms. Give them extra credit. Because only they will have a real grasp of what is actually happening inside men's trousers.

Ladies and gentlemen, please prepare yourself for the most important break-through in scientific knowledge since Darwin looked in the mirror and realised he looked a bit like a monkey. The all-new penile vocabulary.

Of course, I am not the first to attempt to rename the external genitalia. The penis has more euphemisms than you could shake a euphemistic stick at:

Cock, knob, dick, schmuck, rod, tool, Percy, Saint Peter, the bald-headed mouse, the rebellious henchman, Kojak's Moneybox, the ladies' delight, the breakfast burrito, the flesh torpedo, the cherry picker, Nature's scythe, the pink lighthouse that wants to draw you on to its rocks, the kidney scraper, the arrow of desire, the crimson butterfly, the silent flute of love and, of course, Russell the fur-faced chicken.[6]

The testicles too have been imaginatively re-described over the years:

Bollocks, balls, bollards, testicules, vestibules, cobblers, acorns, Christ-apples, eggs in the basket, goolies, gonads, the tadpole factory, nads, Jackson Pollocks, knackers, John Wayne's hairy saddle bags, the Chuckle Brothers' less wrinkly siblings, Mother Nature's maracas and the eerily anatomically accurate, love conkers.[7]

We must make a choice for the textbooks of the future (that's not to say we aren't allowed to use the other names, just that we should adopt official termi-nology for important occasions).

---

6. *If so inclined I could go on with these forever. Many people have been foolish enough to attempt to catalogue them all. This is an impossible and boring task. If you think there are simply not enough euphemisms for the penis in this book then I would refer you to* The Big Book of Filth, *published by Cassell;* Skin Flutes and Velvet Gloves *by Dr Terri Hamilton;* Woody's World of Penis Euphemisms *at http://www.starma.com/penis/penis.html or by far the best of the bunch (as it includes witty definitions rather than just a list of words),* Roger's Profanisaurus *from the boys at* Viz *magazine. If, after all that, your thirst for alter-native names for the penis is not extinguished, then please seek psychiatric help.*
7. *I wonder what Freud would have made of us throwing sticks into trees full of testicles. And then putting the testis on strings and smashing them against each other.*

COCKFACT

Fellas, did you know that if I were to slice open your testicle and stretch out all the tubules inside into one long continuous line, it wouldn't be long before I was committed to the high security ward of a hospital for the criminally insane. As Jeffrey Dahmer, the Milwaukee cannibal, found out to his cost. He was only trying to find out how much there was in there. Simple scientific enquiry. A much misunderstood man.

For me, there is no doubt that the best words for the job are COCK and BOLLOCKS.

They just sound so great together. Say them out loud right now.

I don't care if you're on the train or at your gran's funeral (but thanks for carrying on reading my book through your grief). I want you to utter the words, loudly and proudly this instant. Go!

Sounds good, doesn't it? Cock and Bollocks. They go together like a horse and carriage. Or perhaps more accurately like a horse and one of those two-wheeled chariots at the end of *Ben Hur*.

Cock not only has the right air of authority, it conjures up a delightful poetic image. For what is the cock, if not a bird which rises in the morning, while we are still sleeping, and makes a commotion until someone pays it some attention or strangles it?

Bollocks is the best name for the testicles by far. In fact, you could say that it is the bollocks. It immediately calls to mind a combination of balls and rocks. Or boulders and locks (hiding something mysterious within its impenetrable interior). It is decidedly masculine, unlike the rather effeminate '*testicles*'. (Can you imagine someone having been chastised complaining that they have had 'a right testicling'? It's like being told off by a boss who is more anxious to look like he's your mate as well. Completely ineffectual.)

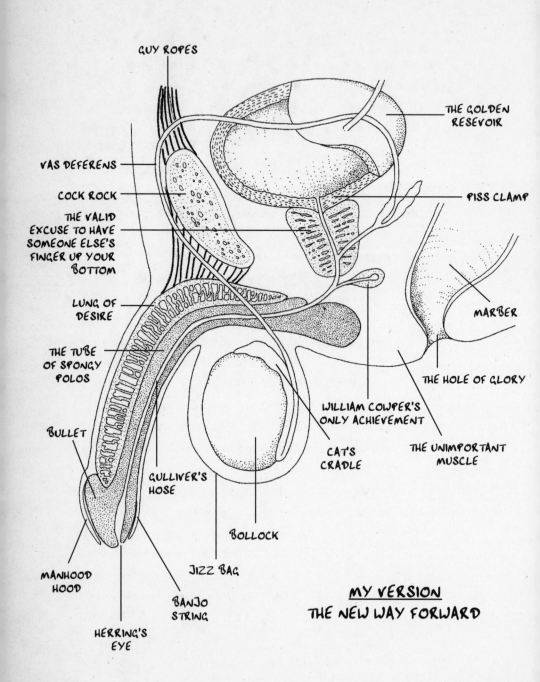

GUY ROPES

THE GOLDEN RESEVOIR

VAS DEFERENS

COCK ROCK

PISS CLAMP

THE VALID EXCUSE TO HAVE SOMEONE ELSE'S FINGER UP YOUR BOTTOM

LUNG OF DESIRE

MARBER

THE TUBE OF SPONGY POLOS

THE HOLE OF GLORY

WILLIAM COWPER'S ONLY ACHIEVEMENT

BULLET

CAT'S CRADLE

THE UNIMPORTANT MUSCLE

GULLIVER'S HOSE

MANHOOD HOOD

BOLLOCK

JIZZ BAG

BANJO STRING

HERRING'S EYE

MY VERSION
THE NEW WAY FORWARD

We have the terms for what's on the surface, but how many alternatives exist for what lies beneath? Not many men have taken the fantastic voyage into the depths of the male genitalia, but only by doing so can we all begin to understand how the sticky wicket works (and why sometimes it doesn't).

Let me take you through a few of those choices:

I have called the *corpus cavernosum* 'the lung of desire' because it almost seems to 'breathe in' blood during arousal. And it holds that breath until its work is done. It's not a 'hollow chamber' as the translated Latin would have us believe. It is full of sound and fury, signifying everything. It's a sensational, expanding hive of blood.

The *urethra* I have dubbed 'Gulliver's Hose' in honour of Lemuel Gulliver's heroic dowsing of the flames at the Royal Palace in Lilliput. It is a hose which can shoot both liquid and foam, making it ideal for conventional, electrical and chemical blazes and is thus the ultimate huge-man-in-a-land-of-tiny-people fire-fighting equipment.

The *corpus spongiosum* ('spongy body' – dear, oh dear) becomes the 'tube of spongy Polos'. All right, it's not a great name, but that is what it most resembles (even down to being a great thing to suck on during a long car journey). In this day and age it is also necessary for schools to make ends meet with some corporate sponsorship and it is partly with this in mind that I plumped for this name. The text books of my new world order could proudly proclaim 'This Cock is sponsored by Nestlé'. I have already written to them to ask them how much they will pay for this wonderful advertising opportunity.[8] If you prefer, you could think of it as that spongy lagging material that some people put round their water-pipes to keep the heat in. The *tube of spongy Polos* is not there to keep in heat, but does protect our water-pipe from being crushed in the event of an erotic thought.

Glans sounds like a tropical disease. It's no kind of label for something so wonderful. But glans is Latin for 'bullet', a perfect term for the tip of the Sex Pistol (as well as bringing a new meaning to phrase 'biting the bullet').

The *rectum* is redubbed the Marber in honour of the curmudgeonly playwright and puppeteer, Patrick Marber. In this way his name will be remembered for centuries, even in the unlikely event that his work falls into obscurity.

---

8. *See Appendix.*

The *Vas Deferens* remains the Vas Deferens. I am not afraid to accept that the old system got some things right. You cannot improve upon perfection.

Finally we come to the *external meatus*, the ridiculous name given to the only part of the prick that is entirely meat-free (though the animal version, apparently, occasionally ends up in sausages). Schoolboys have labelled this aperture 'the Jap's eye', but I find this term offensive to our friends in Japan. So, perhaps arrogantly, I have designated it 'Herring's eye'. Like William Cowper, I think it is only fair that my ground-breaking penile work gets some kind of recognition. It gives me a warm feeling to think that in the future, whenever you look upon this wondrous opening, you will think of my winking eye. Of course, this name also works on two levels. If you prefer not to indulge my vanity then you can think of it as the eye of a fish, which is, in so many ways, even more appropriate.

Rome was not built in a day and throughout the book I will refer to these parts by both their archaic and correct new terms. It would be helpful if you would take some time to digest the new terms and to learn them. There is a test at the end of the chapter. I am taking this seriously. I hope you are too.

I'm sure that you'll agree that my new anatomy is brilliant and awe-inspiring, but it is far from perfect. Reluctantly I have been forced to use the very same excruciating diagram that we all recall from those school textbooks. Not only does this picture fail to capture the true beauty of the skin chimney, more importantly it gives us the impression that the penis is a uniform, never-varying structure. It is always seen as the same length, the same width, the same shape. It has no character, no individuality. If, like my class, you were also lucky enough to have had a biology textbook with a photo of a real naked man and woman in it, this penile template was reconfirmed. The naked man's penis seemed to be dimensionally exactly the same as the drawing. (Not that I was looking at that. No, I only looked at the woman, of course. I have never been interested in cocks. Never, you hear me?)

From very early on we were being educated to expect a norm, we were being told that all penises were the same. There was little effort made to reassure anyone that penises came in all shapes and sizes. It is no wonder that these assumptions remain with many of us into our adult lives, and that any differentiation from this norm is seen as freakish or amusing.

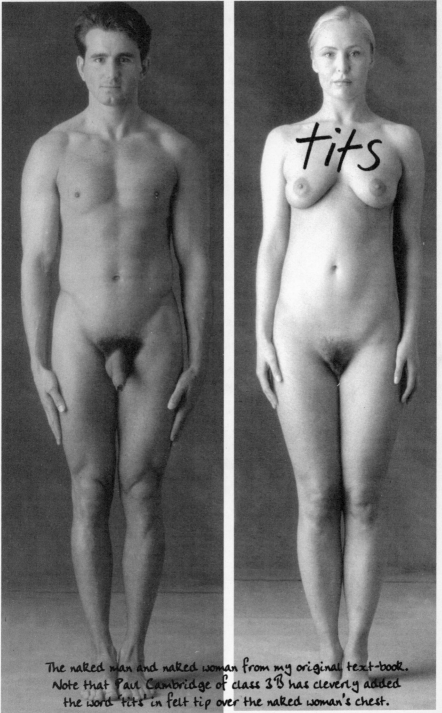

The naked man and naked woman from my original text-book.
Note that Paul Cambridge of class 3B has cleverly added
the word 'tits' in felt tip over the naked woman's chest.

COCKFACT

Ever wondered why it's difficult or impossible to urinate when you have an erection? Sperm is killed if it comes into contact with urine, so to prevent this, an involuntary reflex causes the internal urinary sphincter muscle (or as it is more correctly called, the piss clamp) to shut down. Essentially the tube to your bladder is squeezed shut so nothing can seep out! It's one of Nature's many wonders, but is bloody annoying if you're on for a definite shag and everything's ready to roll, but you need to go for a wee first.

Before I began this project I had happily gone along with this supposition. I had always assumed that all men's penises were pretty much exactly the same as mine … only smaller.

I knew there was a small amount of variety. Indiscreet girlfriends had told me of ex-partners with bizarre equipment and, of course, I had seen some extreme deviations from the average in porn films (that my friends were watching, mum) or on cruel humour sites on the Internet.

But I hadn't seen enough cocks in my life to get any idea of the truth. I had to turn to the experts, who had seen enough pricks to make a judgement. Women. So, on my website questionnaire, I asked them:

 DESCRIBE THE MOST UNUSUAL PENIS YOU HAVE EVER SEEN.

Here are some of the answers:

● **Very thin, looked like one of those long rubber Biros you used to buy when you were little.**

She doesn't say if it had a character from *The Munch Bunch* sat on top of it in eraser form.

- A very, very small penis that belonged to a Dutchman.

Sounds like maybe he just kept that in a box.

- It was fairly normal in size, but the end seemed to have a twist in it so the eye-hole was kind of on the side instead of the top. Made me laugh ... but I sucked it anyway.

- I described him as Mr Walnut Whip, in size and shape, but sadly not in taste.

- It was much thinner at the top than at the bottom, looking a bit like a collapsed anorexic traffic-cone.

- It was the shape of an upside-down banana.

What I want to know is, what's the right way up for a banana to be? I can't visualise it.

Unusual bends in all directions imaginable made up the majority of answers to this question. Perhaps the most impressive was:

- It was bent in two different places and looked like a small flash of lightning.

It's the cock of a superhero!

- My ex's had a huge vein in the shape of a question mark on it.

Whereas this one belongs to some kind of pornographic *Batman* villain. The Piddler, perhaps.

- It was tiny, looked like a baby hamster before they get their fur.

No, don't laugh. That one is just cruel.

- My ex's had two holes in the end and he called his penis, 'the double-barrelled shotgun'.

- My current partner of two years has the most beautiful penis I have ever seen. When he was 15 he had an op to remove his foreskin because it was too tight. This has left him with an unusually textured head (it's just like chamois leather) and a wonderful pad of skin at the back that stimulates my g-spot. Honestly it's like I designed it.

- It was four inches long and bent like a hook.

- My ex-husband's was 9 inches long and never got soft. Never found one like that again.

I imagine that before she left him she'd assumed all cocks were the same as his. But by the time she realised her mistake, he'd found someone else who appreciated what she'd got. You don't miss your water till your well runs dry!

- Looked like a golf ball on a stick.

- Shaped like a doorknob.

- Webbed.

Oh, how I wish she had given more information on that *Man from Atlantis*-style whanger.

- A hemisected one (cut in half lengthways) on a cadaver ... (I am a medical student).

Thank Christ for that. Not for the last time during this project I was on the point of calling the police.

- Foreskin like a sleeping bag!

- Looked like a small mouse in a huge pink anorak.

- I saw one that looked EXACTLY like a baked potato.

But did it have a cottage cheese filling?

- Looked like Gonzo's nose, only not blue (obviously).

No, not obviously. By this stage I am taking nothing for granted.

- It had a giant mole on it (about an inch across) with hair growing out of it. I still have nightmares.

- A guy with two penises.

This is scientifically possible. I have read statistics which suggest that up to one in a hundred thousand men are born like this. It's called being diphallactic or extremely lucky.[9]

But my favourite answer to this question has got to be:

- I've never seen a usual penis.

I would say she's hit the nail on the head (though please remember, that is illegal).

It seems that no two penises are the same. Even if they're both on the same bloke. We should be celebrating that diversity, not expecting everyone to conform to this fascistic penile template.

I've never seen a usual penis.

Remember that. It's important.

Of course, many of those comments are less than flattering. Maybe the reason that

---

9. *This flippant joke rather shamefully ignores the fact that there is nothing fortunate about this condition. Rather than being multi-orifice filling sex machines, diphallactic men are usually both sterile and unable to achieve erection. As with so many supposedly positive cock attributes, the fantasy cock is often much more frustrating than the mundane average.*

women mock and denigrate our genitalia so often, fellas, is because they're jealous of us for having cocks. Because they don't have them and it makes them jealous. That's it, isn't it girls? You feel inferior to us, you haven't got a penis, and you *envy* us.

Well, that was certainly the philosophy of insane Austrian pervert, Sigmund Freud. He argued that women were jealous of him, and his *amazing* cock, and that's why none of them would go out with him … because of the jealousy.

But was he right?

I asked women on the website:

DO YOU ENVY A MAN FOR HAVING A PENIS?
Yes: 480 (21.92%)   **No:** 1,710 (78.08%)   **Total:** 2,190

Over one in five women admitted that they did.

Which seems like a very high figure, until you look at the actual reasons women gave for that envy, which can be summed up by two main answers. About a third of those women said something along the lines of:

● **'Although I don't want a penis, I am curious to know what it would feel like to penetrate someone.'**

Or someone who makes the same point, slightly more crudely:

● **''Cause I'd love to bugger someone up the arse … mwahaha!'**

The 'mwahaha' – very telling there. Essentially, that first reason can be summed up as REVENGE! Getting men back for crimes we may have committed while slightly drunk (as an excuse). Or at the very least, this supposed envy is merely curiosity. I think you'd find that most men would be interested in having breasts for a while (and they'd be staying in for most of that time, in front of the mirror), but that doesn't mean they are all rushing out to the plastic surgeon, or that they are especially envious of women.

In the book *Dick for a Day*, Fiona Giles asked a variety of female celebrities what they would do if they woke up to discover they had acquired a knob for 24 hours. Germaine Greer's comments are interesting and not untypical:

What I would do with it if I had a dick for a day would largely depend on what kind of dick it was. If it was long enough I would probably try to find out whether I was as good/bad a fuck as I was reputed to be. If it came with all its attachments I would probably work on a sizeable donation to a sperm bank, having failed to pass on my genes by any other method. The best bit would be getting rid of it at the end of the day.

The main reason given on my survey for female penis envy (shared by well over half the women who admitted to jealousy) was something along the lines of:

- **I have enough problems with my breasts dangling all over the place, without having another dangling thing, but I do sometimes envy men for having a penis because it means they can piss standing up and so don't have to queue for the toilet.**

Which can also be seen as an avenging desire, as we learn from Tracy Sondern's comment about what she'd do if she had a 'Dick for a Day':

'I'd pee all over the bathroom, the walls, the floor – everywhere. Then I'd make my four brothers clean up, just like I always had to do after them.'

That's it guys, that's the extent of it. That's as far as the envy goes. So much for Freud, the mental twat.[10]

Remember this is a man who was very keen to harp on about the phallic symbols that everyone else was subconsciously obsessed with, but when it was pointed out that his beloved cigars were a bit like cocks going in and out of his mouth on a daily basis, he replied, 'Sometimes a cigar is just a cigar.' The cock-obsessed hypocrite. You do have to wonder about the mental state of someone

---

10. *For further proof of the inadequacy of Freud's theories I asked women:*
As a child did it upset you that you didn't have a penis?
Yes: 164 (7.49%)   *No: 2,027 (92.51%)*   *Total: 2,191*
Women don't want to have a cock, Sigmund. Got it? If you'd just thought to talk to some women about this, you might have saved everyone a lot of time and worry.

who just thinks about cocks all day long. Personally I wouldn't trust a word anyone like that said.

This realisation that women would only want a cock for convenient urination led me to believe that there was a fortune to be made out there for the first person to invent a 'Snap-on Pissing Penis for Ladies'. I had already constructed some unimpressive (and leaky) prototypes when I was informed that someone had already thought of something similar. Kathie Jones from Florida tried to find a way of getting round the unsanitary conditions of public loos, which wouldn't involve the usual undignified squatting over dirty or broken toilets. She set up the Urinette Company in the 1990s which produced a urinal for ladies called, the 'She-inal'. This contraption employed a syphoning attachment to enable women to urinate comfortably in a standing position. The product sold only a few hundred units and the Urinette Company went the way of all urine. Steve Jones, in *Y. The Descent of Men*, claims:

Urinette's mistake was to fly in the face of common sense (and in Texas, where a law against female urinals was passed in 1997, to outrage all norms of society). Everybody knows that men make water while standing while women prefer to squat.

However, I tend to agree with Denise Decker, the author of the Internet site www.restrooms.org/urinals.html who writes:

In my opinion the worst thing about the She-inal was that it required a woman to press a 'funnel-like' thing up against their genital area. Pressing some piece of plastic that other women had previously used up against the vulva had no appeal for most women.

So maybe there is still a gap in the market for my invention, which I envisage as a small detachable penis that a woman can click on when she needs to go, which has the flexibility and directionability of the penis, but which she can take off and clean and then keep tucked away in her handbag until she needs it again. Work continues. Please get in touch if you have the scientific knowhow to make my insane invention work and we can then share the riches that will

Kathie Jones, driven mad by the failure of her female urinal, dances around like a loon amongst row upon row of her unsold product.

be bestowed upon us. And if you are a lady who would like to own such a thing, then get your orders in now. They're going to sell like hot (though slightly damp) cakes.

After reading the women's responses to the idea of penis envy, I had to accept that the vast majority of women are happy with the hand (or rather the crotch) that they've been dealt. But I was still a little curious as to *why* they didn't have one.

I'm sure that many men have thought at some time, 'Why can't women have penises just like us? Wouldn't the world be a better and more joyful place if only they did?'

Most of these men have subsequently found themselves booking a holiday to Thailand.

So why aren't women blessed with cocks as well? Wouldn't it be great if they could join us men as active participants in our cock celebration?

Well, the good news, ladies, is that you kind of can. According to an essay by the late and great Stephen Jay Gould, called 'Male Nipples and Clitoral Ripples', men and women are all built to the same template. For the first few weeks of pregnancy all embryos have the same basic structure, and don't become male or female until acted upon by hormones. Thus in women the breasts will eventually develop, but men still have nipples because they have to be part of the template as women will ultimately need them. Similarly the clitoris and penis are identical to begin with. The same thing. Indistinguishable. But they are later enlarged in male babies by the action of testosterone. So just as nipples serve no evolutionary purpose in men and never have, women have clitorises because men need to have a penis. It's not there for any other reason. The clitoris *is* a penis. It is, Gould says, 'the same organ, endowed with the same anatomical organisation and capacity of response'.

So it hasn't developed for the evolutionary purpose of making intercourse pleasurable for women. Because let's face it, in most cases it doesn't! Women have got it because men need it!

That's not to detract from the clitoris. As Gould argues:

One day if me and men like me have our way,
all women will look like this.

I do not feel degraded because my nipples are concomitants of a general pattern in human development and not a sign that ancestors of my sex once lactated … Why should the dissociation of orgasm from intercourse degrade women when it merely records a basic (if unappreciated) fact of human anatomy that happens to unite both sexes as variations of a common pattern in development?

All I'm pointing out is that women *do* have a penis. A wonderful pygmy, super-sensitive micro-penis. And all men end up with from this are some superfluous nipples. You're the winners here, girls.

In his book *The Prehistory of Sex*, Timothy Taylor says that you could argue that it is the penis that is the functionless, evolutionary offshoot. He points out that there is no need for it to spasm during ejaculation (it could simply deposit the sperm). It is the clitoris (which extends down either side of the vaginal opening) that needs to spasm in order to suck the sperm towards the egg.

The fact is it doesn't matter which organ is functionless in evolutionary terms. It's not a competition over who has the best or most useful genitals. To turn this issue into a battle of the sexes is to miss the point that regardless of what our bits are there to do, men and women are much more similar than we might outwardly appear. Too often authors and comedians have striven to exaggerate those differences. 'Aren't we different? What's that all about?' Yet for the first few weeks of our life we look exactly the same regardless of our sex or race (and often even species). Men and women are composed of the same parts, in a slightly different order. At worst we are merely anagrams of one another. Let's concentrate on what makes us the same, rather than constantly searching for what makes us different.

And the real bright side of all this, fellas, is that if your woman complains that your cock is too small, you can always say, 'Well it's not as small as your freakish, stunted todger.' And that will shut up her complaining.

COCKQUOTE

'The only bodily organ which is really regarded as inferior is the atrophied penis, a girl's clitoris.' – *Sigmund Freud*

You're just digging yourself in deeper, mate.

Please fill in the blanks in the following diagram with the new and correct terms you have learnt in this chapter. Do not read the rest of the book until you have successfully completed this test. No cheating.

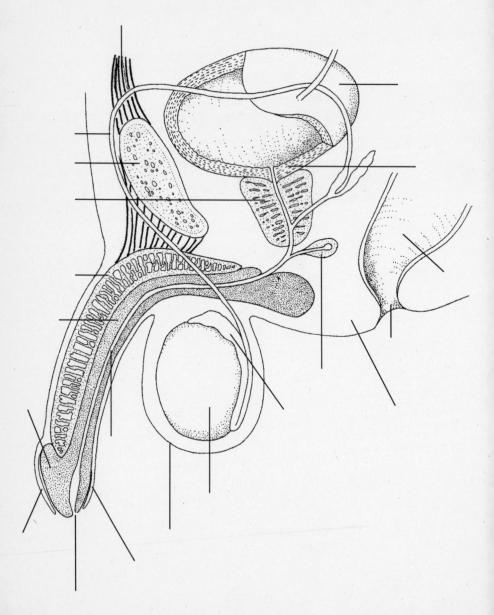

POPSHOTS1

I asked men:

DO YOU HAVE TROUBLE URINATING IN THE COMPANY OF OTHER MEN?

Yes: 1,542 (33.11%)   **No:** 3,115 (66.89%)   **Total:** 4,657

About one in three men suffer from this problem. It's called having a bashful bladder and means you get too nervous to piss if you're standing next to another bloke and have to go into the cubicle (so you see, girls, just having a penis doesn't necessarily mean that you don't have to queue for the toilet!)

No one really knows why it happens. *The Lancet* suggested that it could be something to do with the way that mammals use urine to mark territory. Subconsciously men fear that urinating next to another man will be seen as a territorial affront. Whether this is true or not, it does seem to be a psychological condition.

I'm not ashamed to admit that I used to suffer from this, but a doctor friend told me of a displacement exercise to get around it. Next time you're shoulder to shoulder with a bloke at the urinals and you can't go, what you have to do is imagine that you are urinating through his cock. It's quite important that you just imagine this. Don't stare down at him to help, just do it in your head. For Christ's sake don't hold on to him. Simply visualise it!

It's such a weird thought, that it freaks out your brain and makes it forget about your own weeing problem. I have to say it kind of works.

It's also quite important if you're going to try this that you don't get sexually aroused by the idea of urinating through another man's cock. He might notice and get a bit affronted. You never know though, he may be flattered. You might end up heading for that cubicle after all!

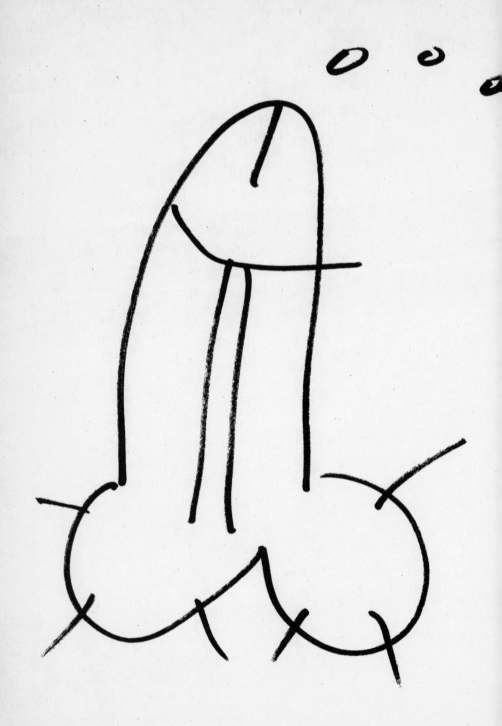

2
THE HISTORY OF MR JOLLY

Of course, the textbook drawing of the dissected penis was not the only lesson in male genital make-up that we got at school. An alternative anatomy appeared felt-tipped on toilet cubicles, chalked on to blackboards,[1] scrawled on to the transparencies of an overhead projector, even traced on to the condensation on the window of a sweaty classroom. It looked something like image opposite.

The beauty of this basic and crude sketch is that it unashamedly celebrates the penis in its engorged state. The cock is not flaccid or cleft in twain. It is erect and complete and usually caught at that instant of epiphany – The Ejaculation. It gives us a flavour of what it means to be human, to be alive and in ecstasy. Something totally lacking in even my textbook version.

But more importantly, unbeknownst to the young artists of such murals, they were joining in a tradition that is as old as *homo sapiens* itself. One of the first things those homos did when they first became sapiens was to get down their local cave and festoon the walls with pictures of tumescent male genitalia.

In the caves of Lascaux, as long ago as 13,000 BC, some randy troglodyte etched this clearly human figure, with an even clearer boner (*figure 1, overleaf*). Other prehistoric etchings show well-hung men having sex with animals (*figure 2*)

---

1. *Most effective when drawn on one of those rolling blackboards which could be pulled down when one surface became full to provide another clean board. Experienced knob guerrillas would draw their cartoon penis and then position the board so it was out of sight. It would then be revealed, in the middle of a lesson, by the unsuspecting teacher. Oh, how the classroom would ring with the laughter of triumph.*

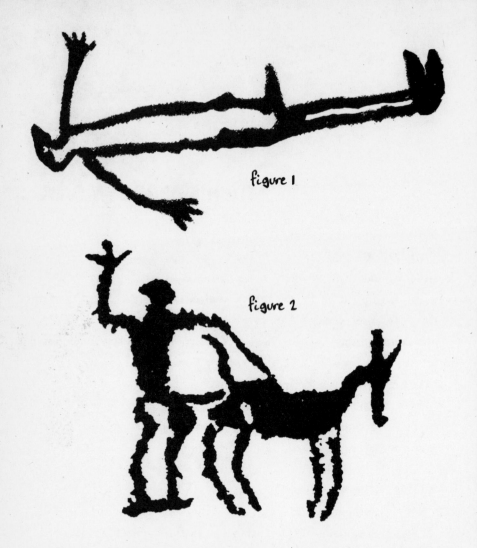

figure 1

figure 2

and well-hung animals having sex with humans. There are even examples of trees sporting erections (perhaps the origin of the concept of 'getting wood').

What were these primitive artists thinking? It's impossible to know for sure. In his book, *The Penis*, Dr Dick Richards (I promise you that is his real name) puts forward some suggestions.

In some cases they were probably fertility symbols or portrayals of fertility rites. Others are examples of parallel magic whereby in some way the picturing of an act or object influenced the happenings in the picture to take place in reality. Some examples, perhaps, are just the wishful thinking of the artist and bear only the same relation to the truth as does the vast bulging graffiti penis drawn on the door of any public toilet in modern day London.[2]

Yet who is to say that the modern day 'cave' artists are not still expressing some notion of parallel magic? There are plenty of more recent examples of the exploitation of penis power. Mark Strage mentions the Kiwai hunter in New Guinea who, before making a harpoon shaft, will press his penis against the selected tree trunk, because, 'he wants his harpoon to be straight, strong and capable of deep penetration and is thus attempting to imbue it with these qualities'.

A couple of interesting anecdotes from the website reveal that men in the Western World are still using their cocks to attempt to influence events:

- **As an adolescent, I used to masturbate, thinking about whatever girl I fancied at the time. When I had come, I would use some of my spunk to write the girl's initials on the wall. I felt that on some primitive, mystical level, doing this would cause the girl to go out with me. To be honest, I have still occasionally done this as an adult. I usually have ended up dating the girl, which might be a testament to the strength of my feelings for them, rather than the magical properties of my semen.**

- **I was chatting up a woman in a crowded pub and offered to buy her a drink. On my way back from the bar, I popped into the gents and dunked my knob into her glass. I was a bit drunk, and I don't know why I did it, to be honest. But I suppose I felt that my cock would imbue the drink with magical energy, and when she'd swallowed the potion she wouldn't be able to resist me sexually. Whether that's true or not, I did end up shagging her.**

I wonder if she'd have been so accommodating if he'd told her what he'd done.

---

2. *Dr Richards is not kind enough to provide you with an illustration, as I have. That's why my cock book is better than his.*

Or would he have had his miraculous 'cock potion' thrown back in his aston-ished face?

So why aren't we generally aware of this link to the past? Once again, in cock terms, our schooling has severely let us down. Any mention of swords or bayo-nets in history lessons would have been strictly in their non-pork or beef varieties. Possibly if you had one of those risqué teachers who wanted to be your mate, you may have heard the rumour that Rasputin's not insubstantial penis had been cut off at his death and was now pickled and last seen in the possession of an elderly female French aristocrat. Apart from that you would think that every man in history had a smooth, hairless groinal area like an Action Man might have, though by the sounds of it, that is how Rasputin at least ended his days.

Even though I studied history at university (though 'studied' might be too strong a word for what essentially amounted to three years of sitting in my room, eating crisps), it wasn't until I began this manhood marathon that I realised to what extent the penis has shaped the world and in some cases, the buildings[3] we live in. Henry Ford was so nearly right. In actual fact, all history is spunk!

As I sat among the bearded nerds that inhabit the reading rooms of the British Library, reading about the history of Mr Happy Helmet, I was amazed and inspired to see how nearly all the great civilisations of the past were not only unashamed of the penis, they actually celebrated, even venerated, it through art, mythology and religion. In our supposed enlightened times, our attitudes have changed so much that when I went on breakfast TV[4] to promote my stage show, not only was I forbidden to mention the impossibly scurrilous title of my work, I couldn't even discuss the subject. Not even if I used the 'correct' scientific names.

---

3. Plans of the Forum of Augustus at the very heart of the Roman Empire show that it consists of a long hall, with two hemispheres at one end. Visitors to the Channel 4 building in London will notice there is a similar (though this time vertical) feature at the front of that building.
4. On a truly awful show called RI:SE on Channel 4, which I can only presume and hope has been taken off the air by the time of publication. It is ironic that Channel 4 are happy to have their HQ festooned with a giant cock, but baulk at saying 'penis' at 7.30am.

But only by understanding the past can we start to understand why the Throbbing Crusader elicits so many contradictory responses. Given that most things that men do ultimately boil down to the interests of their own penis (what is war if not an elaborate attempt to demonstrate who has the biggest cannon?), one chapter is not enough to reveal the whole glorious story. I can only give you a brief history of the hymen-breaker. I will attempt to relate a few of the more impressive and amusing ways that the cock has been celebrated, why too much willy worship can be a bad thing and how it is that the wanger has now become an object so obscene that it has had to be purged from polite society, history books and poor-quality breakfast television. For those of you who find your appetite for cock whetted and wish to discover more about the cultural history of the penis, I heartily recommend the entertaining, illuminating and exhaustive book, *A Mind of Its Own* by David M. Friedman, to which I am greatly indebted.

Prehistory

Earlier I claimed that the artistic schlong celebration is as old as humanity itself, but most historians argue that this is not strictly true. Embarrassingly it wasn't until around 10,000 BC that human beings became aware that pregnancy was caused by sexual intercourse (well, duh! Were the homos really all that sapiens at this point?), so male participation in the creation of life was not appreciated.[5] During the preceding

The Venus of Willendorf – she's not bothered about cellulite, is she girls?

---

5. *Imagine that! A time when sex was completely disassociated from childbirth and people could simply enjoy the act of coitus for what it was, without worrying about the consequences. Sex was just sex and babies appeared by magic like rabbits out of fur-lined hats. Unfortunately once the connection was made between the two events it was inevitable that eventually some people were going to start arguing that intercourse should only occur in order to produce babies. A sad turnaround. Which world would you rather live in?*

20,000 years it was the largely the fecundity and divinity of women that was celebrated by primitive artists. The Venus of Willendorf (*c.* 20,000 BC) is one of the most famous examples. With her pendulous breasts, flabby stomach and massive, great arse, she speaks of a Utopian time for the female sex, where big was beautiful, men had no concept of the potency of their own genitalia and God was a woman.

I have to say that I think men would still celebrate their penises even if we hadn't yet realised that we provide the baby batter in the fishy fry-up that creates life. I can vividly remember being immensely impressed by my own erect penis as a child long before I really knew what that erection was capable of. Several parents have told me of their young lads proudly, even arrogantly, sporting erections in the bath, delighting in the process of its growth, becoming confrontational if chided for their 'behaviour'. Let's face it, the juvenile artists responsible for the illustration at the start of this chapter are celebrating an innate pride in their favourite toy without any real understanding of its more adult function. To quote Carl Jung, 'The phallus functions as an all embracing symbol in the Hindu religion, but if a street urchin draws one on the wall, it just reflects an interest in his penis.'

However, there is no doubting that once primitive man realised that their *baton de commandment* was essential in reproduction, they really began to celebrate their manhood in pictorial and mythological form. The days of the previous matriarchal society were numbered as creation myths slowly came to concentrate on the male role in reproduction.

The Sumerians

One of the first documented examples of the ascendancy of the love muscle occurs five thousand years ago in the ancient Sumerian civilisation (situated between the Tigris and the Euphrates in what is modern-day Iraq). They had a god called Enki, who was known as a crafty god and a trickster (which makes me like him immediately – I love a crafty god, me) but Enki was worshipped primarily for his amazing cock.

This is a Sumerian hymn:

After Father Enki lifted his eyes over the Euphrates,
He stood up full of lust like a rampant bull,
Lifted his penis, ejaculated,
Filled the Euphrates with sparkling water.

Fantastic! That's what I call a hymn. It shits all over 'All Things Bright and Beautiful', doesn't it?[6]

Enki fills a river with his issue (no mere teaspoonful for him, fellas). But not content with creating the Euphrates, without missing a beat and with minimal recovery time he goes on to do the same for the river Tigris:

He lifted his penis, brought the bridal gifts,
Like a big wild bull he thrilled the heart of the Tigris as it gave birth.

He doesn't stop there either. He uses his spurting godhead to dig irrigation ditches (oh yeah, he's helpful), glutting the reeds with an overflow of sperm, creates sexual reproduction and creates the first human (not from dust, but from god-juice), before finally proclaiming,

'Let now my penis be praised!'

That is the kind of god I want to worship. No shame, no prudery. The churches would be full every Sunday, wouldn't they? Think of the sermons:

And Father Enki did say, 'I don't care if you covet your neighbour's ox. I
have but one commandment. Get down on your knees and worship this! It
can dig irrigation ditches.'

If only he'd thought to twist it into the shape of a hamburger, Enki might still be going today!

The moment I first read about Enki, I knew that his proclamation must become a rallying call of modern-day phallic worship.

---

6. *Although it does give cock celebration a go in that verse about 'the purple-headed mountain'.*

'LET NOW MY PENIS BE PRAISED!'

Surely that isn't a statement that should be restricted to masturbating supreme beings. It's not just the penises of the gods[7] that are capable of such creativity. We should all, men and women, be similarly awed by the everyday power of our own genitalia.

The Ancient Egyptians

The Sumerians weren't the only culture to acknowledge that God was a wanker. The Ancient Egyptians worshipped a deity called Atum, who didn't need six days to create the Universe. Six minutes would probably have been plenty for him. Hieroglyphics in the pyramids show him boasting:

> *'I created on my own every being. My fist became my spouse. I copulated with my hand.'*

It makes you wonder if the unsanitary conditions of any adolescent's bedroom could facilitate the spontaneous creation of life. Most of their duvets are practically identical to the primeval swamp.

But the Universe wasn't enough for Atum. Another Pyramid Utterance reads:

> *'Atum was creative in that he proceeded to masturbate with himself in Heliopolis; he put his penis in his hand that he might obtain the pleasure of emission thereby and there was born his brother and sister – that is Shu and Tefnut.'*

Shu and Tefnut must have had some serious psychological issues when they found out where they'd come from. That's got to be the ultimate hand-me-down.

One source even claims that the Egyptian god of creation recrafted the universe on a daily basis, by masturbating, swallowing his own sperm, and then spitting it out. A bas-relief on the walls of the Temple of Karnak suggests that he may have achieved this by sucking his own penis. So we now know how he would have answered at least one question on my questionnaire.

---

7. One of Erich von Daniken's less successful books.

Also at Karnak is proof that the penis was not just seen as a creative force, but one that epitomised the destructive power of masculinity. A Pharaoh called Menephta defeated the Libyan army in around 1300 BC and a victory monument was built which records the rather grim trophies that he chose to keep to commemorate his conquest:

Penises of Libyan generals:	6
Penises cut off Libyans:	6,359
Sicilians killed, penises cut off:	222
Etruscans killed, penises cut off:	542
Greeks killed, penises given to the king:	6,111

I feel sorry for whoever had to do the final count on that one. I can imagine him moving the penises from one pile to another, maybe losing count of the Greek penises halfway through and having to start again. Then getting angry when he discovers an Etruscan penis in the pile of Sicilian ones, 'Who put this here? How am I meant to work under these conditions?'

This ritual emasculation of every defeated enemy warrior (whether killed, injured or just captured) took its origin from the myth of Isis and Osiris. There's a few different versions of this story, so I'm going to try and give you the gist of them all.

The god Osiris was defeated in battle by his brother Set (sometimes Seth or Typhoon) and then cut into 13 or possibly 14 pieces. The bits were scattered all over the world, but then reassembled by Osiris's twin sister, Isis making the world's first mummy. She found everything but his penis, maybe because this had been thrown into the sea and eaten by a fish or alternatively by a Nile crab. Isis reconstructed a phallus, either by crafting a golden dildo or by turning herself into a hawk and then furiously flapping her wings to tease out a new penis. I've seen a lot of adverts for penile enlargement, all fairly fanciful, but none other that employs our feathered friends. I would not recommend it. The hawk might mistake your penis for a worm and it could turn into a gender realignment.

Now, somehow the reconstructed Osiris managed to use his bionic knob to impregnate his sister (I know, it seems distasteful, a woman having sex with her

COCKQUOTE

'He who is abstemious with his phallus, his name does not stink'

– *Ancient Egyptian wisdom text*

And nor does his phallus, presumably.

emasculated, zombie, mummy brother, but different rules apply for gods and apparently they'd already had sex in the womb, so after that anything goes) and the resulting offspring, Horus, then hunted down Set and cut off his knob in revenge. Apparently the fish and the crab got off scot-free (probably by each arguing that it was the other who was responsible).

This confused and insane story[8] was so important to the Egyptians that they re-enacted the event annually, and a gilded representation of Osiris's knob (150 cubits high, equivalent to half the length of Noah's Ark![9]) was carried through the streets by priests. It is my aim to see this tradition reintroduced. It would liven up the parade at your local fête, wouldn't it? I'm not proposing we bring back the enemy cock-cutting-off part though. Only because I know that I'd end up being the one who has to count them.

The extent to which the penis was believed to be invested with power is revealed by Sarah Dening in her excellent book, *The Mythology of Sex*. She writes that 'a sacred king, upon accession to the throne, had to eat the genitals of the one he had deposed in order to absorb the holy power they were thought to contain as a result of intimate union with the goddess-queen'. If only Clinton had known this, he could have claimed that Monica Lewinsky was attempting some kind of *coup d'état*.

---

8. *So much more ridiculous than the things that religious people believe today. In fact many elements and images from this myth resurface, slightly altered in the Christian religion.*
9. *150 cubits = approximately 225 ft.*

Ancient Britain

The ancestors of some of the biggest prudes ever to walk this earth were not against joining in with the phallic festivities. Standing stones and Maypoles both owe their existence to penis worship. I suspect that Morris dancers clacking their sticks together has some kind of homo-erotic cock-based significance, but if not then what are these ridiculous men, if not knobs personified?

But England is also home to what I have always considered to be the greatest cock celebration in all history, and the cover-star of this book, the Cerne Abbas Giant. Sometimes known as the 'Rude Man', his origins are shrouded in myth and mystery, though he may originally date from the Iron Age. Suspiciously, the first documented mention of the figure appears in the mideighteenth century and there is some speculation that the Giant is a sophisticated anti-Puritan hoax. It seems unlikely to me that such a late and sudden appearance would itself go undocumented and most historians agree that the figure is probably a representation of Hercules[10] dating from the reign of Emperor Commodus (AD 180–193).

Carved into the chalk bedrock on a Dorset hillside, the naughty hill-figure stands at 180 ft (60 metres) in height (with a penis that in human proportions comes out at an astounding 14½ inches. Moreover it is standing impossibly

COCKFACT

The Cerne Abbas Giant was camouflaged during World War II to stop German pilots using him as a navigational aid. I think it would have been better to leave him up there. The German pilots would have taken one look at him, thought that he was an average Briton and flown back home with their diminutive German tails between their legs, never to return.

Or maybe it wouldn't bother them; after all they didn't care that their leader only had one testicle.

10. *His cloak having faded into the hillside over the years.*

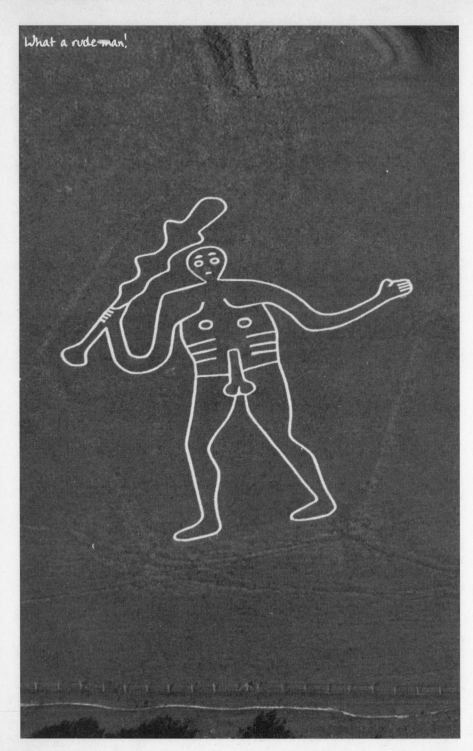

proudly, tight against his stomach and he's kept it like that for hundreds of years. Boy, his balls must ache).

He speaks of a more liberal England of yesteryear. A bloke proudly saying, 'Look at my massive cock, and if you don't I'm going to twat you with this club!'

I remember a childhood visit to Cerne Abbas and how shocking it was to see such a graphic image, so brazenly displayed. It was also funny and subversive, and I liked the idea of the joke stretching through the ages, linking me to my equally puerile ancestors. But there was a part of me that was intimidated (and not just because of the club). Raw masculine power combined with flagrant masculine sexuality. I was humbled and awed. When I began this project it was obvious that Rude Man would make the perfect figurehead for this rude man's campaign.

So imagine how disappointed I was to discover that prior to 1908 his cock was about six feet shorter than it now appears. Because the figure is cut into chalk, the lines have to be re-scoured every couple of decades or the grass grows back and the image disappears. Illustrations from before the twentieth century show him with a smaller (though still supernaturally erect) penis, topped with what is generally taken to be his navel.

So some early twentieth century wag (or incompetent) decided to incorporate the navel into the phallus and one of the earliest and most successful penile extensions has been performed (from 4.8 metres to 7.2 metres).

This seemed to make the carving less emblematic for me. A proportionately more average schlong is less impressive and less humorous and thus the camaraderie I felt with those randy Ancient Britons seemed to be lessened.

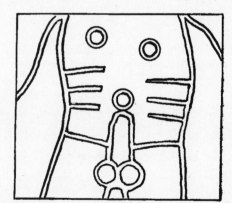 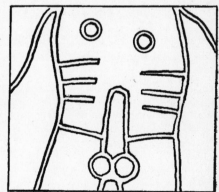

How to add 2.5 metres to your penis without surgery.

Yet looking at the before and after I begin to wonder if that really was his navel. It's awfully big (admittedly so are his nipples, but then he is aroused) and parallel with his ribs. Is it not more likely that what has been taken to be his navel is in fact an impressive bell-end (or 'bullet' to give it its correct scientific name)? We have already read about the cock that looked like a golfball on a stick. Is it possible that this is what we are observing here? Possibly our Herculean giant is still comically large and yet reassuringly unusual.

But even if we accept the truth, that the Giant is closer to the norm in the trouser department (not that he seems to care too much for trousers), it actually makes him a more fitting logo for Cock plc. He becomes a more realistic, less intimidating everyman figure (in all but the angle of his dangle) teaching us that it's not the size of your club, it's the way you swing it, baby.

In any case I don't suppose it matters how big he is or exactly when he appeared. Whatever the truth, for at least the last 350 years (and possibly for over 2,000) the citizens of that small Dorset town have ensured the grass never grows too long to hide the figure or his weapons. So their Jolly Green Giant greets each new day with his growing morning glory.

Nor has his virility diminished. Spending a night sleeping on the hillside (preferably within the borders of the phallus itself) is believed to help a woman conceive, something that can be precipitated by bringing your lover along and doing the deed there and then. No wonder the Rude Man is constantly and impressively erect with all that hot action taking place on his knob.

'Let now his penis be praised!'

Ancient Greece and Rome

It was the Ancient Greeks who had to take the penis celebration too far. Previous cultures had continued to worship female fertility as well as male. But the Greeks made masculine supremacy so complete that women's role in reproduction was demoted to the status of a bag of fertiliser in which the man planted his seed. This seed they believed was a miniature human, that was literally thrust into the furrow, where it grew like a plant. Aristotle likened man to a carpenter creating a baby from the wood that is woman, adding that, 'While the body is from the female, it is the soul that is from the male.' I bet the ladies loved that attitude. I wonder if the homosexuality that was rife in their society came about through choice or necessity.

In under 10,000 years human perception had been skewed from the belief that women were totally responsible for creating life to the 'fact' that men were. Inevitably such ideas were to have an effect on women's place in society (whether they were the cause or confirmation of a paternalistic society) and as you'll see they remained accepted, embarrassingly, until well into the nineteenth century.

The Greeks and the Romans were certainly not afraid or ashamed to revere the purple piccolo. Priapus was a god in both cultures, though embraced more enthusiastically by the Romans. He was dwarfish, with an ugly face and misshapen body, but he had a cock big enough to fill a wheelbarrow!

Which is possibly why they made him the god of gardens. Statues of the Priapus, sporting his enormous stiffy were put in Roman gardens, in the hope of discouraging thieves (I am imagining a pornographic version of Wurzel Gummidge here, and it's not his head that is interchangeable) and were usually accompanied by warnings in verse. Richard Zacks quotes this one in his delightfully rude book, *History Laid Bare*:

When you get the urge for a fig,
And are about to reach out to steal one,
Stare long and hard at me
And try to guess what shitting
A twenty-pound, two foot long turd would feel like.

Although sex and violence were often linked in the Roman psyche, an erection was also heralded as a tool of pleasure. Far from being indecent, they painted and carved tumescent cocks all over the walls of their villas, without so much as a PG certificate. As is seen in numerous statues and reliefs preserved by the volcanic ash which engulfed Pompeii in AD 79.

This is my favourite. Around that same image that has graced both cave and classroom, are the words 'Hic Habitat Felicitas' – *Here Lives Happiness.*

Fantastic.

And remember, you can't spell 'happiness', without 'penis'!

It is clear that up to this point in history the penis was seen as a thing of joy, not a source of male shame. So what's responsible for the change in the penis's standing? Why don't we celebrate it in the same way today?

Judaism

The seeds of change were sown in the strict sexual laws of the ancient Hebrews. The founders of Judaism were more patriarchal than the Greeks and Jewish law regards male genitalia with the highest respect. In fact it was seen as so divine that even to write its proper name might attract evil spirits, which is why the Bible refers to it as the 'thigh' or 'hollow of the thigh'. Solemn oaths were made while placing the hand upon the testicles (which is how we arrived at the modern word 'testify'). In Deuteronomy we learn that 'He whose testicles are crushed or whose male member is cut off shall not enter the assembly of the Lord' (which is really adding insult to injury) and also that a woman who makes a grab for a man's equipment should be punished by having her hand cut off, even if in doing so she was merely trying to protect him. Circumcision was, of course, an acceptable and necessary injury, and more than anything clearly demonstrates the connection between the penis and the divine in the mindset of the Jews.[11]

God had commanded his Chosen People to 'go forth and multiply' and the Jews took this very seriously indeed. Sex for them was primarily a function for creating children and so any aspect of sex for sex's sake was frowned upon. Masturbation, homosexuality and generally spilling sperm anywhere but inside a vagina were all taboo. In effect the penis became so holy that old-style celebration of it (or even deriving much pleasure from it) became blasphemous. The cock was becoming a victim of its own success. Graven images were a big no-no too, so the days of 225 ft cocks being paraded down streets were also numbered. Even stricter rules of morality developed to protect the bloodline of the wandering Jews. Much of this was, of course, at the expense of women, who were, for

---

11. See Chapter 4.

example, ordered to be shunned when menstruating (which shows a certain degree of wisdom in my experience). Patriarchy was now unshakeable and ordained by religious commandment.

Such laws perhaps made sense for the survival of a troubled community with no homeland, keen to protect their genetic identity, and one would not have expected these ancient edicts to influence almost the entire planet. But as Sarah Dening argues, 'These dour attitudes were later to become incorporated into Christianity and were a key factor in the Christian attitude of hostility towards the expressions of sexuality.'

Christianity

Jesus himself had nothing to say directly about the penis. Beyond promoting monogamy, yet still thinking it was a bad idea to throw stones at adulterous women, he didn't talk about sex much at all.[12] It was the people who popularised his ideas who really drove home that sexual desires were wicked and the penis was the instrument of that evil.

The fourth-century bishop Augustine was the prime exponent of anti-prick propaganda. Annoyingly he is one of those blokes who put it around a bit in his youth, then felt all guilty about it, so devoted the rest of his life to telling everyone else they shouldn't do what he'd done. His struggle between promiscuity and monogamy (not exactly a unique experience for a man) is summed up by the prayer he made, while still in his sharking phase, 'God grant me the strength to be chaste … Just not yet.'

He associated sex with guilt and considered the ultimate sin to be 'disobedience in the member'. So if you've ever got a spontaneous erection on a bus, or in your sleep or in your maiden aunt's drawing room, then you are a sinner, my friend. No wonder Hell is such a busy place.

If he had just been an ordinary bloke having these ideas, then Augustine might merely have gone on to create an early version of the 'Wicked Willie' cartoon, which would have given everyone a laugh for a couple of years, before

---

12. *Though he did encourage men to become 'Eunuchs for the Kingdom of Heaven'. Tragically on several occasions men have taken his (presumably) metaphorical words literally.*

The Devil tempts St Augustine with an early edition of Razzle.

deservedly disappearing into oblivion and no one would have thought about him again (except when saying, 'Remember that Wicked Willie thing? Shit, wasn't it.')

Unfortunately he was a bishop. Not just one of the unimportant ones who says stupid things and everyone ignores. He was extremely influential. And the older he got, the more stupid he became.

Eaten away with self-imposed guilt, Augustine advocated stopping having sex at all, and to him even doing your own wife was a sin. He wasn't completely stupid. He knew that without sex, there would be no babies, which is why baptism became paramount. Because genitalia, sperm and sex were all contaminated, the carnal sins of the parents had to be literally washed off the child with special magic holy water (or anti-cock potion, in this case).

You'd think someone would have stood up to this nonsense and bashed the bishop, and of course they did. Bishop Julian of Eclanum brilliantly and eloquently dismissed Augustine's view 'God made bodies,' he wrote, 'distinguished the sexes, made genitalia, bestowed affection through which bodies would be joined, gave power to the semen, and operates in the secret nature of semen – and God made nothing evil.'

Augustine agreed, arguing that it wasn't God, but the sin of Adam that had made all this stuff happen. Even a child could have seen that if God created everything from scratch, then he must have created Adam's propensity for evil, as well as the very concept of evil itself.

Unfortunately the only child available at the time was busy in the town centre pointing out that the emperor had no clothes on, so Augustine got away with it and somehow won the argument. Sworn off sex, Augustine had decided instead to fuck Western culture for the foreseeable future. The fate of the penis was sealed.

As Friedman puts it:

COCKFACT

In the fifteenth century in Arra in India, when men reached puberty, it was the custom to insert tiny bells under the skin of their penis. Any man who did not have these titillating bells would be shunned by the local women. Nicolo de Conti documented this practice:

Either gold or silver bells are bought, according to the rank of the person. The same women who sell them also attach them. They loosen the skin at several places, put the bells in and sew them up … The men decorated in this fashion are held in high esteem by the women, and when they walk through the streets believe it to be a mark of honour if the tinkling of bells is heard.'

This may have been the origin of the phrase, 'Pull the other one, it's got bells on it.'

Once honoured as the engine of life by the men who built the pyramids and the Parthenon, once revered as the god within by the desert tribe that gave the West monotheism and the idea of the Messiah, this sacred staff was toppled from its pedestal and erased from the Western cultural lexicon. In its place came the demon rod, the corrupter of all mankind.

The Middle Ages

Christian anti-cock attitudes did not put a complete stop to penile celebration. Fifteenth-century dandies even emphasised and enhanced their penises with brightly coloured codpieces though there is an argument that these came about in order to prevent the mercury-based unguents used to treat syphilis from ruining the men's fine clothing. People, quite clearly, did not stop having sex and there was certainly much decadence and debauchery still going on (ironically, yet typically, a lot of it committed by the very people who were telling everyone else not to do it).

Virtually all women found guilty of being witches during the Inquisition, along with all the other 'crimes' they admitted to under torture, confessed to having had knowledge of the Devil's penis. Most of these demon whores described Satan's cock as being cold, but beyond that it varied enormously. Some said it was the size of a donkey's knob and ejaculated a thousand times more semen that a man, it was often black in colour and could even be scaly like a fish. Occasionally it was forked and sometimes it was on his behind (as if someone had been playing a slightly unsavoury version of pin the tail on the donkey). These diverse descriptions didn't make people suspicious that the confessions had been forced. As Friedman concludes, instead they 'led a French Inquisitor to guess that Satan served some witches better than others'.

The Age of Enlightenment

One would have hoped that the triumph of science over superstition would rid the world of these ridiculous, judgemental and sexist perceptions about our genitalia. Unfortunately the 'enlightened' thinkers just made things worse.

In 1685, continuing the Greek idea of women as nothing more than grow-

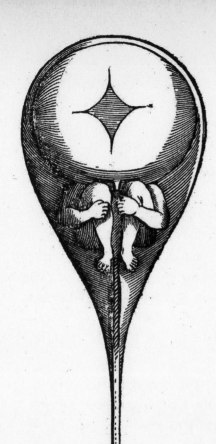

bags, Anthony van Leeuwenhoek declared that he believed there might be tiny preformed men contained in every sperm. Other scientists backed up his assertion, claiming to have observed sperm under microscopes and seen the tiny fellas (or 'homunculi') crouching inside their protective spunk-bubble, ready to be planted in their mums where they could grow into babies.

Even more embarrassingly, it wasn't until 1875 that Oscar Hertwig put forward the theory that babies were actually created by the fusion of sperm and ovum, something proven four years later by Herman Fol, using a somewhat more efficient microscope than his predecessors. As you will see in later chapters, the homunculi were one of the less stupid mistakes made by scientists and thinkers.

It is possibly rash to see a link between Fol's discovery and the rise of the Suffragette movement, but it might hold some indication of the subconscious effect this issue has had on us all. At the very least, the realisation of female importance in reproduction must have done something to raise the battered esteem of womankind.

A homunculus squashed up inside a single sperm. The original boy in a spunk bubble.

The Victorians

It may seem strange that Queen Victoria and her reign are associated with sexual repression. After all, she did have nine children, she must have been a bit of a goer. However, like Augustine, Victoria greatly enjoyed sex in her early life, but after the death of Albert, she turned to supposedly permanent celibacy and po-faced prudery (though rumour has it that she was secretly shagging Billy Connolly). As she outlived Albert by 40 years, her protracted mourning and inhibitions filtered down to the unfortunate populace. Even sex within marriage was frowned upon, which probably explains why prostitution flourished. The influence on the repressed Britain of the twentieth century is not hard to spot.

The modern day

Despite all the shame and confusion, early twentieth-century man at least had the comfort of knowing he was head of his household, and that men ruled the world. The glorious rise of feminism has seen those ideas kicked in the metaphorical nadgers. All those years of patriarchal rule, based on physical strength and a misunderstanding of the laws of reproduction, were coming to an end. Men were also being made to feel personally guilty for the centuries of female subjugation. They were being informed that they were all, at worst, potential rapists and, at best, the useless bit of skin attached to the penis. Religious shame was compounded by social shame, while at the same time men's traditional roles in industry were also being eroded.

When Lorena Bobbitt cut off her husband's penis, it served as a metaphor for the emasculation of the entire male sex in the late twentieth century.

COCKQUOTE

There are very few jobs that actually require a penis or vagina. All other jobs should be open to everybody.

Florynce R. Kennedy – civil rights activist

Not so much for John Wayne Bobbitt.

For him, it was more of a quite unpleasant experience.

But one that I am sure was lessened by his immediate appreciation of the metaphorical significance. And anyway he got to appear in some porno films, so I'm sure he wasn't that bothered.

The worm had turned as Bobbitt's worm was returned.

The cock celebration was over.

Reading back over this chapter, even as a man, it is difficult to feel much sympathy for the male sex and I am sure that many women are, at this point, sarcastically rubbing their eyes and saying 'Boo hoo!'

And while I am personally delighted that there has been a feminist backlash, and that the injustices of thousands of years of patriarchy are beginning to be undone, I don't believe the answer is to replace that patriarchy with a matriarchy.[13]

If you think about it, the thousands of years of belief that men were solely responsible for creating babies were preceded by thousands of years of belief that women alone generated life. The former belief is no more laughable than the latter (OK, it is maybe a bit more laughable, given the obvious origin of all babies, but you get my point).

The reality is that creating a child requires both a woman and a man (at least for the moment). The truth isn't a cue to stop celebrating the penis, it's a cue for us all to celebrate the creativity of our reproductive organs. If all along we had been praising Enki's massive cock, as well as the Venus of Willendorf's capacious cunt, then the world might not be in quite the mess it is at the moment.

This doesn't need to be a competition.

If we use contraception we can enjoy sex for sex's sake like our carefree and ignorant caveman ancestors. If we don't, we can create another human life. If there is a God then surely that is what he intended (unless he is both cruel and insane, as well as crafty). If you think that sex is some kind of corruption, then

---

13. *And nor, I believe, do many feminists.*

this world of rutting animals must be a very miserable place for you, but just close your curtains and pretend it's not happening.

Let's follow the lead of the students who were researching hill figures at Cerne Abbas in the 1990s. Realising we shouldn't be celebrating one sex over another, they provided the Rude Man with the Rude Lady that his tumescent member had been waiting for, for so many years.

POPSHOTS2

I asked men on the website.

HAVE YOU EVER FAKED AN ORGASM?
Yes: 1,161 (30.14%)   **No:** 2,691 (69.86%)   **Total:** 3,852

Thirty per cent of men admit to having faked an orgasm. Which many women might find surprising. Because the stereotype of men is that a gentle breeze can make us come. So why would we have to fake it if that stereotype were true?

Obviously it can be quite tricky for a man to successfully fake an orgasm (especially if he isn't wearing a condom), although one man did tell me of his 'friend', who was having sex with a lady from behind, it was going on for a long time. He knew he wasn't going to come. So he withdrew, and then to simulate orgasm … he spat on her back.

It's a beautiful, romantic story isn't it? Anything to save a lady's feelings.

Most of us are aware of premature ejaculation, which is most easily defined as reaching orgasm before your partner would wish you to. The Kinsey Report in the 1950s reported that 75 per cent of men ejaculate within two minutes of commencing intercourse. In Shere Hite's survey 21 per cent of men reported that they came within the first 60 seconds and 62 per cent would be lighting up their cigarettes within five minutes of starting.

Most doctors believe that premature ejaculation is habitual, and possibly learnt in adolescence by young men who are eager to come quickly as it lessens the chances of being caught. Like most bad habits it can be unlearnt. You can find some suggestions at www.embarrassingproblems.com. Here are a few of their tips:

Common-sense measures for premature ejaculation

● Have sex more often – you are more likely to ejaculate prematurely after a long gap.

● For the same reason, masturbating before intercourse may help.

● Use a condom to decrease sensation.

● Have sex with the woman on top – men are less aroused in this position than when they are on top ('missionary position').

● Learn to control your anal muscles. Contract your buttocks around the anus as if you were trying to prevent a bowel movement. Start by doing this ten times in a row, and increase to 50 times twice a day. Some men find either contracting or relaxing these muscles when ejaculation is near helps them to last longer.

● When your penis is first inside your partner's vagina, try to make shorter thrusts or a circular motion – this can delay ejaculation and you can then progress to the usual in-and-out technique when you and your partner are ready.

The website also has some squeezing exercises you can do to stop the flow!

Delayed or retarded ejaculation is not something that is mentioned so often, but possibly explains why some men need to fake their orgasms. Some men, while being able to achieve erection, will find it difficult to come. This can be due to the fact that men who are used to masturbating may find sex is not frenetic enough to bring them off, or it can be psychological and be based on anxiety or trust issues.

Again it is possible to overcome such issues. More foreplay is one sugges-tion. Some men need to be warmed up just as much as women!

3

FROM**TINY**ACORNS ...

We've seen that the people of the past had no problem with celebrating the penis. And we shouldn't be ashamed to celebrate it today. All of us. Men and women.

After all, we all owe our existence, in part, to a penis.

Every single person in the world began their life by shooting out the end of a cock.[1]

Which might not sound like something to be proud of.

But it is.

Each human being on this planet is the one out of up to 600 million sperm in the single ejaculation that created them, that made it to the egg first. Contemplate the incredible odds of your sperm being the one to make it. How unlikely it is that you should be here? [2]

And you can add to that all the billions of sperm that don't make it anywhere near their target. You could so easily have been one of oceans of sperm that end up in condoms, or handkerchiefs, or mouths.

---

1. *True at time of going to press. But any clones reading this book in the future may correctly feel that they have no connection to the penis at all. And if they are lesbian nuns to boot then they may well be right.*

2. *Then multiply that by the number of sperm that were in the ejaculations that created your parents, and your grandparents and so on all the way back through history when the first amoeba got fed up with living with itself and decided to get a place of its own. The chances of the relevant sperm making it to the relevant egg on every occasion to create you are astronomically huge. So why do people need a God to make themselves feel significant? How much more special and amazing do you want to be?*

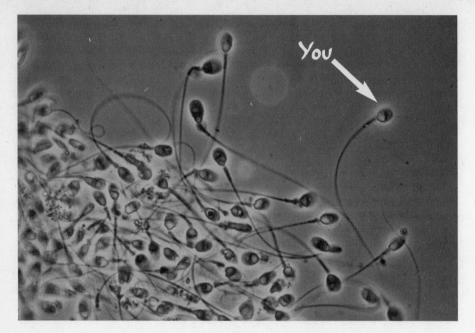

You

Or worse, spat out of mouths. Show some respect.

Or worse still, spat out of a man's *own* mouth. The indignity of it.

You might have been one of the unfortunate sperm that get wasted flying over breasts, chests, buttocks and faces … Though personally I hate to think of those sperm as a *waste*. I see them as more like 'suicide-bomber' sperm. Their sacrifice will never be forgotten. In fact, ironically, the memory of their sacrifice will be used at a later date, to send even more sperm, to an equally meaningless death.[3]

But none of that happened to us. We all shot out of the end of a cock and we lived to tell the tale. We won the cock lottery. We should be proud of ourselves and proud of the cocks that produced us …

Now, we've all just subconsciously thought about our fathers' cocks.

Our fathers' spunking cocks.

Not something you do very often is it? But why not? We should be giving thanks to our fathers' spunking cocks. They created us, they gave us life.

Let now their penises be praised.

---

3. *What we are doing there, fellas, we're satirising the futility of the whole Middle Eastern situation. Coming on your partner is a satirical act. Like something Rory Bremner might do (I mean being satirical, obviously. I am not in any way implying that Rory Bremner enjoys ejaculating over his wife or anyone else and would have no evidence to support such an accusation).*

COCK FACT

The average man will ejaculate more than a trillion sperm in his lifetime. That's 14 gallons of jizz! Given that sperm banks in the UK will pay you up to £15 a shot, you are sitting on a goldmine (though if you're literally sitting on it, you might find that the source of revenue might disappear).

The nausea and discomfort we now feel at the very thought of the specific magic wand that gave us life is not something that we experienced as children. Most men I have talked to admit to nothing but childhood wonder and admiration for their father's penis.

One of my earliest and happiest memories is having baths with my dad. I used to love having baths with him, which is weird, because I'd just find it embarrassing if we were to do it now.

But when I was four, it was the most natural and innocent thing in the world. We were men together and this was a rite of passage, which on some primeval level was a celebration of the bond between father and son.

But I couldn't get over how big his penis was, comparatively. It was like a sea-serpent, bobbing in the waves. Like a Cock Ness Monster, if you will.

I said to him, 'Why are you so big and I'm so small?'

He said, 'Because I am *better* than you.'

I said, 'Will I be as big as that one day?'

He laughed, 'No. You will always be tiny.'

He was right.[4]

We've already seen that as boys, far from feeling shame about our little acorns, we are instinctively rather proud of them. So are the negative feelings we later experience a result of nurture, rather than nature?

---

4. *In fairness to my father I should point out that this conversation (but only the conversation) has been completely fabricated by the author (though I am pretty sure this is what he was thinking). In fairness to myself, I should point out that the thing about my cock retaining its childhood dimensions is also inaccurate. It has, in fact, shrunk.*

Maybe the organ-obsessed psychoanalyst nutcase Sigmund Freud was right about one thing. Maybe the key to men's attitude to their yoghurt-spitting pythons develops in childhood.

Personally, luckily, I had a very happy childhood, though I have to admit that, while I am clearly not obsessed with penises now, I definitely was back then. Not only did I shout out the words 'willie' and 'wee wee' as often and loudly as I could (I can remember the exasperation of my parents at my favourite mantra, 'wee wee, poo poo, bottom!' I still can't understand their problem. It was very funny. But a lot of it was in the delivery[5]), I also used to walk shamelessly around the house naked, no matter what company we had, at many years older than would be considered cute.[6]

And I am not alone. Most men remember the simple pleasures their winkies gave them as boys:

● **I used to run around with my pants round my ankles shouting 'WILLIE-MAN!'**

● **I remember playing it like a guitar and dancing.**

I'd totally forgotten, I used to do that too. You'd stretch it out and strum and jive away. You'd be cocking all over the world. It was amazing, wasn't it fellas? It used to stretch for miles. Or maybe it just seemed bigger, because we were smaller. Like Wagon Wheels.[7]

● **At the age of five at dinner with the whole family, I walked in and**

---

5. *I've moved on a long way, haven't I, Mum and Dad? Who'd have thought I'd end up managing to turn that into a living?!*

6. *I still enjoy walking around naked in my flat, but now I live alone and am unlikely to walk in on my Aunty Jean having a cup of tea and a scone.*

7. *In actual fact Wagon Wheels biscuits were reduced in size in the early 1980s, which means this poor piece of observational comedy is not only hackneyed, but totally untrue. So next time you see a comedian making a joke about this, do be sure to shout out the truth to him (unless it is me doing it, because I already know. And although the audience may laugh when I do the joke in my act, you can be sure that inside I pity them for their stupidity and it is I who is secretly laughing the loudest).*

proclaimed, 'I love my penis more and more and more! (Haven't changed my mind yet, although it can be a bit more love/hate now!)

- I used to piss at the same time as my brother. We used to cross streams. This amused us.

- I used to pretend my penis was the gearstick to my dad's car and practise the gears while I was in bed.

As young boys we see the penis as little more than an elaborate and highly amusing plaything (does anything change?), but we are clearly aware of its comedy value. So how much of our puerile penile merriment is down to the ridiculous prudish attitude of adults? We know it's naughty to talk about them or display them, yet our young hearts tell us that these restrictions are wrong. How can playing your penis like a guitar and dancing be anything but a life-affirming delight? Of course the embarrassment of our parents merely makes our rebellion more amusing. One has to wonder if we weren't faced with this contradiction so early in our lives, would we still be finding the penis as funny as grown-ups? Is it the prudes' disapproval of the knob gag that actually perpetuates it?

Certainly some adults' responses to our childhood exuberance can be, at best, confusing and at worst psychologically scarring:

- My mother threatened to cut it off repeatedly in a joking manner, which prompted raucous laughter from both herself and my sister.

And presumably years in therapy for him, as for the man who said:

- I remember thinking, 'If God created me with a penis, what was so dirty about it? Why must it be shielded from view?'[8]

---

8. *If only that child had been there to back up Julien in his argument with St Augustine, history may have turned out very differently.*

● My father told me it would fall off if I kept touching it.

● When I was about seven, I remember watching *The A-Team* and one of the women on it was really attractive and I got a stiffy. I asked my Dad, 'What this? Why has it gone all hard?' and he told me that it was because I really needed to go to the toilet. So I went off to the bathroom and stood there for ages waiting to wee and I missed the end of *The A-Team*. Gutted!

Some fantastic parenting skills on display there! Although I don't think any of the men above have been damaged by their childhood experiences, one can imagine how associating an erection with urination could become a serious problem in later life. And although the father in that story is trying to save himself embarrassment, there's no need to lie to children about these issues. It's up to the individual to decide how much detail they need to go into, but I think the father in the next anecdote copes with the situation a bit more effectively:

● I panicked at my first erection – in the bath, forgotten what age – I called my dad in and he asked if I'd been thinking about women. He then said it happened to him too and it was nothing to worry about.

Being straightforward and nonchalant is the best approach according to most child psychologists. I am not denying that this is a difficult issue for a parent. As one mother told me:

● Getting the balance right as a parent can be tricky. On the one hand you're conscious that you don't want to make your child ashamed of their genitalia or give them a complex that will haunt them into adult life. On the other hand you don't really want them slapping it out on the fish counter at Sainsbury's every five minutes.

Clearly one needs to impose some restrictions for the sake of decency and hygiene!

Many men told stories of accident and embarrassment. Here are some of the more amusing (in hindsight) and bizarre childhood memories.

- **I used to hide Lego bricks in my foreskin.**

He doesn't say if this was for pleasure or security…. That's got to stop your sister playing with them.

- **The most embarrassing was finding what I thought was a serious illness at the age of seven, and presenting it, in fear, to a group of collected parents, cousins, aunts and grandparents. Turned out to be a bit of fluff from my pyjamas lodged in the end. Aaauuuggghhhh.**

- **Shutting the toilet seat on it when I was five … on purpose.**

The young Marquis de Sade there.

- **When I was six I had a 'pop gun' which fired corks (à la Christopher Robin). You loaded it by breaking the barrel across your knee, putting in a cork and closing it. I was in my pyjamas (swinging free) and I closed it and my foreskin got caught in the gun. Blood went everywhere. My mum threw the gun in the bin. I was gutted because I loved that gun. I wasn't particularly worried about my knob though at the time.**

- **For some reason applying aftershave at about ten.**

- **I remember being about nine, watching Morecambe and Wise on TV with my brother and sister, wearing my pyjamas. Suzanne Danielle was the guest on the show and was wearing a very short skirt and fishnet stockings and I got an erection which shot up through the fly of my pyjama bottoms. I remember my brother and sister and me all really laughing, especially when I commented 'Get down Shep!'**

Although many future problems can be nipped in the bud by talking openly and honestly to your child, I think it would be foolish to conclude that our child-hood relationship with our penises is entirely down to nurture. From a very young age, boys compete with their penises in ways that most certainly haven't been taught them through example.

Personally, I vividly remember having weeing contests at school. A whole row of boys would line up and see who could wee the highest up the urinal wall. (No shy bladders back then, were there fellas? Which is rather telling.) My oh my, how high we weed. It was incredible. Sometimes right over the top of the roofless urinal wall, which must have been a delight for anyone passing on the other side. It's weird though, I can't do that any more. Partly because, as you get older, the water pressure must change or something, I don't know, I can hardly hit the top of the urinal. And partly because if I go into the school toilet and challenge small boys to weeing contests ... It can lead to misunderstandings. The police become involved.

But there are myriad other ways in which young lads can try to establish a pecker-based pecking order:

- **We used to play 'see who can get the quickest erection without touching it' at night in the school dormitory. The winner was highlighted by torchlight.**

- Having a competition with a boy at school who could stick their finger furthest down their penis.

- My school buddies, all 20 of us, wanked off in the school showers together; we aimed to hit the soap bar on the floor with our cum.

- Having a hard-on at a Cub Camp during a 'show your willy' session in one of the tents and then having a brief 'sword fight' with one of the other boys.

- Games of 'goolie fight', with my best friend, which basically involved kicking each other's goolies.

- **Measuring it against the banisters.**

Possibly setting oneself an impossible goal there (depending on how big the banisters were).

- **I was the first kid in my class to get hairy! Hoorah – street cred at last.**

As many of the above examples clearly demonstrate, we soon develop sexual confusion to go alongside the confusion generated by the bizarre behaviour of our guardians. Again shame and taboo make the discussion of these feelings even more difficult and can lead to feelings of unnecessary guilt.

Like most people I remember playing 'You show me yours, I'll show you mine' with a girl from down the street. For me that girl was Susan Evans.[9] This was probably more out of anatomical curiosity than any kind of sexual interest, although we were aware even then that there was something more to it.

As I got older, I recall my bewilderment at some of the things I was starting to feel. At the age of seven, I remember thinking that if I got three wishes, one of them would be to have the blonde one out of Abba appear in my bedroom, just wearing her bra and pants. Yet I wasn't sure why I felt this, and didn't know what I wanted to do once she materialised (though I was pretty certain I didn't want her to sing 'Waterloo'). But I also got similar strange sensations in my stomach when I saw certain celebrities, bizarrely including Nana Mouskouri, the lead singer of Sweet (no, he had long blonde hair and he looked like a lady. I was confused. And Sweet were deliberately playing around with perceptions of gender and so that doesn't make me gay) and Barry Manilow (I have no excuse for that one. Neither in terms of my sexuality or my embarrassing taste in men).

I also recall having some horrible conflicted moments. As I said before, I was amazed and impressed by my own erection and for some unknown reason had a desire to show it to the world. So I would occasionally leave the curtains open in my bedroom (although I think I was always too ashamed and convinced of my

---

9. *Here and in the following anecdotes I have changed names in order to preserve the privacy of people who might not want their childhood foolishnesses printed in a book and sold to strangers!*

own deviancy to parade around for more than a couple of seconds, so no one ever saw). More shamefully, when I was ten, on the way to school, I asked a slightly younger girl (who I'd never talked to before, but who I passed every day) if she wanted to see my willy. Hey! At least I was polite enough to ask.

And it was quite romantic, though. I told her I was in love with her first. I think I'd been having a recurring fantasy about showing my hard-on to her in the long grass by the scout hut, but again with no notion of why I would do such a thing or of anything happening beyond the peacock-like display of cock. But unfortunately she didn't share my fantasy and she understandably ran away. In fact she crossed the street to avoid me for the next three years until her family moved away from the area (hopefully not as a direct result of that incident).

After that I spent years waiting for the knock at the door and the police coming in to tell my parents that I would have to be taken away for my perversity. I envisaged the prison van pulling away from the house, with me looking through the bars at the back to see my parents shaking their heads in disappointment, glad to be rid of their aberrant child.

Of course, while being a stupid and wrong thing to have done,[10] in hindsight it was clearly born out of naïvety and bewilderment about my unexplained, burgeoning sexuality. Again there probably isn't a man alive who doesn't have a similar story of secret shame:

- I can remember watching television in the late fifties, lying on the floor on my stomach while our family watched variety shows and my dick would get hard when some of the dancers would twirl and their skirts would billow up and show their panties.

- Playing 'doctor' with the girl across the street. I was caught eventually.

- Climbing a rope and getting a certain sensation ... typically, in front of the class, although they only noticed that I'd given up climbing halfway.

---

10. *And I'd like to apologise to that girl for any upset I caused her, as well as to all the women in my adult life who I have regaled with similarly crass chat-up lines. Amazingly, 'I love you, do you want to see my cock?' has been known to work in my adult life!*

WHAT DID YOU CALL YOUR PENIS ...

AS A CHILD?	AS A MAN?
Willy	Columbus
Baby Bear	Big Bear
King Henry	Peter Piper
Jeremy	Stevie
Bippie	Little Simon (my name is Simon)
Dinky	Ozymandius
Ping	Thumper
Wee wee	Mr Stiffy
Egbert	Sinbad
My secret	The old fella
Dinger	Sylvester
Loolee	The Captain
My tiddle	Russell the muscle
Budgie	Benson McCarthy
My penny	The Beast
Penis	Little Muley
Ding dong	Dr Wang
Smiley	Polyphemus, the giant Cyclops
My pee pee	Spence (I named it after one of my friends, in honour of him)
Toggle	The boss
Plumbing	Vlad ... as in Vlad the Impaler
Tail	Mein uberpenis
Bug	El Droolo
Winkie	Nothing. This seems to be something only straight men do.
Pipilin	Kipling (after Rudyard, not Mr.)
Elvis	Dave

- Dry humping a 'honey monster' teddy bear at about age ten.

- I remember showing it to five girls from my class at primary school – they went back and told the teacher – I was eight.

- Just lots of wanking. And rubbing it against Brian Whitehouse's cock.

- Got a blow job at 13 from a girl, she gave me a model airplane if I let her.

Well that's a win-win situation if I've ever heard of one.

- Wanking into a sock and thinking 'Christ, my Mum has to wash this!'

Not that that thought stopped him, though!

- Showing it to Sarah Dingford.

- I remember learning to masturbate at summer camp from other guys there, and being aware enough of my penis that I wanted to 'acciden-tally' have it be seen in public (like going to the window with my robe 'accidentally' opened).

Like many men will at some point in this book, I find myself thinking, 'Phew, so it wasn't just me, then.'

Again it is our difficult parental duty to walk the tightrope between discour-aging the more antisocial aspects of this behaviour, while still letting our chil-dren know that such notions are not unusual or unnatural. I think it is useful to recall our own confusion and misunderstandings, and attempt to help our youngsters through a very difficult time. If you're too shy or embarrassed to do that yourself then why not buy them a copy of this book! You'd better get them their own book, don't share yours with them. If they're anything like I was when I was an adolescent then their copy is going to fall open at the page with the naked woman on it. Or worse, not open at that page at all.

It is sometimes easy to forget, but our penises can be used not just for pleasure and pissing, but to help create another human life. How does this god-like ability make men feel? I asked men:

HAVE YOU EVER FATHERED ANY CHILDREN?
Yes: 737 (18.82%)   **No:** 3,179 (81.18%)   **Total:** 3,916

I asked:

HAS THIS ALTERED YOUR PERSPECTIVE ON YOUR PENIS? HOW DID HAVING CHILDREN MAKE YOU FEEL ABOUT YOUR PENIS?

Most fathers were overwhelmingly positive about the experience:

- Yeah, made me feel a man.
- It made it more important, as I realised its true purpose in life.
- My penis is not my whole world.
- I felt fertile and potent with a different kind of confidence after I had kids but after 20 years, I realise that it really was only a psychological hurdle that I passed.
- Proud. I feel I should spread my virility to the less fortunate. Maybe give a few eggcupfuls to charitable causes.
- Having kids meant to me that not only was my penis a wonderful source of personal joy but it also provided my wife and me with the fulfilment and love that can only be felt by someone experiencing the birth of children within a happy relationship.

Some men don't feel overawed by the creation of a new life:

- **No perspective alteration. Having the children did not cause any revelations about how they were made.**
- **Not really. Having two boys perhaps made me more aware of its size, as they constantly comment on it.**

While others bemoan what they have lost:

- **It hasn't altered my perspective, but after the children have arrived, I feel kind of sorry for my penis (and me) because sex with the missus is not as frequent as pre-children.**
- **I thought it would drop off once it served its purpose. Sadly it just sees less use.**
- **It made me learn a penis can be expensive.**

Children can be a cause of regret and mixed feelings:

- **Yes. Ability to change things in such a large way. Unplanned pregnancy; messed up relationship – I caused this with my penis. I still love my son – how can you not? But Christ, what a mess.**
- **Having children didn't change any thoughts of my penis except I should pull out sooner.**

Interestingly it helps some men to overcome any image problems they had previously:

- **Whatever it looks like, it works!**
- **Absolutely – I breed therefore I am. It may be titchy, but as the advert said, 'Small ones are more juicy!'**

4

THEFIRSTCUTISTHEDEEPEST

For one in five men in the world (some 700 million in total) the penis will undergo a rather significant alteration in infancy or childhood (and occasionally later in life), when they are the recipients of a surgical procedure known as circumcision. This entails the removal of part, or all, of the prepuce (what you probably refer to as the foreskin or, as medical science will soon be calling it, 'the Manhood Hood').

As an intact man this is not an issue I had considered very greatly before I decided to devote a year of my life to the penis. I remember when I was about 12, a gaggle of giggling girls at my school (who had clearly just discovered this new and rude penile variation) ran up to me and splutteringly asked, 'Have you been circumcised?'

At the time I had to confess that I wasn't sure. They decided this meant that I didn't know what the term meant and ran off laughing and trilling, 'Richard Herring doesn't know what circumcision is!' to anyone who would listen, even though they themselves had clearly only found out in the last 24 hours. Not that I'm holding a grudge or anything. The slags.[1]

In fact I was broadly aware of what the word referred to, but I was still confused over whether I'd personally been 'done'. I assumed that I hadn't and my parents had never mentioned it (though I wasn't convinced that that proved anything as it's not something they would have talked about), but I had

---

1. *Oh I waited, but now I've got my revenge on them in book form. I bet they're sorry now. Whoever they were. I can't quite remember. And nor can they probably. But still it's a moral victory.*

wondered if I had because usually my foreskin did not completely cover the head of my penis. I didn't know if this meant that part of the hood had been removed or whether I was just deficient in some way.

As I now learn, almost a quarter of a century later, this is fairly common (and I should stress that I did in fact work out that I was not circumcised some time ago[2]) so I needn't have worried. I suppose the story highlights both the reluctance we have to talk to our kids over such issues, but also how mysterious circumcision is. It is something that happens to us (usually) as babies and that we will thus have no memory of. Yet it can have repercussions upon some men that will last for their entire lives.

Since I'd established that I wasn't circumcised it hadn't been a subject that had taken up many of my thoughts. As far as I was aware it was merely something that some religions expected of their male members, and I didn't think it mattered much beyond that.

So when I started up my website questionnaire I was quite astonished to find out how contentious an issue circumcision is. Some men were furious that it was done to them, others claimed it was the best thing that ever happened to them in their lives (what lives they must have led).

The answers were varied, passionate and often contradictory, as you can see from this sample:

- I'm Jewish. It is fine. I'm not upset or anything. It's good to feel I'm part of a tradition.

- 'Routine infant circumcision' – in other words, there was NO REASON for it. If I knew who did it, I would kill him/her.

- Tradition. I love my penis the way it is. It is VERRRRY sensitive.

- Parents did it. I've had problems with delayed orgasm, I sometimes wonder if my penis would have been more sensitive if I were uncircumcised.

- My parents butchered me because that's what middle-class Americans do.

---

2. *I was 28 years old at the time.*

- Apparently my foreskin was too tight as a child so it had to go. How do I feel about it? Well, it's cleaner, I don't have a sensitive bell-end, and since most 'lifelike' vibrators are circumcised, I actually feel more 'normal'. My only regret is that when my mates at school found out (during a fit of 'be mature and honest and everyone'll be mature and understanding'), I got stuck with the nickname 'Rumple Foreskin'.

- Religious at eight days of life. I'm glad I am. I've seen studies and heard women comment that they prefer circumcised penises. I am a physician. I have many forthright friends. I've known many men who are hostile to the idea of circumcision. These men are invariably uncircumcised. I've never met a circumcised man who was hostile to the idea. I must conclude that the hostile men are all jealous.

- Family tradition. I feel very angry, abused, raped, insulted, cheated. Although I don't hate my (now dead) parents for it, I am still unable to forgive them doing that to a baby with no say in the matter. It's wrong.

- I am very pro-circ. So pro-circ, in fact, that I elected to have it done voluntarily only about 12 months ago after a lifetime of wondering what it would be like to own a circumcised penis. Having experienced both the cut/uncut state as an adult I know I have made the right choice, for me at least.

- I don't mind being circumcised, it's a lot cleaner, healthier, less smelly and less bother – I certainly am not worried whether a partner has a foreskin or not (as long as it's not rank under there!) But some people are very fussy and will not have sex with circumcised men.

- Done at birth. Women like it.

- Rapacity and idiocy of the medical profession who disregarded their ethic: Primum non nocere (First do no harm). I have never forgiven either my parents or the medical profession for condemning me to a third-rate sex life. I have now achieved some peace of mind from restoration, giving me a normal-looking foreskin, but without the vital nerve endings which were thrown in the bin 66 years ago.

- I feel girls like it more – cos I've sucked a guy's cock who hasn't been circumcised and it was pretty revolting. Turned me straight!

Hold on! Surely it's just a little flap of skin, isn't it? It can't be that important whether you've got it or not.

To attempt to make sense from this quagmire of emotion, we first need to understand how this practice began in the first place.

Having part of their penis cut off is not something that most blokes would queue round the block for. There are very few spam emails asking you if you would like to have the size of your penis decreased. So why did all this foreskin slashing start?

The simple answer is that the origins of circumcision are so shrouded in mystery that no one can be sure.

In the Western world we can trace the practice back to the Ancient Egyptians. A carving at the necropolis of Saqqara, dating from 2400 BC is the oldest surviving depiction of circumcision.[3]

The inscription on the bas-relief reads, 'Hold him and do not allow him to faint.'

As the circumcisee is a young adult, and from the obvious pain he is experiencing, we might surmise that the Egyptians saw the procedure as a rite of passage. Alternatively, it may have begun as a status symbol, possibly among the priesthood, but which was later adopted by the members of other élites.

But why cut off part of their cock? Who thought of that? And why didn't anyone else just say, 'No, let's not do that, can't we just demonstrate our higher status by wearing a special hat or having softer toilet paper or something?'

---

3. *Though mummified remains found elsewhere in Egypt show that the procedure was being undertaken at least 1,500 years before that date.*

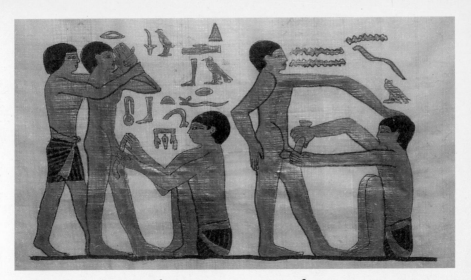

An artist's rendering of the Saqqara carving - forget the circumcision, what worries me is the length of the arm of the guy standing on the right..

David L Gollaher, in his excellent book, *Circumcision*, argues that the Egyptians were obsessed with bodily purity and that cutting off the foreskin would help limit the build-up of smegma, the unpleasant-smelling cottage-cheeselike secretion which appears under the foreskin if a man decides he doesn't need to wash his penis on a regular basis. Contemporary Greek historian Herodotus also suggests that cleanliness was the primary motive, sarcastically commenting, 'Other people leave their genitals as they were at birth,' but the Egyptians claim they 'prefer to be clean than of seemly appearance'.

The fact is any attempt to work out how or why circumcision began is based mainly on guesswork. Although we can trace Egyptian influence to the subsequent circumcision rites of Judaism and Islam, it is a practice that has emerged independently in several (but by no means all) tribal cultures.

Some Australian Aborigines cut the penis all the way up the shaft from the bollocks to the bell-end, opening the urethra (Gulliver's Hose). Some commentators believe by doing this they are trying to mimic the bifurcated or forked penis of the kangaroo; others that they see the bleeding that resulted as being akin to menstrual discharge, thus ridding the body of evil substances. Possibly, to some cultures the shedding of the foreskin may have been influenced by the way a snake sheds its skin.

Alternatively, notions of masculinity may have brought this weird ceremony into being. Removing the foreskin gives the impression that the penis is permanently erect and thus could be said to make a man more masculine. Alternatively it might be argued that early circumcisers of men and women were simply removing the parts that were reminiscent of the genitalia of the opposite sex. Hence women had their penis-like clitoris removed and men lost that somewhat feminine flap of skin. It is interesting and ironic that men so feared the idea of being mistaken as female that they were prepared to remove part of the male sex organ. Surely if men were confident of their sex and their sexuality such a bold statement would not be necessary.

In some cultures the removed foreskin is consumed after the ceremony. In Persia, for example, the mother ate it to ensure fertility, whereas in Mali several freshly harvested foreskins are ground up and added to a mixture which is then made into what you might call cock cakes. Three days later, the men who provided the secret ingredient get to consume these delicacies. It's a very elaborate way to end up with another man's dick in your mouth.

Whether such ceremonies were forerunners of our own Eucharist are lost in the mists of time, along with whatever insane reason or reasons our primitive ancestors had for voluntarily disfiguring themselves and their children.

Many people who are circumcised today are doing it because they believe they have been ordered to by God, as reported in Genesis:

> God said to Abraham, 'For your part, you must keep my covenant, you and your descendants after you, generation by generation … You shall circumcise the flesh of your foreskin, and it shall be the sign of the covenant between us. Every male among you in every generation shall be circumcised on the eighth day, both those in your house and any foreigner, not of your blood but bought with your money.[4]

As we've already seen, the Jews had good reason to distinguish themselves from other races in order to protect their bloodline. Clearly this penile adaptation

---

4. *You might wonder why God created the penis with a foreskin if he was just going to get you to chop it off so soon after you were born, but it is not ours to question His majestic wisdom. It's clearly because He is insane, so don't make a fuss or He'll get you.*

COCKQUOTE

'If God had wanted us to be uncircumcised, we'd all be born with foreskins.'

J. D. Ahmanson

would help this sense of identity, though it wasn't just the Jews who entered into this covenant. Abraham was the father of Ishmael, who founded the Arab nation. Consequently Muslims also practise circumcision.

One has to wonder if God was just dicking around with Abraham and seeing what he could get him to do. 'All right, Gabriel, just for a laugh, I'm going to tell him that if he loves me so much, he's got to cut part of his cock off. Ha ha, he'll never do that and … blimey he has. OK, I'm going to tell him he has to sacrifice his son for me, no one could like me that muc … In the name of Me, someone stop that lunatic!'

Tragically, history records numerous cases of this ease of identification being used against Jews in particular. Jewish legends tell of Roman soldiers dismembering Israelites, while they were still alive, and then throwing their severed penises skywards, shouting to the Jewish God, 'Is *this* what you have chosen?' In second-century Judea, mothers who allowed their babies to be circumcised were garrotted and then hanged upon crosses, with their strangled infants tied around their necks.

Given that so much of Judaism passed down into Christianity, you may wonder why the ceremony is not part of any Christian faith. After all Jesus himself was circumcised.[5]

The cut-off point (or not, as the case may be) came with St Paul's crusade to bring the new faith to the non-Jewish population. He realised that potential

---

5. *In the Middle Ages there were at least a dozen holy relics purporting to be part or all of the Holy Hood. One of them was used by Queen Catherine of England to ease her delivery pains as she gave birth to Henry VI.*

Greek and the Roman converts would find such an operation unseemly and refuse to have anything to do with a religion that practised it. Instead, employing spin that would even impress a New Labour government, Paul neatly claimed that the covenant between God and Abraham had been usurped and replaced by a new covenant between God and Jesus. Circumcision was thus an irrelevance that was no longer required. The Gentile vote was won!

Whatever you think about the origins of the operation, at the very least you can understand why Jews and Muslims continue to circumcise their children. Not only is it a tradition, they believe they have been ordered to do it by a Higher Being.

So why are so many men in the world today who are neither Muslim nor Jew circumcised? Why until recently were practically all American boys circumcised regardless of religion?

It is usually argued that the Americans embraced the operation for reasons of hygiene. A penis without a foreskin is easier to clean. But I ask you fellas, how hard is it really to clean a penis that has a foreskin? Quite hard judging by a lot of the comments I've had from women (and men) on the survey regarding oral sex.

That truly is disgusting. If you learn just one fact from this book, gentlemen, please let it be this:

WASH YOUR PENIS ON AT LEAST A DAILY BASIS!

If you remember that, then my work here is done and the women of the world should get down on their knees and show their eternal gratitude to me.

Don't worry, I practise what I preach!

It's true that some nineteenth-century doctors argued that germs harboured in the foreskin were responsible for rheumatism, asthma, liver disease, impotence, syphilis and cancer. A doctor called Lewis A. Sayre came to the slightly bizarre conclusion that removing the prepuce could cure paralysis, hernias and even constipation. I would guess if the surgery was performed without anaesthetic even the most bunged-up man would be shitting himself.

There was also a theory (championed by a physician called Peter Charles Remondino) that the foreskin (like the appendix) was a vestigial organ, a redundant by-product of man's evolution that now no longer served any purpose (he concluded that naked primitive man would have required it to protect his glans as he foraged around in the prickly undergrowth! Not something modern man had to worry about in most normal circumstances, unless he goes brambling in a nudist camp).

However, hygiene wasn't the main reason that circumcision became so widespread in the States. Somewhat tangentially, the surgery became so wide-spread in the hope that it would discourage masturbation. As you'll see in the next chapter, from the eighteenth to the twentieth century there was a belief among the medical community that taking part in Onan's Olympics would lead to moral, mental and physical decay. The Americans were particularly impressed by these arguments and, in an attempt to make it more difficult for infants to defile themselves instinctively, the foreskin was removed.

Circumcision came about, therefore, to stop America turning into a nation of tossers.

So that worked then.

Only in the last 20 or 30 years has there been a backlash against circumcision in the USA. As you can see from the responses from the questionnaire, it is a revolt of some pain and fury. Some men feel they have been mutilated and abused. Others argue that surgeons only continue with the practice because of the money they make from performing it. There have, it is true, been very occasional cases of circumcisions that have gone disastrously wrong, where more than the foreskin has been taken off, even occasions where the operation has

COCKQUOTE

'I think circumcision is a good idea ... However, it is not absolutely necessary.' (1946–68)

'I think circumcision is a good idea ... However, it is not necessary.' (1968–74)

'I strongly recommend leaving the foreskin alone.' (1985)

Dr Benjamin Spock, Baby and Child Care

been so botched that gender realignment has been necessary (i.e. a little boy has become a little girl). In the past doctors argued that babies were too young to feel or understand the pain of the operation (carried out usually without anaesthetic), although nowadays it is accepted that such arguments are nonsense. Nowadays many worry that it is not only physically painful, but psychologically scarring. Should the first experience a baby has involving its penis be pain? Marilyn Milos, a nurse who went on to found the National Organization of Circumcision Information Resource Centres (NOCIRC) in 1986, described the first circumcision she attended:

> *We students filed into the newborn nursery to find a baby strapped spread-eagle to a plastic board on a counter top across the room. He was struggling against his restraints – tugging, whimpering, and then crying helplessly …*
> *I immediately asked the doctor if I could help the baby. He told me to put my finger into the baby's mouth … He began to relax and was momentarily quiet. The silence was soon broken by a piercing scream – the baby's reaction to having his foreskin pinched and crushed as the doctor attached the clamp to his penis. The shriek intensified when the doctor inserted an instrument between the foreskin and the glans (head of the penis), tearing*

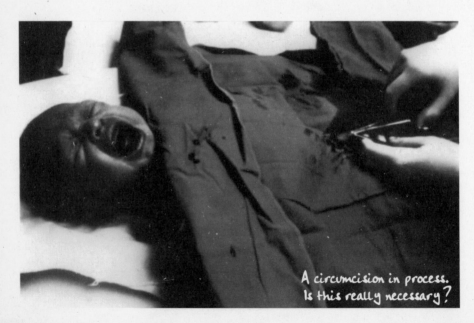

A circumcision in process.
Is this really necessary?

the two structures apart ... The baby started shaking his head back and forth – the only part of his body free to move – as the doctor used another clamp to crush the foreskin lengthwise, which he then cut ... The baby began to gasp and choke, breathless from his shrill continuous screams. How could anyone say circumcision is painless when the suffering is so obvious? My bottom lip began to quiver, tears filled my eyes and spilled over. I found my own sobs difficult to contain. How much longer could this go on?

During the next stage of the surgery, the doctor crushed the foreskin against the circumcision instrument and then, finally amputated it. The baby was limp, exhausted, spent. To see a part of this baby's penis being cut off – without an anaesthetic – was devastating. But even more shocking was the doctor's comment, barely audible several octaves below the piercing screams of the baby, 'There's no medical reason for doing this.'[6]

The language is emotional (possibly a little melodramatic), but she is at least accurate in her description of the procedure and it would be hard to argue against her desire that such an operation should not be performed on a child who didn't actually require it.

So is there any reason, beyond religious belief, to carry out this operation?

Is the foreskin a redundant and useless flap of skin?

No. It has several functions. It protects and lubricates the head of the penis (without the hood, according to some, the glans loses moisture and hardens and becomes less sensitive). The prepuce also contains many touch receptors and nerve endings, which supposedly make sex more pleasurable. Anti-circumcision campaigner Dr Peter Ball argues:

Circumcision has removed the most erogenous tissue of the penis. The fore-skin contains the Ridged Band.[7] *This structure, which is to be found just*

---

6. *Marilyn Milos, 'Circumcision: What I Wish I Had Known'; www.nocirc.org*
7. *See http://research.cirp.org*

*within the opening of the foreskin, generates voluptuous feelings as the fore-
skin moves over the glans.*

Some studies claim the foreskin helps to regulate the depth of penetration
during sex. It also helps the penis glide into its chosen orifice, rather than creating friction. However, I am not sure how significant these differences are.
Personally I have never noticed any great sensations emanating from my foreskin during sex and it is obvious that most circumcised men (and their partners)

A protestor from NOCIRC makes a valid point.

COCKFACT

Traditionally, as part of the élite, the male members of the British Royal Family are circumcised. However, Princess Diana declined to have the surgery performed on her sons. So Charles has been done, but William and Harry remain intact. It's the Roundheads and Cavaliers all over again.

have perfectly fulfilling sex lives. In fact, some women (and gay men) stated they preferred 'cut' partners (while some prefer 'uncut' and most don't really care). If there is a slight decrease in sensation when you're circumcised that isn't always such a bad thing anyway, as this man observes:

- **I understand the head of my penis would probably be more sensitive if I was uncircumcised … on the other hand, being able to fuck for longer is more fun.**

Is the surgery ever necessary for health reasons?

It is true that circumcised men very rarely get cancer of the penis. It is also true that cancer of the penis is an incredibly uncommon disease anyway. In fact it occurs so infrequently that it is difficult to come up with any valid statistics about it. There is evidence that it may be more prevalent in uncircumcised men who allow their penises to get especially dirty (wash them daily, have you got it?!) Gollaher points out that a lot of skin cancers develop on the nose, but we don't cut that off at birth to prevent their occurrence. The number of men who get cancer of the penis is around the same proportion as those that get their penises damaged in botched circumcisions, so what you save on the swings, you lose on the roundabouts.

Some people still claim that circumcised men are less likely to contract sexually transmitted infections. Older studies failed to take into account the fact that Jewish men tend to be more monogamous and better educated, and more recent studies have found that the issue makes no real difference, one concluding that

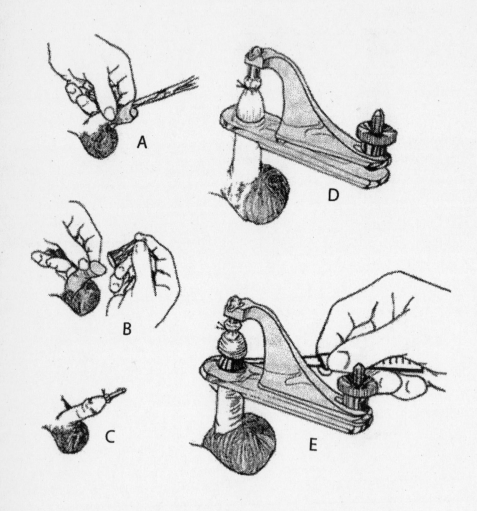

Circumcision made easy (or more terrifying depending on whether it's you having it done) with the Gomko Clamp.

'we found no evidence of a prophylactic role for circumcision and a slight tendency in the opposite direction'.[8]

A study in Africa in 1996 found that male circumcision did give some protection against HIV infection. This could possibly be because there is less skin and thus less vulnerable tissue and also because the glans will have hardened without the protection of the foreskin and be less likely to be injured. But the study was small and may have been influenced by cultural factors. It is certainly still possible to be infected with HIV if you are circumcised.

There are occasions when the circumcision is a surgical necessity. The adherence of the manhood hood to the bullet-head of the cock can be a problem for a minority of men. Circumcision can rescue them from a life of painful erections and urination. Yet it is worth noting that as babies we are born with the foreskin sealed on to our tiny acorn (it helps protect the sensitive bullet-head from the copious amounts of piss and shit that babies seem so fond of creating). For some years it can be tricky to pull back the hood of the pink anorak. On average, in fact, the foreskin is not fully retractable until we reach the age of ten.

Is there any health benefit in being circumcised at all?

There is, but not necessarily to yourself. Tissue scientists have found a way of using discarded foreskins to help heal wounds and provide grafts for burn victims. Steve Jones says 'a baby's foreskin placed in a nutrient solution grows to make a sheet of tissue, which, because it comes from a child whose immune system is not yet mature, is accepted by people in need of a skin transplant'. Marie Burke of Advanced Tissue Sciences boasts that 'With one foreskin, you can grow about six football fields worth of skin through current cell culture techniques.'

But then who wants to play football on a pitch made of skin? I think that's a misuse of ATS's resources and that they should concentrate on using it to cure burns and stuff.

---

8. *From tests carried out by Edward O. Laumann, a sociologist at the University of Chicago.*

I want my foreskin back. Any chance?

If you're really bothered about the loss of the hood to the pink cagoule, and you've got some time and patience, you can return to a semblance of your complete self, by restoring the foreskin. The National Organisation of Restoring Men (NORM) is one of many organisations devoted to recreating the prepuce. Dr Peter Ball who is a member of NORM UK explained how it's done:

> *The principle is that new skin can be grown by subjecting it to steady and prolonged tension. The facsimile of a new foreskin is produced by attaching adhesive tape[9] to the shaft of the penis and using this to pull the skin towards and eventually over the glans, until sufficient skin has been grown to cover it when no longer under tension. This takes from 1 to 2 years or longer. ... Restoration has transformed the lives of many men. They walk tall, have more confidence in social relationships and often a more successful and fulfilling sexual relationship. They can urinate in the stalls instead of retreating into the cubicles. Changing in public sports halls and swimming pools is done proudly and openly. Sex becomes a joyous and fulfilling experience.*

Like I say, if you're that bothered then stretch away. Personally I feel that the loss of this (not entirely insignificant, but not totally essential) flap of skin is not important enough to get this worked up about. You should learn to love whatever penis you've ended up with. I think we've already established that when it comes to the trouser trout there is no norm.

Dr Ball and his colleagues disagree and they are very sincere in their beliefs. If you want to find out more then visit *www.norm-uk.org*

From being fairly ambivalent about circumcision, after my research into this bizarre ritual, I do feel it is something that you should think very carefully about before inflicting it on your own child. At the very least you have to ask yourself, 'If I do go ahead and circumcise him ... where on earth is he going to hide his Lego bricks?'

---

9. *They never used it for this purpose on* Blue Peter.

Various pieces of apparatus designed
to help restore the foreskin. I could
tell you how each of them works, but
I think it's more fun for you to try
to figure that out for yourself!

At the end of the day it's a matter of personal choice (though not one that the person involved generally has any say in), but I don't really think it makes any significant physical difference if a man is circumcised or not.

Psychologically, however, it may do.

You only have to look at the vehemence of some of the men's testimonies earlier in this chapter to realise that. I have to say though that I find many of the anti-circumcision arguments slightly hysterical. For example, some of them attempt to equate the operation with the substantially more barbaric incidence of female circumcision. As this generally involves labial mutilation and loss of the entire clitoris I think the male equivalent would be loss of the entire genitals.

I also feel that the men who claim they hate their parents for allowing it to happen, or who wish revenge on the surgeons are failing to understand that everyone was merely acting on the information available at the time. They almost certainly thought they were doing it for the best.

What is particularly interesting for me for my Cock Trek (a one-year mission to boldly go where no man has been stupid enough to go before) is the way that the controversy over circumcision reveals just how much men identify and define themselves through their penis.

Gollaher argues that because nearly all American men were circumcised, in America the circumcised penis has truly become a badge of status and national identity. That's certainly backed up on the survey by some very sad stories:

- I wasn't circumcised, but I moved to North America in the 1970s, where/when approx. 95 per cent of boys were cut. I felt tremendously inferior and embarrassed when I found out and unfortunately my dad wasn't around to make me feel better about myself. Then I found out at church that even Jesus had been circumcised, and so I prayed nightly to be miraculously and painlessly made like all the other boys ... Sadly, for 20 years I kept my feelings of inadequacy hidden and tried several times to alter my own appearance by pretending in toilets and locker rooms to be cut. In the end, my foreskin lost its elasticity and I effectively circumcised myself. I'm rather embarrassed about it still. I'm somewhere in the middle.

I also got a response from an American man born in 1952 who had been circumcised, but whose penis still had the appearance of an uncircumcised penis (an occasional complication of the operation, sometimes referred to as 'concealed penis'). It maybe doesn't sound all that important, but because he was different from all the other boys in the locker room he spent a lot of his life feeling he was defective. This part of his story is particularly telling.

● **Shortly before my eighth birthday we moved to Taiwan. I was quite pleased to see that ALL the Chinese kids looked like me. Despite the fact that I am of northern European descent, my logic told me that since my parents could speak a little Chinese and I had a Chinese penis, then obviously I was a 'little bit Chinese'! OK, maybe I was not a very bright eight-year-old. However, the point is that much of my identity was defined by the appearance of my penis. For a while I did not feel as 'defective' as before.**

It's quite an extreme case, but I think, to some extent, that all men define themselves through the appearance of their penis. Any differentiation from the perceived norm (whatever that is in your culture and it can vary massively – the Ancient Greeks for example prized a slender penis above all others) is seen as being a bad, a shameful thing. The irony in this case is that the guy's penis just looked like a penis is supposed to look naturally. He says:

● **I wish that my parents had had the sense to send me to someone who could explain my anatomy to me. It could have saved me 30 years of worry and frustration.**

I think it's important that we all remember these words:

I've never seen a 'usual' penis.

But in remembering those words, we shouldn't forget these:

Wash your penis on at least a daily basis.

POPSHOTS4

I asked men:

 IF YOUR PENIS COULD SPEAK, WHAT WOULD IT SAY IN TWO WORDS?

Wash me.

More please.

Wank me.

Want vagina.

More! More!

Need piss.

Dirty bastard.

Let's wrestle.

Hello ladies.

Lemme out.

Thank you.

Looser pants.

You wanker.

Suck me.

Do her.

Feed me.

I stink.

5

SHAKINGHANDSWITHTHEUNEMPLOYED

We have already seen how confusing the sexual feelings that we develop around puberty can be. Luckily it is not long before adolescents discover a way to channel them.

We learn to bash the bishop, milk the one-eyed aphid, prime the spunk gun, choke the Chihuahua, whittle the gut stick or as the disingenuous language of science would have it, 'masturbate'.

This is a book which celebrates the penis, and masturbation is the ultimate cock celebration, one that can be enjoyed by any man, regardless of his sexual attractiveness, any time, any place, anywhere. It can turn any bedroom, toilet cubicle, hermit's cave or airing cupboard into a cock shrine. An altar on which to sacrifice your precious gametes to the Lord God Enki.

Given that there can't be a human being alive who hasn't, at some point, manipulated their own genitals for sexual pleasure, it is strange that we all still use the terms 'wanker', 'tosser' and 'python strangler' in a pejorative sense.

Most of us accept that it will not send us mad or blind or give us hairy palms and that it is in fact actually a healthy and normal thing to do. So why do the negative connotations still persist, and what is their source in the first place?

Perhaps the questionnaire can provide some insight into this.

I asked men:

AS A CHILD WERE YOU DISCOURAGED FROM MASTURBATING?

Yes: 681 (14.49%)   **No:** 4,019 (85.51%)   **Total:** 4,700

Unsurprisingly perhaps, older correspondents experienced more youthful chastisement (only 10 per cent of the under-20s admitted to having been discouraged, rising to 32.99 per cent for the over-50s) often from official sources:

- When I was a child it was common knowledge that it was bad for a boy to 'abuse' himself; blindness and hairy palms were only the start of it. But I was astonished when, during my National Service in the RAF in the late Fifties, we trainee wireless fitters were assembled for a lecture on the dangers of self-abuse by the Medical Officer!

- I recall archaic little pamphlets that had been printed during the war to encourage young boys to play manly sports rather than masturbate.

These older men are not alone – younger men also recall dire warnings of what would happen if they squeezed the salty salami:

- I was told that if you masturbate too much, you could get overly tired and not do well in school.

- They said it was bad and that you can 'get homosexual' by doing it!

- I thought that maybe it was wrong, because if you weren't liked at school people would call you a wanker.

Parents, it seems, were one of the top anti-wank propaganda merchants:

- I remember, lectures, scenes ... once my mother sewed up the fly of my pyjamas. She was off her nut.

- Parents tried to discourage the reading of dad's porn – oh, the hypocrisy.

- They told me I would go blind. It was not true. I just need very strong glasses.

- My mom told me my hands would rot off and that every time I masturbated it made Jesus cry … She freaked me out for a long time.

Jesus wept! And presumably, given the prevalence of tossers in the world, he has never stopped crying for a single second. He's bawling his eyes out as we're emptying our balls out.

Unsurprisingly, religious condemnation figured in the vast majority of responses to this question, the Catholic faith seemingly more disapproving than any other.

- Catholic parents put glow-in-the-dark Jesus by our beds just to remind us of the mortal sin we were so frequently committing.

- I went to a Roman Catholic school where not only the teachers but even the boys thought it was wrong. The boys used to say that your balls would not drop if you masturbated, as the weight of the semen pulled them down.

- I was told that it would bring on T.B. of the spine by clergy.

- For several years I masturbated only on Saturdays, because I was sure that God would punish me with a bad mark in school if I had masturbated the previous day. And after Saturday comes Sunday so he couldn't punish me.

Personally I think God may have been clever enough to be able to see through that plan and perhaps punish a Saturday transgression on a Monday. But then Sunday is a busy day for him, so he might have forgotten. That young log-flogger, however, was not the only one who foresaw dire consequences for his masturbatory habits:

- Due to the fact that I was brought up in a very religious household, I thought that wanking would have serious and disastrous effects on the ones you loved – e.g. car crash, etc.

Once again the penis becomes an object of totemistic power. Perhaps aware of the wrath of God, I myself recall going through a difficult couple of months when I was about 13. I became convinced that the world would end if I masturbated a hundred more times. Although this did cause me to cut down temporarily (to about eight times a day), I am ashamed to say that I put my own fleeting pleasure above the continuation of the human race and carried on regardless. God, in his wisdom, saw fit to spare you all.

One can't help thinking that over the years religious condemnation has just made people *more* aware of the practice of wanking:

- I was raised Catholic, and chastisement came from all sides, all the time. So naturally it was all I could think about.

Those naughty vicars certainly know how to get us going. And possibly themselves too. These next comments aren't untypical:

- The Catholic Priest used to make me feel guilty in the Confessional at church by making me explain in great detail what I did, whether I used pornography and what happened when I had an orgasm. (What a pervert!)

- As an enforced Catholic churchgoer in my youth, my priest Father Maloney would talk to the boys, warning us that we would burn in Hell! Didn't put us off though. Besides one of the lads had seen him doing it in the confessional.

You may be surprised to learn that the Christian Church and the Bible have very little to say on the whole subject of milking the cow with one udder. There is the case of Onan, the Biblical character who famously spilled his seed on the ground and thus gave rise to the posh word for wanking, Onanism. This is how Genesis tells it:

COCKFACT

I do have to warn any wankers among you that, according to some Eastern religions, masturbation is a form of psychic rape, because you're having sex with someone in your imagination without their consent. So if that bothers you, next time you are planning to use someone in your Onanistic fantasies, do make sure you ring them up first and get their permission for whatever scenario you are about to conjure up in your mind. I imagine your end of the conversation might go something like this:

'Hi there, it's Ian from Accounts here ... no, you've never met me, I've just seen you in the canteen ... yeah, I suppose I am the one who stares ... look, I'm a bit bored at work today, I was just about to have a wank ... the reason I'm ringing, I was planning on imagining coming on your face. Would that be OK? ... I see ... yeah ... all right ... calm down ... Fair enough ... If you prefer the tits, who am I to argue?'

COCKFACT

In 1012, Burchard of Worms listed the required penitence for 194 different sexual sins: those found masturbating were required to do penance of 20 days on nothing but bread and water.

Masturbation with a sex aid such as 'a hollowed out piece of wood or some device' received the same punishment despite being naughtier, surely.

To put that in context, wanking wasn't as bad as fornication with a nun which would get you a 40-day penance (small price to pay in my opinion), but was worse than having doggy-style sex which would get you a mere ten days.

It doesn't say what would happen if you masturbated over a nun, before having doggy-style sex with her, but my guess is you'd be on bread and water for at least 70 days, though with a good defence your punishments might be allowed to run concurrently.

And Judah said unto Onan, Go in unto thy brother's wife, and marry her, and raise up seed to thy brother. And Onan knew that the seed should not be his; and it came to pass, when he went in unto his brother's wife, that he spilled it on the ground, lest that he should give seed to his brother. And the thing which he did displeased the LORD: wherefore he slew him also.

But most commentators agree that he probably wasn't masturbating at all. The most common reading of the relevant passage suggests that Onan was shagging the wife of his dead brother, Er[1] and merely withdrew at the last minute.[2] Although God did not approve of such wastage of sperm,[3] I would argue that Onan was being quite responsible. He could easily have shot his load inside his sister-in-law and left her to cope on her own with any resulting offspring. Instead he did the honourable thing, curtailed his pleasure and pulled out just in time (even being respectful enough to come on the ground, rather than over the lady's belly. He didn't even wipe it on the curtains). To add insult to injury, he wasn't merely punished with death for this kindness, he has also gone down in history as the biggest wanker of all time. It's time for a reappraisal. Onan was a great bloke. Please name your sons after him. Don't worry, it's not like they will get teased or anything (no one reads the Bible any more).

While the church had always believed that every sperm was sacred (and yet at the same time strangely evil) there are very few examples of explicit references to the dangers or dire consequences of masturbation. According to

---

1. *That may have been his name, or possibly no one could ever remember what he was called – 'And this is … er…'*

2. *Or more interestingly he possibly chose to take her up the tradesman's entrance. According to Thomas W. Lacquer his real crime was not the spilling of the seed, but his blunt refusal to impregnate his sister-in-law Tarah, and thus take his place in the lineage that would eventually lead to the birth of the Messiah. He was shirking his duties and that's why God slew him. In the end Onan's dad Judah fulfilled the job that both Onan and his brother (whose name escapes me) had fallen short of. Don't you just love those crazy Bible days?*

3. *Even though He himself created a system where for every sperm that makes it to an egg, several hundred million more are 'wasted' and achieve nothing. If he didn't like wastage why not just make one super-efficient egg-seeking sperm of about the size of a trout, that doesn't ever die? It is not ours to question why.*

Thomas W. Lacquer in his academic tome *Solitary Sex – A Cultural History of Masturbation*[4] before around 1712 nobody was very concerned about wanking at all. We've already seen how it figured in the creation myths of early cultures, but to ancient Greeks and Romans it was seen as an activity that was not suited to a noble person, the humorous implication being that it was something one only did if they were unable to find a willing woman (or in the Greeks' case, young boy).

Lacquer argues that to Jews and Christians before the eighteenth century masturbation was only ever mentioned as a very minor sin, the fear being that the narcissistic practice of making love to oneself might somehow inevitably lead to homosexuality, in the same way that many reactionaries argue today that marijuana use will result in eventual heroin addiction. Possibly priests didn't mention it for fear of putting ideas in people's heads. Maybe they realised there was no point in preaching against something that everyone did, but which had no witnesses.[5]

I am not totally convinced by Lacquer's arguments, as it is clear that the Church has historically made people feel guilty for doing anything that was fun (especially if that fun involved the release of sperm). Friedman notes that there was a prevailing belief in the Middle Ages that sperm spilled through masturbation was used by Satan to impregnate women and create demons. Also equally worrying for the priesthood was the fact that there was no jurisdiction over what sins people committed in their imagination as they tugged one off. If to commit adultery in your mind was an offence to God, then how would he feel about your conjuring up an orgy involving all the women in your village as well as some of the livestock? For a priesthood that liked to control every aspect of people's lives, this freedom (as well as its implicit secrecy) must have been at least a worry.

---

4. Imagine writing a whole book about wanking. The man is obsessed. Obsessed, I say. At least I've only got a chapter on it. See, Mum, I know I'm not writing a book about Shelley like my schoolfriend Steve Cheeke, but at least I haven't spent years of my life producing a book about tossing off. Mrs Lacquer must be very disappointed.

5. If you want to find out about the history of masturbation in intricate detail (and one has to ask oneself why you would want to – I had to read it, I was writing this book!) then you'll have to read the whole of Solitary Sex. *To really appreciate it you should read it while alone.*

COCKSTAT

I asked men:

 HOW MANY TIMES A WEEK DO YOU MASTURBATE?

The highest answer given for this question was **322**, which sounds like a lie, but it's a suspiciously precise figure. Why would you make up that exact number if you hadn't been keeping a tally?[6]

The minimum number of weekly wanks was **0**.

I can only presume that that man's cock has fallen off at some point. Possibly that was the week after the 322.

The average number, funnily enough, came out at exactly **6**.

Well, even God needed a day off.

Lacquer is certainly correct that it wasn't until the Enlightenment that the extreme anti-wanking propaganda that still resonates today became prevalent.

I have to admit that I was astonished to learn that it was (once again) supposedly liberal philosophers and scientists, rather than religious zealots, who transformed the five-knuckle shuffle into an energy-sapping, brain-rotting, sight-impairing malady.

In the early eighteenth century a tract was published in London which, according to Lacquer, 'not only named but actually invented a new disease and a new highly specific, thoroughly modern, and nearly universal engine for generating guilt, shame and anxiety'. The pamphlet was called *Onania; or, The Heinous Sin of Self Pollution, and all its Frightful Consequences, in both SEXES Considered, with Spiritual and Physical Advice to those who have already injured themselves by this abominable practice. And seasonable Admonition to the Youth of the nation of Both Sexes.*

---

6. *Another correspondent claimed an average of 150 wanks per week, and reading the rest of his questionnaire I have to say I believe he is telling the truth.*

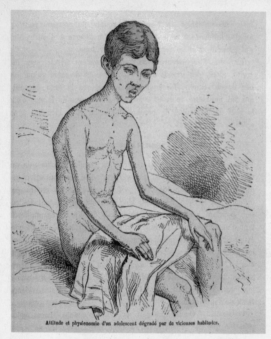

Attitude et physionomie d'un adolescent dégradé par de vicieuses habitudes.

N° 1

Representing the debilitated state of the body from the effects of Onanism or Self-pollution.

Some contemporary drawings show the supposed terrible effects of masturbation. At least the first fella's brought a towel to mop himself up with.

Possibly thanks to the catchy title the pamphlet was a massive success.

Part harbinger of disease and death, part titillating pornography (thus cleverly helping to spread the very disease it warned against), suspiciously the pamphlet was sold hand in hand with the medicine required to cure the many maladies that self-abuse supposedly caused. It was blatant and obvious quackery.

The Kinsey Report of 1953 concluded that 90–95 per cent of men masturbate in their teens and twenties. Kinsey claimed there was a minority of men who choked the chicken (not his term) more than 23 times a week, with no noticeable ill effects.

Considering this, it is amazing that over the next few decades the ideas in this ridiculous pamphlet were embraced by science and medicine. The work that would most influence thought on the subject was *Onanism: Or a Treatise on the Maladies Produced by Masturbation*,[7] written by a reputable Swiss doctor,

---

7. *He chose to go for a shorter title, which might be why he had more success.*

Samuel Auguste-Tissot in 1758. Friedman summarises the work, listing the consequences of self-pollution as a weakening of the digestive and respiratory apparatus, sterility, rheumatism, tumours, gonorrhoea, priapism (prolonged erection), and an often irreversible decline of the immune system, up to and including blindness and insanity. One of his patients dried out his brain so thoroughly via masturbation, Tissot said, it could be heard rattling around his skull like a rotten walnut.

Tissot's views were embraced by such luminaries as Rousseau and Diderot and his work became an international bestseller. One might wonder how such educated and enlightened men could make these nonsensical claims. The theory derived from a belief in the power of sperm. Perhaps noting how all men are weakened and lethargic after orgasm, it was a small leap to argue that the unnecessary and regular loss through masturbation will have a cumulative effect. Tissot called semen 'the most important liquor, which might be called the Essential Oil of the animal liquors'. He claimed that the loss of one ounce of semen was equal to the loss of 40 ounces of blood. How he arrived at such a spurious figure is not particularly clear, though one might observe that someone can bleed a fair amount before they collapse, whereas one good orgasm can usually do the trick. If you keep exhausting the supply before it could be replenished (which is obviously eminently possible through masturbation – how many men remember those glory days of youth when the sixth wank in an hour would seemingly produce little more than a spray of dust?), then you were heading for disaster. And according to Tissot, masturbation was 'more pernicious than excesses with women' because it relies on imagination, leading to overheating of the brain.

Tissot's views were particularly embraced by the Americans, which as we've seen in the last chapter led to the unexpected and not insubstantial effect of the routine circumcision of the Yankie whanger. There was another surprising influence on the diet of the Western World. John Kellogg theorised that bodily overheating could be kept in check by eating uninteresting and bland food. He invented Kellogg's Corn Flakes (and for similar reasons his contemporary Sylvester Graham came up with Graham's crackers[8]) in order to diminish sexual

---

8. *Graham controversially claimed, 'Health does not absolutely require that there should ever be an emission of semen from puberty to death ... though the individual live an hundred years.'*

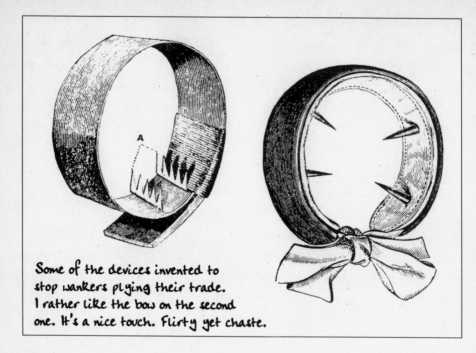

Some of the devices invented to stop wankers plying their trade. I rather like the bow on the second one. It's a nice touch. Flirty yet chaste.

feelings and masturbation. It is surprising that Kellogg's don't use this fact in their advertising campaigns.

'HAVE YOU FORGOTTEN HOW BLAND THEY TASTE?'

'KELLOGG'S CORN FLAKES. THE ONE THING GUARANTEED TO GET YOU DOWN IN THE MORNING.'

It is fittingly ironic that the logo for Kellogg's Corn Flakes is a gigantic cock.

Thankfully medical science eventually moved on from such theories (though as we have seen above, the rumours still persist to this day). The true cause of tuberculosis, one of the most commonly espoused consequences of wanking, became known. Neurology moved on and so mental disorders were better understood. It's also worth remembering that in the eighteenth and nineteenth centuries infant mortality rates were much higher. As these came down, it became clear that bacterial infections, not masturbation, had been the real cause of early youthful demise.

Guilt and shame still persisted well into the twentieth century, as did the old-age notions of masturbators being lowly perverts who couldn't get it

COCKSTAT

I asked men:

AT WHAT AGE DID YOU START MASTURBATING?
Max: 35   Min: 4   Total: 12.16

You might be surprised at how low the minimum age is, but the fact is that many of us (men and women) discover the pleasure of touching ourselves as babies. In fact ultrasound scans have revealed that some of us even begin playing with ourselves while still in the womb. Which rather puts paid to the argument that masturbation is something we learn through nurture. Clearly it is the most natural thing in the world.

Personally I am more astonished by the maximum age for this question. Thirty-five years of abstinence. I wonder what finally made him give in to temptation. Talk about back pressure build-up!

anywhere else. Freud added his unhelpful tuppence-worth. 'Masturbation,' he opined, 'contributes to the substitution of fantasy objects for reality.' This is rich coming from a man who believed that he lived in a world where all women envied men for having a penis.

Despite the proliferation and success of pornographic magazines and websites, many men still fear admitting that they have partaken of this harmless occupation. It is the self-love that dare not speak its name.

Perhaps it is the fact that we carry it out in private that makes the discovery all the more shaming.

I asked men:

HAVE YOU EVER BEEN CAUGHT MASTURBATING?
Yes: 1,614 (33.86%)   **No:** 3,152 (66.14%)   **Total:** 4,766

Which proves that two-thirds of men in the world have worked out how to use a lock.

Yet even those who are caught in the act will try to pretend there is a perfectly innocent explanation. Here are some of the more imaginative and improbable excuses:

- Aged about 15, I was at it in my bedroom when my mum burst in unannounced. I managed to cover up, but it was still pretty obvious that my jeans were undone. She asked, rather naïvely 'What are you doing?', to which I replied slightly weakly, 'Just tucking myself in'. Fortunately, she was too embarrassed to point out that it would be somewhat unusual to tuck myself in while lying spread-eagled on the bed.

- My mum walked in. Fortunately I was slightly out of her line of sight, kneeling on the floor behind my bed. She said, 'What are you doing?' and I said, 'Getting changed,' and she made a sort of sour dog face which meant, 'Yeah, right'.

- Mother saw the silhouette of me masturbating through the blinds of my bathroom window. My brother made an excuse for me ... he said I was texting on my phone.

- Female friend saw me through the window; I claimed to have been 'playing Tetris'.

I think we have just witnessed the birth of a fantastic new euphemism.

Of course for those of us in relationships, being found in the throes of self-fulfilment can be seen as a terrible insult.

- An ex-girlfriend walked in – she was a bit fucked off as we hadn't had sex in a while and took it as a sign that I was losing interest in her. I tried to explain that it had about as much significance as brushing my teeth.

It can be hard for a woman to realise that for many men, a wank is just a way of passing some time and is not necessarily a reflection on their sexual attractiveness. Surprisingly it's not just women who think this though. Men can be just as guilty of this jealousy:

- The only person who caught me has been my partner of nine years. It was soon after we'd started dating. He had a key to my apartment and showed up unexpectedly. I guess I was so into stroking my cock that I didn't hear him enter. When he walked into my bedroom and saw me masturbating to a gay porn mag, he was shocked and hurt. He wanted to be the only one to turn me on.

Occasionally we can be insensitive to the feelings of our loved ones.

- I was caught wanking by a girlfriend during the free ten minutes of porn on satellite. She was upset but I still finished. You only get ten minutes.

Some men had more understanding partners, and are possibly more secure in their relationships:

- My girlfriend saw me, lost her smile, and told me to go on as she watched.

- Girlfriend has caught me loads of times, which was nice!!! She always finishes the job off for me!

- Only by wife. She took over or made me cum over her bum.

Take note, jealous lovers. I'm guessing these guys will never leave their partners!

Perhaps what is challenging to the more insecure lover is the power of the masturbatory imagination.

I remember being asked by one girlfriend if I thought about other women while I was masturbating. I refused to answer the question for fear of incriminating myself. I didn't have the heart to tell her that not only did I do this, I also often thought about other women when we were having sex.

In any healthy relationship I think both partners have to understand that fantasy is a normal and harmless (and probably helpful) release valve. A person who is too insecure to acknowledge that you will never be sexually attracted to anyone else is deluding themselves. It's whether you act on that fantasy in reality that is the real issue. And I think if we're honest many of us would baulk from actually going through with most of the disgraceful things that our minds can envisage while in the grip of masturbatory reverie!

Yet, after all my research, what I find interesting is that for all the opponents of masturbation – whether they be priests or scientists, parents or lovers, insane psychoanalysts or manufacturers of tasteless cereals – the recurring reason for their objection is the power of the imagination. Practically all opposition is based on the inability of others to control what goes on in our heads. Our parents are uncomfortable with the idea of us approaching sexual maturity and will sew up pyjama flies to try and maintain our childhood innocence; the religious resent our ability to break every law in the book without fear of being observed; our lovers know we can betray them in our minds; even the liberal thinkers of the Enlightenment saw it as a challenge to intellectual purity. Perhaps the army in the 1950s continued lectures on the danger of self-abuse because it was the one arena that they could exert no control over their unwilling recruits.

So, ultimately, far from being physically or psychologically damaging, 'playing Tetris' is the ultimate expression of personal freedom. It is a private and harmless revolution against the restrictions of State, Church and Spouse.

While it is not as emotionally or spiritually satisfying as making love with another person and thus should not become one's only sexual outlet (for the record I think that 322 times a week should be considered excessive), it is nonetheless a great way to relieve the tensions of modern life and fill in the time between the end of *Neighbours* and the start of *The Simpsons*.[9] If nothing else it is great practice for when you get the opportunity to try the real thing (and even the most successful athletes have to practise every day).

Learning to love yourself is the greatest love of all. There's no shame in being a wanker.

---

9. *Or if you're a teenager the time between your eleventh and nineteenth birthdays.*

"IT'S MY LATEST INVENTION. YOU PUT YOUR WANG IN HERE..."

MENWILLFUCKMUD

However liberating masturbation is for the imagination and the soul and the testicles, for most men Madame Palm and her five daughters will never be quite enough. Generally men are on a constant search for something more satisfying.

I asked men:

 ## WHAT PLACES HAVE YOU PUT YOUR PENIS FOR SEXUAL SATISFACTION?

You know, I really wish I hadn't asked that question.

The very first person to respond to this questionnaire replied:

● **In a vagina … Where else is there?**

I wish that unimaginative man could read the 5,000 answers that immediately follow his, perhaps answering his question in a bit too much detail. Here are just a select few, a *pot pourri*, if you will.[1]

● **A milk bottle.[2]**

---

1. *To be honest, I am surprised that pot pourri isn't included here.*
2. *For aficionados here's a more detailed version from someone else:*
Empty milk bottle filled with warm water. Inserted flaccid penis and allowed it to harden inside neck of bottle and proceeded to masturbate into bottle and water.

- In a shampoo bottle.

- In a glass of wine.

I believe this is known in the trade as a *cock au vin*.

- Raw steak.

- Jelly spooned into a toilet roll.

Now I don't know about you, what delights me about that answer is that the jelly is very specifically spooned in. You can't pour it in just before it sets. That wouldn't work. The consistency would be all wrong! You can't scoop it in with your hands. You don't want to get jelly all over your *fingers*. That would be disgusting. You have to spoon it in with a spoon. The more I think about that answer, the more I get a very clear mental image of the bloke actually doing that. There's a look of anticipation, maybe even frustration, on his face. He's been waiting a while for that jelly to set. But now he's going to show that jelly who the daddy is.

- In a Hoover.

Oh, of course, in a Hoover, we've all done that.

- Between a mattress and the metal frame of the bed.

Which comes up disturbingly frequently.

- Through a hole in the fence.

Everybody needs good neighbours.

- It's been rubbed against a whole variety of surfaces – trees are quite nice.

- On ice cubes.

- Pot of honey, etc.

I just like the etc. on the end of that one. As if 'pot of honey' is normal and automatically suggests all the other places he's used.

- Various teddy bears as a child.

Various ones. Not all of them, some of them he didn't fancy. He doesn't want us thinking he's a teddy bear whore.

- Loo rolls ... Not very good.

Of course not, he forgot to fill them with jelly. A schoolboy error ... Don't forget, you have to use a spoon to get it in there though!

- Inside the top of a novelty shaped bubble bath ... (it was shaped like the children's character, Noddy).

As if that additional information somehow excuses his behaviour. 'He was looking at me with those big eyes, his bell. What man could resist?' It makes it worse that he's a Noddy, he's just a little boy. If it was Big Ears then that would be fair enough. He knows what he's doing and he clearly wants it.

- My fella's mouth, hand, arse ... and even once or twice in a ... oh God I can't say it ... a v..vv..vv...vagina.

Out of all this long list it is ironic that only the vagina seems to elicit any shame!

- The back of a folding metal chair.

Dangerous, but not as dangerous as:

- In a car exhaust pipe.

- Inside a child's buoyancy aid.

That's an armband. I'm hoping to God that there wasn't a child in it at the time.

- Into a toilet roll with the inside lined with sandpaper.

Otherwise known as a 'Dick Emery'. I can understand why you'd want to put it in a jelly-filled toilet roll if you'd tried the sandpaper version first.

- In a hollowed-out cucumber.

I think that one disturbs me the most. What kind of world is it where a man hollows out a cucumber … not the strongest of vegetables even when it has its filling in it … in order to make (presumably) gentle love to it? Was there nothing else more suitable? Could there be anything more inappropriate and against nature?

- Small melon with the seeds taken out through a hole, then filled with Swarfega. Heard someone say it was good … but it wasn't.

In answer to my own question, apparently there is.

- Everywhere I can think of without hurting it.

By which I think he means his penis rather than the receptacle. So I wonder if he'd put his in:

- A food mixer.

- Blow up doll, pocket vagina, my hand, a snowball, my beagle licked it when I was young.

- My sister's knickers (I was quite young and she wasn't wearing them).

Then no one can claim you have done anything wrong!

- Into the bottom of a Vosene bottle (neatly cut off and moulded over the kitchen stove), with a little soap for lubricant.

That's not one that you just chance across, is it? You don't trip and fall on to one of those. That's years of experimentation, leading to what I'm guessing is the perfect simulation of the vagina. If that news gets out, ladies, then you might become obsolete. But buy shares in Vosene. You'll be sitting pretty.

And perhaps most worrying for me:

- Rubbed against my computer screen, while filling in this questionnaire.

Oh dear God, no.

I could fill this entire book with the answers to the 'where have you put it for fun' question. There are thousands more, but I'm going to spare you the terrible details of what I have had to endure on your behalf, the psychological scarring. I've stared into the abyss. Knowing that someone, somewhere has probably tried to put his cock in it.

As the results of the questionnaire rolled in, my initial response was horror, as well as a mixture of laughter, disbelief and disgust. The list seemed to confirm the stereotype that when it comes to sex, men are worse than dogs (though some beagles are just as dirty apparently) and that Lenny Bruce summed us up perfectly when he said, 'Men Will Fuck Mud'.[3]

I certainly had never anticipated such a rich variety of answers, possibly because aside from the usual human orifices the only other slightly unusual

---

3. *To which I reply that Les Grey was quite attractive when he was younger and I wouldn't mind having a go at the one with the long hair and the big earrings who dressed like a woman (as you might have guessed from my previous revelation about Sweet) but I wouldn't touch the others with a bargepole.*

COCKFACT

The average speed of ejaculation is 28 mph and the furthest medically recorded ejaculation is 11.7 inches. Though I'm sure I used to do a lot better than that as a young man. I seem to remember hitting the ceiling a couple of times.

Girls, there's only 36 calories in a teaspoon of spunk, making it an ideal snack for anyone on a diet.

place I can remember putting my penis for sexual satisfaction was when I masturbated into a condom as a teenager (otherwise known, of course, as a 'posh wank').

This happened when I was around about 14 and my mates and I discovered a broken condom machine in a local pub toilet that was dispensing its contents for free. I returned home with a pocket bulging with prophylactics. One of my friends told me that wanking into a condom was exactly like having sex, so I gave it a go ... several times (which was just as well, because those condoms would have passed their sell-by date long before I ever got a chance to use them for their intended function). It is only in hindsight that I realise how wrong my friend was, although it is true that I learned the value of practising safe sex even when working alone.

Considering the bizarre admissions from the survey more carefully, one realises that men have put their penis into everything that could possibly accommodate a penis (as well as many other things that couldn't possibly accommodate a penis, but have been made to accommodate a penis, nonetheless). As a rough estimate, I would say 80 per cent of the 4,790 men who answered this question have put their penis somewhere that might be considered 'unusual' for sexual satisfaction. How many of the others neglected to mention or had forgotten some weird peccadillo of youth? If such a vast majority of men have experimented in this way it ceases to be a catalogue of perversion, rather one of normality.

Clearly, we are naturally predisposed to attempt to achieve sexual satisfaction in whatever manner we can (and many of the above ideas are triumphs of the imagination), at least when the ultimate prize of a willing human partner is unavailable to us.

So while a man who can only become aroused by having sex with a car exhaust pipe might need to seek some professional help, a man who gives it a go (in the privacy of his own garage) is at worst going to realise that his cock isn't quite as big as he imagined (although if the engine is running it could conceivably be more serious).

None of the above examples directly affects another human being, so why are such stories frowned upon? And why do the unfortunate men who end up at Casualty with a Hoover attachment attached somewhere to which it was never meant to be attached attract such universal derision? Are some men laughing a bit too hard and thinking 'there but for the grace of God'? Is their only crime to have been caught?

And where is the line drawn that makes one sexual act normal and another perverse?

Of course, our political and religious leaders have historically had much to say on this, setting down the limits of acceptable behaviour in religious law, legal statute or merely in speeches and sermons.

Yet one doesn't have to look very far to see that many of these pillars of our society were flouting their own rules in ways that their public could never imagine (and how many others got away with it without being found out?)

Suetonius in his *Lives of the Caesars* reveals that:

Nero practised every kind of obscenity and after defiling almost every part of his body, finally invented a novel game: He was released from a cage dressed in the skins of wild animals, and attacked the private parts of men and women who stood bound to stakes. After working up sufficient excitement by these means, he was dispatched – shall we say? – by his freedman Doryphorus.

Nero smiles to himself as he imagines a new act of sexual depravity that he can commit with a harp.

Bishop Johann Burchand attended a party held by Pope Alexander VI (otherwise known as Rodrigo Borgia) on 30 October 1501 at the Apostolic palace, where among the guests there were 50 prostitutes and where prizes of silk mantles, pairs of shoes and headdresses were given to those 'who had carnal knowledge with the greatest numbers of courtesans'. That's a party held by the leader of the Christian Church. Hypocritical? Is the Pope Catholic? Suddenly that becomes a difficult one to answer. Not in his sexual tastes apparently.

Let's face it, modern history is littered with priests caught fiddling with themselves or their choirboys and 'family-values' politicians cheating on their wives or swallowing oranges and choking themselves to death for sexual kicks.

Does church or state have any right to pontificate or legislate against any kind of consensual sexual behaviour in any case?

Until shamefully recently, homosexuals were imprisoned in the UK for their sexual preferences (witness the tragedy of the disgrace and demise of Oscar Wilde) and round the world gay men are still persecuted and killed by people who are in no way affected by their actions.

In the early nineties a group of British men who enjoyed nailing their penises to pieces of wood were imprisoned for the practice (though one has to question whether sending sadomasochists to prison is any kind of punishment at all). To me the crime is its own punishment, but if those men wanted to do that then I think they should be allowed to. We don't imprison the millions of people who chose to harm themselves daily through the use of alcohol or tobacco.

Surely what we choose to do in the privacy of our own homes, alone, or with consenting adult partners, is no one's business but our own.

Equally though, are there not some sexual practices which are unquestionably morally wrong?

Bestiality, for example.

The Bible is very clear on the issue. Leviticus states 'if a man lie with a beast, he shall surely be put to death: and ye shall slay the beast'. That seems a bit rough on the animal who is surely the wronged one in this case.

But other cultures while not exactly approving of love between man and beast, have been prepared to make exceptions. A Hittite law tablet from around about 1400 BC details the punishments for sex with various different animals. Before you read this, it is worth remembering that horses were the main form of Hittite transport. And that the Hittites would often travel vast distances with only a horse for company:

> If a man does evil with a head of cattle, it is a capital crime and he shall be killed.
> If a man does evil with a sheep, it is a capital crime and he shall be killed.
> If anyone does evil with a pig, he shall die.

If a man does evil with a horse or mule, there shall be no punishment.

If an ox 'leaps at' [i.e. attempts to mount] a man, the ox shall die, but the man shall not die. A sheep may be proffered in the man's stead and they shall kill that.

If a pig leaps at a man there shall be no punishment.

Again a bit unfair on the sheep that had nothing to do with the ox's crime and there is a clear double standard that neither the pig nor the man (nor even so much as a sheep) dies if the pig does the raping. But it's clear that animal sex hasn't always been a completely cut and dried moral issue and also that it has always been reasonably common if it needs to be legislated against in such enormous detail.

COCK**FACT**

According to the Kinsey Report, 26–28 per cent of American males had masturbated animals while also masturbating themselves. This figure rose to an astounding 65 per cent in some areas of Western United States.

Just as straight men are prepared to indulge in gay sex when locked up in prison, why do we not accept what the Hittites clearly knew thousands of years ago. If a man has nothing but an animal for company for a long period of time, there is a point where that animal is going to start to look attractive to him.

Yet bestiality is illegal and people are still sent to prison for the crime, which is weird as millions of animals are murdered and eaten every single day and no one gets into trouble for that. It's obvious that there's a double standard when it comes to animals. Killing and eating, OK. Fucking – absolutely not. Kissing – all right as long as it's a dog, cat or pony. It would be easy enough to construct a philosophical argument that denied there was anything immoral about bestiality, just as most of us can comfortably justify imprisoning, killing and eating them.

Indeed there are people who seriously argue that it is possible to have consensual sex with animals, such as the anonymous author of the website www.dolphinsex.org (go and have a look. There are no unpleasant images and I am pretty sure that no one can arrest you for just reading it!)

While I acknowledge there is a possibility that this site is a spoof (but if it is it is one written by someone who has thought the mechanics of making love to a dolphin through to such a degree that one begins to assume he must have actually done it), I have no doubt that there are men in the world who genuinely believe in the sentiments expressed within it.

The creator of the site describes himself as a Delphinic Zoophile and defines zoophilia as 'a love of animals so intimate that the person (and the animal) involved have no objections to expressing their affection for one another in a sexual fashion'. He adds, 'This is not to be confused with bestiality, where a person forcefully mates an animal, without their consent, and with no mutual feelings whatsoever.'

It offers advice on how to sex a dolphin and how to masturbate them and (in the case of the female dolphin) how to go about having sex with them. Consensually, remember. It also advises you to remember to cuddle them afterwards and show them you care, 'Like a way of saying that this wasn't a one-night

A dolphin yesterday. Look at the little minx. It's asking for it, quite clearly.

fling.' Which is good advice for any sexual relationship, really. Even if it *is* just a one-night fling.

There are also warnings. Although you can lick a dolphin's penis while masturbating it, you mustn't have your face in the way when it comes because the force of ejaculation is so strong that 'a male dolphin could snap your neck in an accidental thrust, and that would be the end of the relationship'.

It should be noted that when looking for a dolphin partner 'Aquariums are a bad choice … Too public, the dolphins are not in their natural habitat, night visits are impossible, etc, etc.'

But are dolphins intelligent enough to make a rational judgement about consensual sex, or are they in fact just animals, freed from constraints of morality, and thus seemingly happy to go along with something that is physically stimulating? To be honest it is such a palaver to have sex with a dolphin (as you'll see if you read the site) that one would have to question the sanity (and desperation) of anyone who decided to make them their sexual partner of choice.

Personally, I believe the anonymous amphibious mammal lover is fooling himself. Both in his assumption that a dolphin can consent to sex and in his wish to have sex with a dolphin in the first place. But at the very most I would only suggest he seek counselling to see why he wants to do this. I don't think he's hurting anyone, except possibly himself (I mean psychologically, rather than through dolphin ejaculation-based injury).

Perhaps in a hundred years' time, the persecution of zoophiles will be seen as similar to the treatment of homosexuals in Victorian times.

But probably not.

Whatever the truth, the author seems sincere in his beliefs when he concludes:

> *You should love a dolphin, not because of the sexual relief they can provide,*
> *but because they are a unique animal, one of the few wild animals that seek*
> *the company of man by their own initiative. This is special. Do not abuse it.*

In his mind at least, what he is doing isn't immoral.

Personally I believe that bestiality is strange and cruel and that anyone who thinks animals are capable of consent is deluding themselves. The point is that morality is a man-made concept, and there are no rules handed down to us from a higher authority. We need to make our own decisions as a society about what is acceptable and what is not.

Clearly there are some sexual acts that a civilised society must legislate against. Just as it is in the interest of us all to live in a world where our instinct to kill people we don't like is made illegal, we must have laws to protect exploitation of the innocent and of those unable to make their own decisions, as well as to prevent anyone being coerced into participating in something they don't want to do. I don't think it's too much to ask that society should expect people to express themselves sexually in private (though I suspect most of us have got carried away at some point and at least put ourselves in danger of being discovered).[4]

If I want to staple my penis to an oven glove, cover it in Angel Delight and then stick it down the neck of a frozen chicken, then no one should be allowed to stop me ... I don't want to do that though. And I never have done it. And anyone who says that I have and that they have got photos of it, is lying.

Morality is clearly a shifting entity. To the ancient Greeks, for example, sex between men and boys was not only legal, but institutionalised and encouraged among the élite. Pythagoras, Socrates and Plato were among those who saw nothing morally wrong with pederasty. Though I am happy to use Pythagoras's theorem, and employ Socratic irony and watch Plato in those Disney cartoons, like most people in the modern world I find their sexual activities abhorrent. Yet to them it was normal.

Obviously we have to make decisions about sexual boundaries based upon the world that we live in today. So, just as we can reject the excesses of the Greeks, we should not live our lives by a sexual code that was largely designed by a tribe of wandering Jews anxious to preserve their bloodline. We can make our own rules. And they should be rules which allow sexual autonomy in all instances of consensual sex with adults.

To end this chapter I think it is fitting to relate one more astonishing case of how far men will go for sexual satisfaction.

---

4. *And didn't that make things even more exciting!*

You'd imagine that when you've spent the best part of a year thinking about cocks, reading about cocks, looking at pictures of cocks in various states of arousal or disease and reading thousands of responses to a long questionnaire that you've set up which is all about cocks, you would pretty much know everything there was to know about cocks. That there wouldn't be a function or a use or a sexual preference that hadn't at least crossed your mind.

But you'd be wrong.

In the late stages of writing this book I was perusing some new cock-sources at that font of penis knowledge, the British Library (though they keep the really dirty stuff separate and you have to view it at a special table, so it doesn't infect all the nerds who are researching fourteenth-century hats, who are quite clearly all virgins), and chanced across a use of the penis that had never even fleetingly occurred to me. I was reading a book about penises (good) and vaginas (no interest to me. I don't want to look at pictures of vaginas. It's cocks that I like ... on a purely academic level ... oh, I'm so confused), called *Skin Flutes and Velvet Gloves*. This was written by a Dr Terri Hamilton. (I was reading it under duress because at the time I firmly believed that there should be a law that people called Terri can't become doctors. I believe there may be such a law in the UK, but this Terri comes from America.)

It is a good book, packed with facts, many of which by this stage were familiar to me. But then, on page 66, I read about something so unexpected and new to me that it sent my mind spiralling. It was this:

Approximately 1 in 100 males is capable of self-penetration (inserting his penis in his own rectum).

Well, bugger me!

Surely not, I thought. That can't be possible, unless your penis is about 25 inches long and curves down and around on itself like an inverted jester's shoe. I mean, how would it even work if you could get it all the way round and in? Surely you couldn't thrust backwards like that? Could it be anything approaching fun to do so (unless you were turned on by your genitalia being in extreme agony)?

Let's just suppose there is some freak in the world who can manage that; surely he is alone. This can't be a 'gift' given to one per cent of the male population. Have one per cent of the male population even considered it as a possibility and attempted it? If only I had asked that on my questionnaire (but at the time I'd felt like I was pushing back the boundaries of imagination by asking if men had ever tried to suck their own cocks).

Later on the very same day, I read about a documented case of what I now learnt was called auto-eroticism. You wait a year for a story of self-buggery and then two come along at once.

I was reading *The Male Member* by Kit Schwarz who related the story of Dr Mikhail Stern, a Russian psychiatrist imprisoned in Kharkov in the late 1960s. One of his fellow prisoners was an auto-sexual – 'a man whose penis was both flexible and rigid enough that he could insert it in his own anus, and by contracting his anal sphincter and his groin and buttock muscles could bring himself to orgasm'. Dr Stern commented that the auto-sexual was 'virtually autistic; he says very little or nothing at all, and he rarely seeks out the company of his fellow inmates. He lives in absolute solitude but never seems affected by his loneliness.'

Well I guess if you had that as your party trick you wouldn't have much call for friends. Quite possibly they wouldn't really want to hang around with you. 'Oh yes, that's my mate. Yes, the bloke sitting on his own penis and rocking back and forth. He's great.'

Even with this additional evidence I still found Dr Terri's bold assertion somewhat implausible. There was only one thing for it. I would email her and ask from what source she had derived this information.

Thanks to the wonders of modern technology I had my reply within 48 hours. Here's what Dr Terri had to say:

As to the reference for the self penetration figure — btw, the practice is technically referred to as 'autopederasty', and involves pushing aside the testicles and stuffing a well lubricated semi erect glans into a well lubricated anus – my first citation of the figure dates back some 25 years to a workshop with William Hartman, Ph.D., a noted sex researcher in Southern California (I did my first round of sex therapy training with Dr. Hartman and his partner, Marilyn Fithian). It was an entry among other notes involving various unusual physiological 'acts and antics', including fisting, self fellation, etc. Hartman and Fithian did quite a lot of research in their own lab, and also had associations with Kinsey, Pomeroy, and other pioneers of the time, so I'm not sure if it was based on their own work or derived from other existing data. The figure has also been cited by 'penis researcher' Gary Griffin in his books (Penis Size and Enlargement, etc.).

The citation mentioned in the Schwartz book actually refers to a very rare type of autopederasty ... a man who not only could get his penis in his anus, but could also bring himself to orgasm. Be aware that men who can do the former (more than a few) generally cannot do the latter (hardly anyone!)

What a fantastic woman. I take my previous Terri prejudice back and will take this opportunity to recommend that you buy every book she has ever written and visit her website at http://www.terrihamilton.com

And if you try to bugger yourself and get into trouble, then blame her, not me.

A better man than me summed up the message of this chapter in only 15 words and without direct recourse to swearing or discussion of dolphin-fellatio when he said, 'Judge not, lest ye be judged.'

And added, 'Let he who is without sin cast the first stone.'

It's amazing how many of the people who follow everything that guy said (some of them almost religiously) seem to forget those central tenets.

I've always found it interesting that even Jesus (yes, that's who it was, in case you hadn't realised) didn't feel he was in a position to cast that stone.

So why do we continue to judge each other?

'Men will fuck mud.' Let's not use that to abuse them or call them perverts if they do. Let's use those words in a positive way. Let's accept that it is an inclination in all men to satisfy themselves sexually by any means necessary. And let us celebrate the fact that most of rise some way above our base urges and refine our sexual behaviour so that we largely have sex with human beings that we love. And failing that, a Vosene bottle that we have a lot of respect for.

POPSHOTS5

I asked men:

WHAT IS YOUR SEXUALITY?

Straight:	3,611 (69.26%)
Bi-sexual:	659 (12.64%)
Gay:	944 (18.11%)
Total:	5,214

So approaching 20 per cent of men said they were gay, which is higher than other surveys on this subject (suggesting gay men are more inclined to fill in a questionnaire about cocks). Almost exactly one in eight men admitted that they were playing for whichever team is winning at the time, one man claiming:

● **I'm not actually gay, but I don't mind helping them out when they're busy.**

But seven-tenths of men are straight down the line, completely straight, one hundred per cent heterosexual. They've never had a gay experience, never had a gay thought, never had a gay bone in their bodies ... quite literally.

It seems that for most straight men, the idea of being perceived, or mistaken for a second, as one of the gays would be the worst thing imaginable because it somehow brings their masculinity into question.

Despite the fact that 70 per cent of men have tried to suck their *own* cock and that 99.99 per cent of them spend an hour a day playing with their *own* erect penis, to share those things with someone else would be embarrassing. Of course!

I might be wrong, girls, but most of your boyfriends are obsessed with getting you to have anal sex. Do you recognise this phrase, 'Can we just give it a go? It is my birthday! Oh go on, just the tip.' But to do those things with a man would be unnatural. Unlike heterosexual anal sex as nature intended.

The only reason straight men are so vociferous and outspoken about this issue is because we know in our hearts that there's a part of us that is gay, there's a part of us that is at least curious, there's a part of us that has probably experimented to some extent. I think it's just sad that we can't admit that, that we carry on with this macho charade and feel unable to admit the sexual duality within us all. It's pathetic.

For example, I had a taxi driver the other day ... well, I didn't have him. I'm not gay ... I was in his cab and the driver said to me:

● **That George Michael, all that money and he still chooses to put his cock in a man's hairy arse.**

As if George Michael's sexuality was somehow a financial issue. As if before he was famous, he was in his bedsit, having anal sex with a man and thinking, 'God this is disgusting, I'll be glad when I have some money and can stop doing this for fun!'

What really interests me about the taxi driver's statement is that the arses in his anecdote are very specifically 'Hairy'. He's really thought the scenario through in quite some detail, hasn't he? A suspicious amount of detail for someone who wasn't interested in taking part in the act.

He's thought, 'Urgh, having sex with a bloke ... well it might be all right actually, it'd probably be the same as having anal sex with a woman. Possibly better, because a man would be more muscular, you'd have more to push against and ... oh no hold on, there would be more hair. A man's arse would definitely be more hairy than a woman's arse. It might have 50 more hairs on it ... although the hair might improve things. I don't know, the friction might make it better. If you got bored you could at least stroke it ... But the hair might make things worse, that's what I'm worried about ... Yeah, well, I suppose if I was rich, I could afford to buy a razor and then make my decision once I got there.'

I have to say I envy gay men their sense of identity. After years of being judged and literally condemned for their sexuality, they've reached a point where they know who they are and what they want. And they don't give a fuck about what anyone else thinks about them. They have a pride that I think is lacking in most straight men at the moment.

Self-respect. Self-belief. Self awareness.

Surely these are the things that make you a man regardless of whether you choose to put your dick in a woman or in a man or in a Noddy-shaped bubble bath. As long as you've got your self-respect.

In terms of this book all gay men are cock heroes. This project is all about celebrating the penis. Not content with celebrating your own cocks, you want to celebrate everyone else's as well.

I salute you, fellas, for your commitment to the cause. Every struggle needs extremists.

7

THENAUGHTYNAZISALUTE

I've been thinking a bit about that hollowed-out cucumber from the last chapter. Do you remember it? I was quite dismissive of it at the time.

But I suppose the positive thing about making sweet love to a hollowed-out cucumber is that it isn't going to get upset if it fails to arouse you.

Of course not. Because the cucumber is aware it is of a different genus to you. You're not supposed to find it sexually attractive, so it won't be offended.

Don't get me wrong. The cucumber is adventurous. It'll give it a go. It'll say, 'What? You want to hollow me out and have sex with me? OK, why not? I'm game for anything. I'm a cucumber, my life is quite dull.'

But if you both give it a go and you can't get an erection, the cucumber will be philosophical. He'll say 'Well, to be honest, I'm not that surprised. I thought it was a slightly queer notion when you mentioned it. The way I look at it, I'm a vegetable, you're a mammal. I would say our love was never meant to be. Why don't we just go back to using me in salads as before? We *both* enjoyed that.'

Unfortunately, the same can't always be said of human partners.

I asked women:

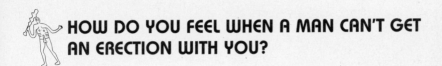 **HOW DO YOU FEEL WHEN A MAN CAN'T GET AN ERECTION WITH YOU?**

Some blame themselves:

- I feel I must be fat.

- Worried, self conscious, undesirable, ugly.

- Honestly? Deeply unattractive. Like he finds me repulsive.

- Like ending my life.

- Gutted. Feel very unattractive. I once heard about this bloke who was giving it to some bird from behind, who put a copy of the *Sun* on her back so he could get hard looking at Page Three girls. I'd rather a bloke just left than do that.

Some women, on the other hand, blame the men:

- I think he must be gay.

Of course! That's the only possible explanation. What he was doing naked in your bedroom in the first place, God only knows!

- He's a prat who's out of touch with his feelings/reality.

- I feel fine, but I think 'What a loser' about him.

- He's being lazy.

One respondent was simply incredulous:

- Hard to believe. I have 48DD tits.

Whereas others see the positive:

- Time for a blow job.

- Hey it's cool. I like it when it's soft, to play with and check it out.

- Try harder! If still unsuccessful shrug it off and get the toys out.

- I imagine I would feel it's time to have a sandwich instead.

I was disappointed to see that a few women were totally unforgiving:

- I will dump that boy.

- He exists no longer.

- Murderous.

Yes, threaten him with death. That's going to get him bouncing back!

Though most were kind enough to acknowledge the debilitating effect of intoxicants:

- If he had drunk 15 pints, I don't think I would be so upset.

- I shouldn't have bought him so many drinks to get him into bed.

- Guilty and unattractive … unless he's drunk or stoned in which case I think, 'Nice going, asshole.'

- Mad that my boyfriend has snorted all the coke without me.

A few women made rather sweeping judgements which show a misunderstanding of the psychology of erection:

- Utterly devastated. You can get stiffies at the most inopportune moments – why not in bed with me, dammit?

- I feel like there is a medical reason for this.

- He's not in control of his body.

- It only happened once, and I blame the Scandinavians.

What all of them? I wonder what they did.

Some are perhaps too knowledgeable:

- I'm a neuropsychologist, so know the plethora of reasons why this can happen. But you can hardly say, 'Don't worry darling, this is simply a result of the fact that your peripheral nervous system isn't functioning correctly ...' Now get down there and lick my minge.

Oh, no, sorry. She didn't actually say that last bit about the minge. She should have said that. She should have *just* said that.

And some women are less sensitive about it, such as the woman who simply wrote this:

- Ha ha ha ha ha ha ha ha ha ha ha ha ha ha ha ha ha ha ha ha ha ha ha ha
ha ha ha ha ha ha ha ha ha ha ha ha ha ha ha ha ha ha ha ha ha ha ha ha
ha ha ha ha ha ha ha ha ha ha ha ha ha ha ha ha ha ha ha ha ha ha ha ha
ha ha ha ha ha ha ha ha ha ha ha ha ha ha ha ha ha ha ha ha ha ha ha ha
ha ha ha ha ha ha ha ha ha ha ha ha ha ha ha ha ha ha ha ha ha ha ha ha
ha ha ha ha ha ha ha ha ha ha ha ha ha ha ha ha ha ha ha ha ha ha ha ha
ha ha ha ha ha ha ha ha ha ha ha ha ha ha ha ha ha ha ha ha ha ha ha ha
ha ha ha ha ha ha ha ha ha ha ha ha ha ha ha ha ha ha ha ha ha ha ha ha
ha ha ha ha ha ha ha ha ha ha ha ha ha ha ha ha ha ha ha ha ha ha ha ha
ha ha ha ha ha ha ha ha ha ha ha ha ha ha ha ha ha ha ha ha ha ha ha ha
ha ha ha ha ha ha ha ha ha ha ha ha ha ha ha ha ha ha ha ha ha ha ha ha
ha ha ha ha ha ha ha ha ha ha ha ha ha ha ha ha ha ha ha ha ha ha ha ha
ha ha ha ha ha ha ha ha ha ha ha ha ha ha ha ha ha ha ha ha ha ha ha ha
ha ha ha ha ha ha ha ha ha ha ha ha ha ha ha ha ha ha ha ha ha ha ha ha
ha ha ha ha ha ha ha ha ha ha ha ha ha ha ha ha ha ha ha ha ha ha ha ha
ha ha ha ha ha ha ha ha ha ha ha ha ha ha ha ha ha ha ha ha ha ha ha ha
ha ha ha ha ha ha ha ha ha ha ha ha ha ha ha ha ha ha ha ha ha ha ha ha

ha ha ha ha ha ha ha ha ha ha ha ha ha ha ha ha ha ha ha ha ha ha ha ha
ha ha ha ha ha ha ha ha ha ha ha ha ha ha ha ha ha ha ha ha ha ha ha ha
ha ha ha ha ha ha ha ha ha ha ha ha ha ha ha ha ha ha ha ha ha ha ha ha
ha ha ha ha ha ha ha ha ha ha ha ha ha ha ha ha ha ha ha ha ha ha ha ha
ha ha ha ha ha ha ha ha ha ha ha ha ha.

Thanks very much. That's really helped matters.

Clearly there is some confusion about why men sometimes can't get an erection, but not only from women. Men are just as ignorant of the truth and yet are probably more damaged by its occurrence. For most of us, failure to execute the naughty Nazi salute is an ego-crushing disaster because it once again brings our (oh so important) masculinity into question. This condition used to be (and to many still is) known as 'impotence'. The loss of power (and masculine power at that) was thus implicit on every level.

Even with the less judgemental new descriptive term of 'erectile dysfunction', most men this happens to will still feel alone and emasculated. We are aware that most partners will be at best disappointed and at worst derisory. We may even feel that we are the only one that this ever happens to.

But I asked men:

HAVE YOU EVER BEEN UNABLE TO GET AN ERECTION WHILE WITH A PARTNER?

Yes: 2,115 (45.94%)   **No:** 2,489 (54.06%)   **Total:** 4,604

Nearly half of men admit to having had a problem and the other 54 per cent of men are fucking liars.[1]

---

1. *Unsurprisingly the percentage of failure increased with age, with 63.21 per cent of men over 40 admitting to it. Which still leaves an astonishing 36.79 per cent of over-40s who claim never to have experienced it. Indeed over a third of men over 60 also claimed to have never encountered the problem. (Though according to Steve Jones, one in six men over 60 are unable to maintain an erection.)*

To understand why an erection sometimes fails, we really have to understand what goes in to making a successful stonk-on.

The truth is that an erect penis is a miracle of mechanics and hydraulics. Had it been designed by Isambard Kingdom Brunel there would be hordes of Japanese tourists clambering all over it, taking photos.

And for a few lucky men there are.

But even today all the wonders of the erection are not fully understood by science, though we have come some way since the eleventh century when Constantinus Africanus came up with this theory in *De Coitu*:

Three things are involved in intercourse: appetite (created by the fancy), spirit, and humour. The appetite comes from the liver, the spirit from the heart, and the humour from the brain. When appetite rises in the liver, the heart generates a spirit which descends through the arteries, fills the hollow of the penis and makes it hard and stiff. The delightful movements of intercourse give warmth to all the members, and hence to the humour which is in the brain; the liquid is drawn through the veins which lead from behind the ears to the testicles and from them it is squirted by the penis into the vulva.

How I wish it was as simple as that.

In the sixteenth century Costanzo Varolio opined that men got stiffies thanks to 'erector muscles'; others believed that an erection was caused by the penis filling with air.

The truth is perhaps more bizarre and wonderful than that and the first inkling of what really causes men to get wood came in 1863 when Conrad Eckhard attached an electric current to nerves in the sacral spinal cord of a dog (one hopes this was in the spirit of scientific enquiry, but he may have just been a bit drunk after a party at the lab and thought it might be a laugh). The dog's penis became hard (a case of giving a dog a boner if I ever heard of one) and the neurological erection connection was made.

Arousal is a thus complicated process dependent on all kinds of psychosomatic conditions coming together and can be initiated by touch, sight, smell or even sounds (studies involving men with damaged sacral spinal cords demonstrate that there are two different types of erection, one caused by imagination, the other by manipulation. How kind of God to provide a back-up system for such an important function).

As you may recall from Chapter 1, the bulk of the penis is made up of three tubes. There are two lungs of desire (otherwise known as a *corpus cavernosum*) and one tube of spongy Polos (*corpus spongiosum*). The lungs of desire are like expanding hives of blood, as they are filled with what Steve Jones describes as 'a net of flexible reservoirs, held in a mesh of smooth muscle'. This hive is not made up of hexagonal, honeycomb structures (nor does it produce honey, despite what some men may tell you, girls), but is formed from a series of corkscrew-shaped vessels. In between the lungs is the Polo tube which contains and protects Gulliver's Hose (the urethra) allowing the free flow of sperm despite the Incredible Hulk-style metamorphosis that is about to occur.[2]

Blood enters the penis through a network of arteries which lead into the reservoirs in the lungs of desire. As with the other organs of the body a series of veins takes the blood away from the penis. The blood vessels are quite thin in this limp state and so not much blood comes in and out and so your Hampton remains small.

If you watch a cock become erect you can understand why scientists of the past may have thought it was filling with air. It does apparently inflate like a balloon. The lungs of desire seemingly breathe in blood. And the way that the 'air' is kept in the balloon is quite amazing. Rather than having to tie a knot at the end, the blood-flow is controlled by muscular valves which surround the arteries. Usually these are tense and closed, but when they become relaxed the arteries open (and they also become wider).

Imagine the penis is the popular department store Harrods on New Year's morning and that your blood cells are millions of expectant shoppers who have been queuing outside for days on end waiting to see what bargains await them inside. The muscular valves are like bouncers, keeping the rabble at bay. All night they have been tensing their biceps and kept the doors to the shop tightly closed.

---

2. Please note that my Hulk-based analogy only works up to a point. If your cock turns green when you get a hard-on then there is something badly wrong going on.

But when Mohammed Al Fayed (the brain) starts to get excited at the prospect of all the money he is about to earn, he sends a signal to the doormen to open up the shop. The hired muscle relaxes and the doors open allowing the shoppers to rush in. Very quickly every department in Harrods is full to bursting with shoppers and Mohammed Al Fayed has a metaphorical and literal erection.

Mohammed Al Fayed achieves another successful 'January Sale'.

COCKFACT

According to the Roman poets Ovid, Martial and Columella, cress possesses awesome erotic power. They were backed up by a Roman doctor called Marcellus Empiricus who recommended three scruples of cress, three of red onion, three of pine seed and three of Indian nard as a cure for impotence.

I hope to see the Cress Marketing Board promoting these properties in its next campaign.

Incredibly the veins that drain the penis of blood are compressed by the pressure of the inflated organ and become blocked so much less blood can leave. Thus with most of the blood trapped, an erection is maintained. Only when the brain sends the required chemical message do the muscles around the arteries tense up as usual. No more blood can get in, the pressure gradually decreases, the veins are unblocked, blood escapes quicker than it is getting in and you, my friend, have a flop-on.

Like any piece of machinery, after years of service there will be some wear and tear. Clearly some cases of failure to raise the Titanic are due to physical and medical reasons. Some say it's around 10 per cent of cases, others more like 90 per cent. Generally the drug manufacturers tend to emphasise the physical causes, while therapists see it as mental influences. We thus prove that commerce is still an important factor in scientific research (I should point out that I've been paid to say that).

The survey threw up some good examples of genuine medical reasons for saying hello to Mr Floppy:

- **I have experienced several months where this has happened regularly and subsequently went to the doctor who found that my testosterone was low. He put me on monthly testosterone injections. These have helped but I still don't always get erections as hard as when I was younger.**

Testosterone replacement therapy is a controversial procedure and one which most doctors don't recommend as a routine solution, although it is considered to be reasonably harmless.

- **Being an insulin-dependent diabetic, I can be occasionally prone to it going limp unexpectedly if my blood sugar level becomes low. This then leads to paranoia in whichever partner I happen to have been with at the time (they assume I am no longer sexually attracted to them). A Mars Bar and a ten-minute rest soon disprove this new-found theory.**

Presumably he means he would eat the Mars Bar himself, but many women would probably be happy if he just used it as a substitute. In fact according to a recent survey 70 per cent of women prefer chocolate to sex, so maybe you're better off just letting her eat the Mars Bar while you get some sleep.

More than 50 per cent of men with diabetes have problems with their erection, because it both accelerates arterial disease and makes muscles unable to respond to nerve signals. Losing weight is the best way to avoid the onset of diabetes and hopefully that is a good reason to lose your gut, fellas.

If you care about maintaining a fully functioning cock you might also want to consider quitting smoking. The urologist Dr Irwin Goldstein writes that 'In addition to damaging blood vessels, smoking may damage penis tissue itself, making it less elastic and preventing it from stretching.' So much for smoking making you look sexy.

Another side effect of smoking and poor diet is high blood pressure, which can inhibit the flow of blood into the penis, making erection impossible. Exercise can also help prevent that, as well as clogging of the arteries. The more active you are the cleaner and more flexible your internal plumbing will become. According to a recent study men who walked two miles a day had half the erection problems of couch potatoes.

But if you are about to become a health freak for the sake of your love life you may want to avoid cycling. *The European Journal of Urology* revealed that a long bike ride can lead to erectile dysfunction, because sitting on a saddle pushes the penile arteries against the pubic bone (cock rock) and can starve your prick of oxygen. Dr Goldstein explains, 'When a man sits on a bicycle seat he's putting his entire body weight on the artery that supplies the penis. It's a nightmarish situation.'[3]

Using a wider saddle or standing as you pedal can help prevent this.

But a bicycle (or any other) accident can lead to more permanent damage. It is possible to rupture your lungs of desire (*corposa cavernosa*) and if the injury isn't treated within a day, the scar tissue will lead to a loss of elasticity in your knob, causing curvature and cock malfunction. According to *Men's Health* magazine, 'It's estimated that more than a third of impotent men have a history of penile trauma.'

---

3. *Goldstein is somewhat controversial among urologists and most doctors argue that the health benefits of cycling far outweigh the risks.*

Tragically, like any piece of machinery, the wear and tear of a long life will affect the efficiency of the penis. All of our muscles, arteries and even our skin become less elastic with age, and our cocks don't escape this decline and fall.

Throughout history people have searched for remedies for the physical causes of impotence.

Pliny the Elder suggested that wearing the right testis of a donkey as a bracelet would increase sexual potency (though he also contended that smearing someone with the excrement of a mouse would make them impotent – at the very least it would probably make them too unappealing to get a shag).

Unsurprisingly Constantinus Africanus had some interesting recipes to provoke desire in the impotent man. In *De Coitu* he advises you to

Take the brains of thirty male sparrows and steep them for a very long time in a glass pot; take an equal amount of grease surrounding the kidneys of a freshly killed billy goat, dissolve it on the fire, add the brains and as much honey as is needed, mix it in the dish and cook until it becomes hard. Make into pills like filberts and give one before intercourse.

If Sainsbury's reports an upsurge in the sale of sparrow brains, then I will know what you lot have been up to.

In the nineteenth century, the limp-cocked had electric currents applied to their (non-existent) erector muscles, using a machine that Friedman sees as being reminiscent of 'restarting a car battery with jumper cables'.

In the 1910s, Bernarrd MacFadden invented the Peniscope, which you have to admit is a fantastic name. It was a glass tube, with a pump attached. The man inserts his penis and then creates a vacuum in the tube. A negative pressure around the knob, causes blood to rush in (where angels really do fear to tread), and the erection is maintained by a tight ring worn around the base of the shaft. Not only did this cause the penis to become starved of oxygen, it also resulted in a somewhat unappealing cold erection. With no blood circulation there was nothing to keep it warm.

The 1940s saw the advent of the penile prosthesis. Essentially inflatable cylinders were placed inside the lungs of desire, which were connected to a pump which was located inside the scrotum (jizz-bag). The pump was in turn

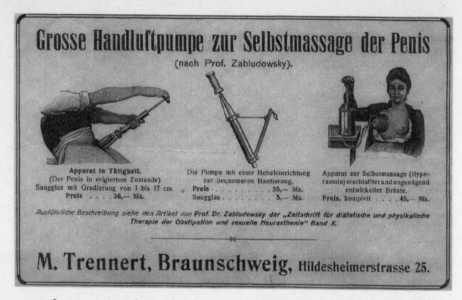

Grosse Handluftpumpe zur Selbstmassage der Penis

(nach Prof. Zabludowsky).

Apparat in Tätigkeit.
(Der Penis in erigiertem Zustande)
Saugglas mit Gradierung von 1 bis 17 cm.
Preis . . . . 36,— Mk.

Die Pumpe mit einer Hebeleinrichtung
zur bequemeren Hantierung.
Preis . . . . 35,— Mk.
Saugglas . . . . 5,— Mk.

Apparat zur Selbstmassage (Hype-
raemie) erschlaffter und ungenügend
entwickelter Brüste.
Preis, komplett . . . . 45,— Mk.

Ausführliche Beschreibung siehe den Artikel von Prof. Dr. Zabludowsky der „Zeitschrift für diätetische und physikalische
Therapie der Obstipation und sexuelle Neurasthenie" Band X.

M. Trennert, Braunschweig, Hildesheimerstrasse 25.

Proof that even before the Internet, penis and breast enlargement were big business for sleazy advertisers. If only the modern day hucksters followed M. Trennert's example and put their address on their emails we could all go round and beat the shit out of the bastards.

connected to a saline-filled reservoir which was put into the unfortunate man's abdomen. Arnold Melman explains how it worked:

> When a patient desires a tumescent phallus, the bulb is squeezed five or six times and fluid is forced from the reservoir into the cylinder chambers. When a flaccid penis is wanted, a deflation valve is pressed and the fluid returns to the reservoir.

Alternatively men could have a pair of semi-rigid rods inserted into their useless dicks, which had hinges on them so that this constantly erect penis could be hidden from the public gaze by being bent down or up against the body when the man was clothed.

Not surprisingly, these devices often went wrong and there were many complaints from dissatisfied (and unsatisfied) customers.

In 1985 *Vogue* magazine reported a return to the use of electricity in the treatment of impotence when it described an 'electrostimulatory device to be inserted in the anus before intercourse and controlled by a ring or a wristwatch-like switch so that patients can signal appropriate nerve to produce an erection'. I'd quite like one of those, regardless.

Other men solved their difficulties by injecting certain erection-creating drugs directly into their deflated horns. So mankind doubtless gave an audible sigh of relief, followed by a roar of delight when an oral treatment for ED came on to the market.

The wonder pill. The salvation of mankind.

Viagra!

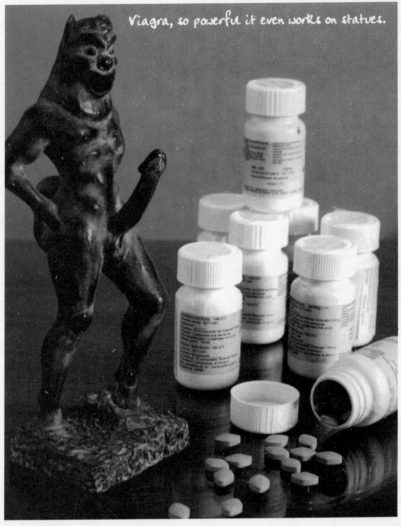

Viagra, so powerful it even works on statues.

I asked men:

HAVE YOU EVER TAKEN VIAGRA?

Yes: 298 (7.55%)   **No:** 3,650 (92.45%)   **Total:** 3,948

Here are some of those men's verdicts on this miraculous drug:
Some loved it:

- **A cosmic experience like seeing stars.**

- **Fucking brilliant. Really intense sensations for hours. My cock was hard enough to dent a car. Explosive ejaculations.**

I hope the manufacturers of Viagra will use that quote on their advertisements from now on. If you do, can you also include this next one:

- **Bloody good. Turned me into a 4 hour porn star. The wife told me to 'fuck off and go to sleep' in the end.**

You can't ask for a better endorsement than that.

- **Great, but still needs the mind to be aroused.**

Indeed, it is worth remembering that Viagra is not an aphrodisiac and you still require sexual stimulation to become erect.
Some experienced side effects, though to be fair most of them weren't that bothered!

- **I am lucky as due to having diabetes, I can have Viagra prescribed free of charge![4] It worked on making me erect, but the side effects were unpleasant. Headache, raised blood pressure, blocked nose, sinuses.**

---

4. *I am not sure about that as a definition of luck. And I don't want any of you attempting to get diabetes in order to get free Viagra. It really isn't worth it.*

- Made me very hard. Also made me have a red face and sleepless night ... but it was great.

- Gave me the worst headache ever. Worked great though, dick was so hard it could cut diamonds.

Am I the only one who wonders if such a penis might appear in a gay-porn version of James Bond? But this time Bond is strapped to the table face down. And he doesn't escape at the last minute, before the probe can pierce him.

- I was drunk. My lips got erect. My penis didn't. It was hilarious.

- Not desperately interesting and it inflamed my nasal passages so that I got what felt like terrible hay-fever.

- Worked great ... however it gave me a terrible headache ... but next time I took Viagra, I took two aspirin beforehand and had no problems. It does make my face turn red, and when wearing contacts, it makes them a little uncomfortable because the blood vessels in your eyes also swell a bit.

- Got stuck in my throat. I had a stiff neck for ages!

Very amusing. There were other negative remarks:

- Infuriating. My wife fell asleep, I woke up with a tent impression, begged her to let me fuck her, then it refused to go down for six hours. I was scared I had rigor mortis but I was still alive.

- By the third time, it was literally like fucking with someone else's equipment. I was still erect but the sensation was the same as after two consecutive and particularly bludgeoning wanks.

- Intense, vascular, heart pounding, but not sexual for me. In fact, it was somewhat of an inhibitor.

It isn't a drug that will work for everyone.

- Crap – hardly made any difference.

- Well it felt like I had a rubber glove and it was super huge and almost purple ... I couldn't come ... no matter what ... I finally gave up.

- Too expensive.

Though, for most men who suffer from erectile dysfunction, I suspect that you couldn't put a price on a functioning erection. There have been reports that Viagra may have had a part in the deaths of a handful of men who have taken it (and it shouldn't be taken by men with coronary artery disease, or by anyone taking nitrates), but I still think that if you hadn't had a stiffy for a decade you'd be happy to take that chance.[5]

It is worth emphasising that Viagra is not a drug that should really be used by those without a medical reason for doing so. I have heard a story of a healthy man taking too many pills and getting an erection that wouldn't go down for days, causing him great pain and risking permanent internal damage and gangrene.

The fact is that most young men who occasionally fail to get an erection are not suffering from erectile dysfunction. It is interesting that although both men and women accept that drinking too much alcohol is a valid cause of 'marshmallow penis' (and one that neither casts aspersions on the attractiveness of the partner, nor the masculinity of the man himself), most people seem totally unaware of the thousands of equally valid reasons for a temporary failure.

---

5. *Please read Friedman's* A Mind of its Own *for a very intelligent discussion on the implications for mankind because of the advent of Viagra (and other treatments for ED). In fact, you should just read the book anyway. It is really great.*

It can be due to drugs, illegal or prescribed:

- I was on Prozac which can cause erectile dysfunction ... I thought the stuff was supposed to cheer you up!

- I take medication for enlarged prostate and my partner knows that it can 'restrict' my sex life. Usually I get hard-ons but I don't always shoot.

- Blame Colombia.

Makes a change from blaming Scandinavia.

Simple overuse can cause it.

- I couldn't get it up. But then I had already masturbated 322 times that week which might be something to do with it.

- It *was* after several hours of non-stop shagging. All good things must come to an end.

- Yeah. Dammit. Though I had cracked off twice that day – so it was understandable. Look I was doing an essay, OK? You've got to reward yourself every 2,000 words or so.

By that reckoning I would have masturbated 40 times during the work on this book. It's been more like every 25 words for me ... Excuse me a second.

Even if you've saved yourself up for a special occasion, events can conspire to thwart you:

- Once went to visit a Czech girl I met in Ios the year before. It was meant to be a naughty week in the sun with plenty of sex. After 8 hours on the ferry in the blistering Greek sun I turned up, red with sunburn and woozy with sunstroke. We found our pension, kissed and got naked. I couldn't get it up for the next 2 days. She went home early. I was stuck on that rock for another 5 days. Alone. How did I feel!? Emasculated. Awful. Sick. Gay.

Sometimes an inappropriate situation can cause it:

● **She didn't mind. I felt stupid … but I was driving … so it was probably for the best.**

Yeah, probably!

● **It was under awkward circumstances. We were in a cinema watching a movie and she wanted to blow me, but I felt uncomfortable with that. I didn't really mind about not being able to get an erection because I didn't want it then, and my partner was satisfied when I told her I'd stick it in her later.**

● **I was with a woman I'd just met. I was absolutely pissed, she was on top, and I felt a tug on my leg. I looked over and a little boy (maybe 4 years old) met my eyes expectantly and said 'Daddy?' That pretty much took it right out of me.**

That'd put anyone off their stride.

The wrong ambience can also be a terrible passion killer, especially it seems when the music is wrong:

● **It was the music he insisted on playing. I told him it made me feel like I was at work, and he didn't believe me and about ten minutes into it I got a flop on. I don't think he understood cos he was only nineteen and thought the music at my work (a gay nightclub) was great. Ugh. Poofs are annoying.**

Not just poofs.

● **She wanted to listen to fucking Celine fucking Dion while we were doing it. That stopped me in my tracks.**

I personally had a similar experience with a girl who insisted on playing that awful Enya track, 'Sail Away', during sex. It was impossible to get any kind of rhythm going to it, and I couldn't stop thinking about the music and how much I hated it. So it wasn't just the sail that went away.

Undue pressure or depression can be equally devastating:

- **We were trying to make babies and I was getting so stressed up about having to perform over and over again at just the right moment, etc, that I eventually called it a day.**

- **It's intensely undermining. I understand that it's not unusual for divorced men to go through this. Prior to my divorce I had never, literally never, had any problems getting or maintaining an erection. Subsequently, apart from the obvious embarrassment with a partner, it's made me worry about my potency and virility, and affected my feelings of self-worth. Mind you, it was a pretty fucked-up divorce and still quite recent, so everything's still tangled together there.**

- **While waiting for my wife to 'get ready' (a lengthy, bathroom-based process) I heard on the news that a famous Welsh historian had died. I tried to go through with it for Gwyn Alf's sake, but it wouldn't happen.**

I think I love that story as much as anything you will read in this book.

Similarly guilt can bring the Leaning Tower of Pisa crashing down, both from ingrained religious beliefs and also from infidelity:

- **Normally when I was being unfaithful and knowing I had to get home. I kept trying but gave up. Has happened several times.**

Getting into a sexual rut can be the passion killer as well:

- **I felt upset and my partner didn't help initially, as she took it personally. We discussed it and decided that sex was getting a little too** repetitive and predictable. Eventually, she was understanding and helped by getting dressed up in skimpy riding gear when I got home from work. Problem solved!

A minority of men do try to blame the woman for the problem:

● **I didn't care. I was drunk and she was a munter.**

● **Relieved. She was a moose. How she felt was not of great concern.**

But one suspects that these (presumably gorgeous and super-fit) men are trying to pass the buck. After all they both got to the point where they were able to fail to get an erection. Their charming remarks suggest that the women involved might have had a lucky escape in any case!

But sometimes our brain may wish to experiment, but our body doesn't play along:

● **My only ever full on homosexual experience. I decided that I'd better stick to women in future. I suspect that, if you'd asked him, he'd have agreed.**

Even thinking about it too much can cause a man to lose his pride, as happened to this anonymous correspondent:

● **I am currently writing a book entirely about penises. I've set up a questionnaire and everything. It's taking over my life. Consequently, whenever I am about to have sex I can't stop thinking about the mechanics of what's going on and I can't get it up.**

What a sad case ...

But thinking about it too much can cause a man to lose his erection. Which possibly explains why some men seem to shut themselves off emotionally in sexual scenarios. We *can't* think about it, because we might lose it.

And as I've already mentioned, getting an erection isn't something that we can control through an act of will. We have not direct control over it at all.

Go on, if you are a man, try and get an erection right now. No touching yourself, no looking down the top of the person next to you, no naughty thoughts, no throwing your hat in the air and watching it fall ... Simply command your penis to become erect.

I'm presuming you haven't managed it (though if you have, a job in the porn industry awaits you).

This is because your erection is controlled by your peripheral nervous system and is dependent on a chain of chemical reactions, rather than on conscious thought.

When we are stimulated sexually, nitric oxide is released from the blood vessels over the entire body, but particularly in the penis. Other chemicals are in turn activated which cause the arteries to widen and so begins that marvellous process that we are already familiar with.

However, the body also has enzymes which are there to stop an erection developing or to get rid of it quickly if circumstances dictate that it isn't required. Adrenalin is particularly effective in disrupting the hydraulics of the erection.

It makes sense for us to lose our erection if we become anxious or afraid, because when primitive man was on the savannah and in danger of being eaten by sabre-toothed tigers or pterodactyls (if you believe the chronology of the *Flintstones*) at any moment, this immediate shrinkage would allow him to flee if he was caught on the job.

Because running with an erection ... It's a bit like taking part in a three-legged race.

Well, it is for me, girls, if you see what I'm implying.

I'm not sure I've made it totally clear what I'm implying.

I'm implying that I've got a 28-inch penis.[6]

So this is why the men above needed to feel they were in a safe environment (not a moving car), where they felt at home and comfortable (with no Celine

---

6. *I know, I have got very short legs, haven't I? But you know what they say, 'Short legs, 28-inch penis!' Well, I say that quite a lot. It doesn't seem to work very often though.*

Dion music playing) and where they weren't in danger of being caught by the modern-day version of the pterodactyl – the wife.

Although it makes sense for the survival of the species that anxiety causes us to say hello to Mr Floppy, the implications for modern men are quite profound. Because we are secretly increasingly anxious about our sexual performance. We've read your magazines, ladies, we've watched *Sex and the City*. We're aware that women's sexual expectations are rising all the time and it puts the fear of God into us. We can't admit it, but it's true.

I asked men:

 ## DO YOU FEEL UNDER PRESSURE TO PERFORM?
Yes: 1,668 (43.3%)   **No:** 2,184 (56.7%)   **Total:** 3,852

Almost one in two men feel under pressure to perform. Not something you would hear most men openly admitting to, because being a man is supposedly about confidence. Knowing what you're doing in bed is another quality which defines masculinity.

I admit that I have had a few problems in this area, when I've been to bed with someone new. It was very reassuring to discover that first-night nerves are extremely common:

● I felt terrible – completely useless. It's a vicious circle as well. The reason I couldn't get it up was because I was nervous – then I was even more nervous the next time and so on – it kept happening for about two weeks. And to make things worse this happened the first time I tried to have sex with my current girlfriend (who I like more than any girl I've ever met). My girlfriend thought she wasn't sexy enough. I even started to doubt my straightness. BUT I got over it and we've been making up for that lost time ever since.

● It happens nearly 100 per cent of the time when attempting to have sex for the first time with a new partner. Unless there is no love interest, but I have only had one casual shag in my life.[7] The partners in question are already my girlfriend when this happens. Most of them have found it touching, that it wasn't just about the sex. It's made it much better when it works on the second occasion. One partner seemed offended. But she was the exception.

● I had been anxious to have sex with a particularly attractive friend and when the opportunity to fuck him arose I went limp and couldn't recover my erection.

So to all those women who think that a man's failure to rise to the occasion is a comment on their attractiveness, it appears that there is actually a good chance that he can't get it up precisely because he thinks you're gorgeous and wants to impress you … either that or it's because you're making love in the tiger enclosure at the zoo.

And fellas, the puncturing of your party balloon doesn't make you a loser or unmanly or gay, if you're straight (or straight, if you're gay) or mean you're out of touch with reality. In the vast majority of cases you just need to take a look at your surroundings and work out what it is that's making you feel uneasy.

And here's a novel idea, rather than getting angry, or upset, or trying to blame your partner, why not have a go at explaining to them what is wrong. I think the vast majority of women will be quite flattered if you tell them that you are nervous because you want to impress them. And the ones that aren't probably need to look at their own preconceptions about masculinity.

Don't fret about it (it'll just make things worse), don't feel you're a freak (because you're certainly not alone on this one), look on the funny side (if you can both laugh about it, it's not such a problem) and wait and see if you feel that conditions improve a bit later on (or another time). If nothing else, most women will feel they have cut their losses if you get down there and lick her minge!

Girls, you can help us, too, by understanding that despite their macho

---

7. It's interesting here that the implication is that being able to get an erection with a new person is almost more insulting than not. It means that this man doesn't really care about who he is with. I think a lot of men can probably identify with this paradox.

posturing, men have exactly the same emotions and insecurities as you, by reassuring us and helping us to relax, by turning off your fucking Enya CD.

And most importantly, by *not doing this*:

- Ha ha.

A pornographic game of Quidditch.
The winner is the one who grabs the golden snatch.

8

LETNOWTHEPENISBEPRAISED

Forty-three per cent of men feel under pressure to perform.

A third of men have faked an orgasm.

A third of men can't even urinate standing next to other men.

It seems men are not as cocksure as they might outwardly appear. In fact there is a great deal of cock-uncertainty.

The more I read of the survey results, the more surprised I was to discover the extent of this secret male vulnerability.

Yet, why was I so astonished?

I'd felt under pressure to perform sexually on many occasions. I had experienced trouble while trying to urinate next to other men. And although I had never attempted to fake an orgasm there had been plenty of times when I hadn't been able to have one. (If only I'd thought of spitting on my partner's back.) Yet like all those other men I kept quiet about these flaws for fear of appearing unmanly.

I didn't conform to the stereotype and rather than making the obvious mental leap and concluding that the stereotype was wrong, I had decided that there was something wrong with me, so I'd better pretend that I conformed to the image that was expected of me.

Unlike most stereotypes, the stereotypes of men aren't just tolerated by men: we seem happy to perpetuate them. We will laugh along with the jokes that present us as insensitive, sexually obsessed, predatory, ignorant, selfish, childish and violent, and will even make those jokes ourselves.

Throughout my life, at one time or another, I have exhibited all the unpleasant qualities in that list above, but so has almost every human being on the planet, male or female. Those attributes don't define me, nor when I think about it, any man alive.

You might say that it's not important. It's all just a bit of a joke. But is it really? Is this blank acceptance of an unpleasant generalisation just another indication of the lack of pride most men are suffering from? Do some men conform to the men-behaving-badly laddish stereotype that is prevalent at the moment because they are irresponsible or because they have realised that they have nothing to be responsible for?

The results from the survey seemed to confirm that secretly many men were feeling the same confusion as me. It is clear that men of the twenty-first century are having a serious identity crisis. None of us know what our role is in this changing modern world.

Machines mean our brute strength isn't needed for industry – we're not defined by our bread-winning status any longer; computers and technology have downgraded our importance as soldiers – we're not the warriors we once were; science is reaching a point where men aren't even necessary for reproduction.

Are we approaching a future where men exist only as sperm-donors?

Where women will keep us chained up and milk us like aphids?!

Like most men, I bloody well hope so. Oh, brave new world that has such dungeons in it!

I think the fact that I'm still making those kind of jokes demonstrates just how much this attitude is engrained in men, our self-image is so low, our need for acceptance is so important that few of us are going to be prepared to rock the boat and look at the positive things that men can do. To focus on all the men who are good fathers, good lovers, good friends. The majority of men who use their dicks for good, not evil.

My mission to celebrate the Fuckingham Phallus had only been up and running for a month or so and I had already found a god who embodied my penis-praising, Enki, and a graphic representation of what the penis stands for in the

Rude Man of Cerne Abbas, but what use were they? One was imaginary and the other was made out of chalk. They weren't any real use as figure-knobheads.

I have to say that in those first few weeks the constant barrage of happy-lamp-based information had got to me a little. I was having cock thrust down my throat, again and again, over and over. It was unbalancing my life. I would bring up a new piece of research at dinner parties and be greeted by a barrage of spat-out canapés and shocked expressions.

Well, I would have been if I ever got invited to dinner parties, but that was never going to happen. 'And this is Richard, he's writing a book about cocks. No, he doesn't have a girlfriend.' That would be social death. Instead I was eating pizzas at home and reading books about the history of circumcision. It was a bit depressing to be honest. I was thinking of jacking it all in. I considered jacking it all off, but that would mean further interfacing with a penis and I wasn't sure I could face it.

I was feeling alone. It seemed I was the only person in the world to be taking such an interest in this subject. Sure, there are plenty of people out there happy to celebrate the penis in a sexual way, but that wasn't what *Talking Cock* was about. It had a higher purpose. I needed to know there was someone else out there like me, a living, breathing embodiment of jigger jollification who would inspire me to push onwards in my quest.

I wanted to find a kindred spirit, a person in the world who saw the penis for what it was and would praise it, in all its many forms.

Finding someone to fit this bill was more easily said than done. Celebrating the penis is not something that anyone admits to very readily.

COCKFACT

The Japanese are among the top penis celebrators of the modern world. As well as many penis shrines throughout the countryside, there is a phallus festival each year, where a seven foot (only 5 cubits) penis is hewn from a cypress tree and carried by a dozen men (it weighs around 700 pounds) from the Kumano Shrine to the Tagata shrine. It's about a mile, so several groups of 12 men take it in turns, in a relay race with a most unusual and unwieldy baton.

There was one obvious candidate, Cynthia Plaster-Caster,[1] the woman who famously made plaster-casts of the erect penises of some of the world's most famous rock stars.

I visited her website at www.cynthiaplastercaster.com to find out more about her. She described the genesis of the idea. It all began when she was a teenager in the Sixties and was finding herself somewhat aroused by the music and musicians of that swinging decade. Yet hard as she tried to meet the objects of her lust she found that there was a lot of competition from other girls who wanted a pass that would allow them to access absolutely all areas.

She continues the story, 'One fateful day in college, a homework assignment from my art teacher to plaster cast "something solid that could retain its shape" changed my life forever.' She asked Paul Revere and the Raiders if they would be up for it. They weren't, but Cynthia reveals she did lose her virginity (whether to Paul Revere or one or more of his Raiders isn't made clear).

Cynthia Plaster-Caster with one of her works of art. I am more impressed by the size of her ring.

1. *Possibly not her real name.*

Cynthia was happy. 'We had found ourselves the perfect gimmick – something that could make us stand out from all the other teenyboppers and groupies.'

After a couple of years searching for the correct moulding material Cynthia discovered a dental mould called alginates and the first rock star to pose for her was none other than the impressively cocked Jimi Hendrix. The resulting statuette was beautiful, but a little cracked and thus became known as the 'Penis de Milo'.

Other castees included Jello Biafra of The Dead Kennedys, Pete Shelley of The Buzzcocks (though she fucked up the mould for this one – maybe his cock did actually buzz), Anthony Newley (slightly incongruously), Zal Yanovsky from Lovin' Spoonful and Chris Connelly of The Revolting Cocks (possibly Cynthia was drawn to bands with the word cock in them, or perhaps she just wanted to see how revolting Chris's cock really was).

The collection wasn't actually exhibited until the year 2000 and Cynthia now tours universities and rock clubs 'talking dick' (what a pathetic way to make a living). Plus for $500 she offers to take two lovers, gay or straight, through the whole process, though only as an observer. If you want to take advantage of this, email her at casterd@aol.com

Much as it would have been interesting to talk to such an historic figure, and possibly have my little chap preserved for posterity,[2] I felt that Cynthia, legendary and admirable as she was, did not fit the bill as a modern-day, non-imaginary Enki.

First her motives (at least initially) were sexual. By her own admission she saw her hobby as a way of meeting rock stars in the hope of sleeping with them. This implied she was more interested in her own desires than in cock celebration. More importantly she was only concerned with penises that 'are attached

---

2. *Though I think I may have declined even if she'd offered. I was given a similar opportunity in Melbourne in April 2003, after the patrons of an establishment called Bodybitz came to see my show. A lady called Susie Bodybitz (maybe not her real name, or perhaps people with these unusual surnames feel it is their inescapable destiny to make moulds of tumescent knobs) offered to do a casting of my privates for nothing. Part of me felt that I should do it for the sake of art, posterity and to give me something to write about in this book. But part of me thought, 'But I'd have to get an erection in a room of strangers which might be a bit strange, and how would I get through customs?' So unfortunately I wimped out. But if you are braver than I, you could also visit www.bodybitz.com to find out more.*

to rock stars and other talented earthlings'. It was what the cock was connected to that interested her most. I wanted to find someone for whom the cock was the celebrity, not who was only interested in the cocks of celebrities. Someone who was equally fascinated by every penis on the planet, regardless of its size, shape or species. Someone who saw the penis as a thing of beauty and a joy forever, while not being swayed from this pure and true path by sexual desire.

I needed to find a Prick Professor, a Cock Curator, an Acadickmic.

My only hope was the Internet, though I was already wary of putting the word 'Cock' into a search engine and seeing what popped up.

I went to Google and typed in 'Penis University'.

I got directed to a site entitled 'Penis Action – Thousands of XXX clips, Hottest Teens – No Credit Card' (not the higher plane I had been hoping for), a joke about why the top of the penis is wider than the base (it's not worth the effort of telling it) and a rather more promising link to the Penis University of West Florida.

This led, disappointingly, to a list of web addresses about penis enlargement. I get enough of those in spam form in my email inbox, thanks very much (I'm hoping it's not just me that they send them to, but now I've had that thought I'm beginning to worry).

As there was no joy with 'Penis University' (and with a little consideration, I'm not that surprised), I typed 'Penis Museum' into my search engine. This was a lot more fruitful.

I was presented with a list of several sites about something variously described as the penis museum, the Phallus Palace or the Icelandic Phallological Museum.[3] I read of a man called Sigurdur Hjartarson who had been collecting animal penises since the 1950s. According to Internet news-site, Ananova, he was now searching for a human penis for his collection and an 85-year-old Icelandic man called Pall Arason had promised him his (when he died). On another site a weblog entry by (I'm guessing) an American tourist described it as 'totally the worst museum ever, and I really made an effort!' A 'reporter'

---

3. *As it turns out there is no need to use the word 'Icelandic', as there isn't one of these anywhere else in the world. And 'phallological' isn't actually a real word. But it is a museum. One out of three ain't bad.*

called Josh Schonwald (who was definitely an American) detailed his attempts to interview Mr Hjartarson by email, which had been curtailed rather abruptly when Schonwald told him that all his friends had assumed that a man running a penis museum must be gay. The American took the Icelandic man's offence as being a sign that he was homophobic, but it was more probably that Hjartarson was affronted by the juvenile line of enquiry (which to be honest implied that the host of such a museum must have a sexual interest in animals). Unlike Josh Schonwald I already liked this unusual Icelandic man.

Everything I read made me more and more certain that I had found my cock hero. It was obvious that I had to visit this controversial museum myself and meet the man who had collected these specimens over so many years, to find out what his real motivation was. I found his email address, told him of my cock quest and he got back to me very promptly and we arranged a mutually convenient date for an interview, the afternoon of 18 June 2002. I was going to Reykjavik in Iceland. Not to look at the geysers or the glaciers, but to look at a room filled with severed animal penises.

I began to wonder if I was taking my work a little bit seriously.

Especially when I discovered the only flight available on the dates I required was in business class and I wasn't going to get much change out of a grand. The hotel (which at least promised proximity to the city centre) was also almost prohibitively expensive. I consoled myself with the fact that it was at least tax deductible. I just hoped the taxman didn't contact me to find out what the purpose of my business trip had been.

I arrived in Iceland in the afternoon of Monday, 17 June. From the air, it seemed barren and rocky and surprisingly free of ice. As I exited the terminal the weather was overcast, but the light behind the clouds seemed strangely eerie and bright. I already had that sense of displacement that comes with foreign travel, but there was something even more unsettling that I couldn't quite put my finger on. Was it just because I was travelling alone or did I feel a little uneasy because I was about to visit with a man who had confessed to wanting to detach and display the penis of another bloke?

The cab to my hotel seemed extremely expensive. Maybe I had done my conversion sums incorrectly, but it appeared to have cost me over £80 and it hadn't been *that* long a journey. Had word got round already? 'There's a bloke coming over just to look at the penis museum. He's obviously some kind of idiot. Overcharge him for everything.' At least my hotel should be pretty luxurious for the amount I was paying. Of course, when I arrived I saw that it was extremely average and more annoyingly a good 25-minute walk from the town centre. Maybe I was being paranoid, but it seemed the whole country was out to fleece me.

I was alone and disorientated in Iceland and the only person I knew here was a man who collected severed penises. I gave him a ring to confirm our meeting. Half of me was hoping he might invite me round for dinner, but the other half was a bit concerned about what might be on the menu. As it happened we had a perfunctory conversation in which we made a loose arrangement for me to arrive at the museum some time the next afternoon.

I wandered into the town centre, along a long busy road which overlooked the sea. The water looked grey, cold and uninviting. I watched it crash against the shore. The eerie daylight did not play across the waves as if in a cosmic ballet. Instead the light seemed to be swallowed by the murky ocean. I felt the sea wished to devour me as well. I wished I'd brought a friend with me, maybe even turned the trip into a romantic sojourn. Then I remembered what I was doing here and was pleased that I had come alone.

Once I arrived in the heart of the city I was surprised at how small it was. It didn't seem like the capital of a country. If anything it reminded me of Weston-Super-Mare, but a Weston-Super-Mare that had been plucked from the banks of the Bristol Channel and dropped on an isolated stretch of coastline in the Hebrides (which is something I am planning to have done to Weston-Super-Mare if I ever earn enough money – however unfair this would be on the people of the Hebrides).

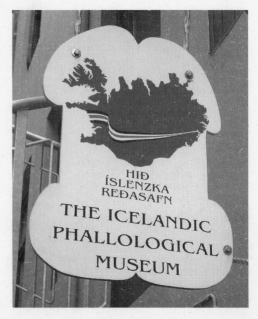

I had been worried about locating the penis museum, but passed it almost immediately. An amusing penis-shaped sign hung in the street above a small arched alleyway. My Holy Grail was located just a few steps away. I couldn't resist going to have a look, but it was early evening and the museum was closed. The glass in the windows was frosted. I had no clue of what to expect.

I popped into a bar, thinking I would drink beer till nightfall. I had an odd feeling of nervousness, loneliness and dislocation and was half hoping I might meet someone to talk to but the

Temple of God or Icelandic Penis Worshippers' HQ.

other half of me was hoping I wouldn't. Otherwise they'd ask me what I was doing in their country and I would have to tell them. So I read a book about penises instead. Which would just make it doubly worse if anyone began a conversation.

It was Monday night in Reykjavik and I have to say that the joint wasn't jumping. Not surprising given the fact that beer was equivalent to £5 a glass. Or at least it was £5 a glass to the penis guy! Thank God I had decided to get a cab back to the hotel the minute that it was dark.

I kept reading and drinking and reading and drinking, then the print started to get blurry so I stopped the reading and replaced it with more drinking. I smiled at some pretty local girls in the bar, but by this stage I was drunk enough for that smile to actually register as a leer and they didn't talk to me. I looked outside. Dusk hadn't even arrived. I would have one more beer. Then I looked at my watch and realised it was approaching midnight, and remembered that when you get this far north the days are long in summer and short in winter. I had 40 pounds' worth of beer sloshing around in me. Anywhere else in the world the sheer volume of 40 pounds' worth of beer would have killed me. But this was 40 pounds' worth of expensive Icelandic beer. I had room for some chips. They only cost a pound. A pound a chip.

I resolved to go to sleep and prepare for my day of destiny.

In the morning I walked into town again, feeling a bit foolish over the previous day's paranoia. As if the whole city was colluding to trick me! I did some sightseeing. The cathedral, I thought, had a somewhat phallic tower and even the adverts for children's snacks seemed preoccupied with the penis. Maybe it wasn't just Mr Hjartarson who was obsessed with penises, maybe it was everyone in Iceland. Perhaps they did all know who I was and had been biding their time

Harmless advertisement for hot dogs or perverted publicity for skateboarding cocks!

and were going to kidnap me and use me as a sacrificial lamb (or more likely, cock) in their bizarre Icelandic Phallalogical Cult.

Why was I so freaked out by this place?

I sat in a café and drafted some questions for Mr Hjartarson. What could I ask him that he hadn't been asked before? I made a note not to ask him if collecting severed penises made him a gay.

A few coffees later and it was afternoon, but I found myself overcome with shyness. It was a bit like being on a date. A date which starts by asking the other

COCKFACT

Proportionate to body size, man has the biggest penis of any of the primates (which includes all lemurs, monkeys and anthropoid apes). So it is after all man that is the King of the Swingers. Despite all those monkeys' boasts in song. No wonder they want to be like us!

person if I can see their genitals. Very much like a normal date for me then. Except for once they were going to let me.

I didn't want to turn up too soon, all keen. I would make him wait. I ate a lunch of traditional local Mexican food and then made my way into the (I now realised) vagina-like alley that led to the Icelandic Phallus Palace.

It wasn't really what I expected at all. It was just two very small rooms, lined with display cabinets, which housed jars filled with strange white lumps of flesh. A man, who I presumed was Sigurdur, was talking to the two other visitors who were in the museum, so I had a brief look around as I waited to talk to him.

Far from feeling at home, or having found the Cock Camelot, I felt a bit nauseous. Seeing so many dismembered animal genitals was slightly unsettling (especially after eating an Icelandic version of the burrito). The room was so small that it almost felt like one had stumbled across a bizarre shrine created by some strange serial killer, or the laboratory of a perverted Dr Frankenstein. But those weren't brains in those bell-jars. Not unless it's true we all think with our dicks. I thought about how far I had travelled and how much I had spent, about the

Sigurdur Hjartarson - Please note his penis shaped phone on the wall beside him. The man is obsessed with cocks. It's sad.

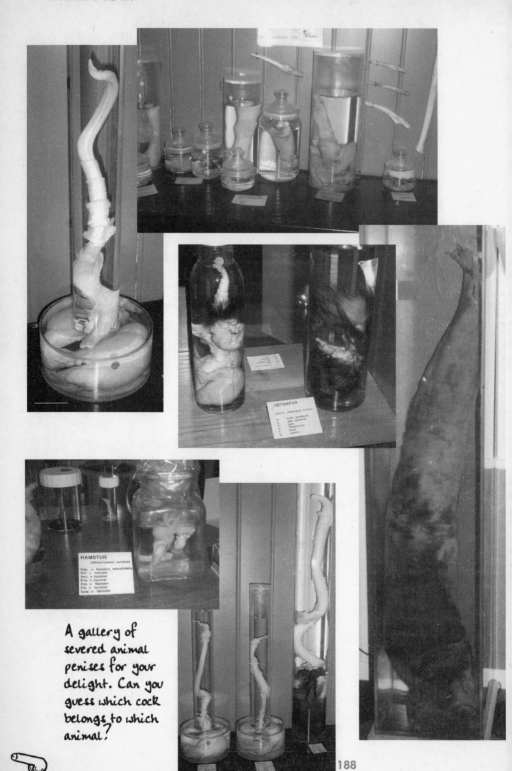

A gallery of severed animal penises for your delight. Can you guess which cock belongs to which animal?

high hopes I had had of finding a modern-day Knob God and I thought maybe I had made a terrible mistake.

Mr Hjartarson was now free to talk to me, but I was a bag of nerves and my throat was dry as I introduced myself. What was this man all about?

He looked like any normal, middle-aged man, a little portly, yet he was sterner and more formal than I had imagined he'd be. He seemed distant, even a little humourless. Worse still, he didn't seem to know who I was, even though I had spoken to him just 12 hours earlier. I hadn't expected a fanfare or dancing girls, but I had come all this way to see him. Surely he could have got a bit excited. Was he the freak I had been trying to convince myself that he wasn't?

Then again I was a nervous-looking Englishman who had probably turned a bit white (or green) and who had been emailing and ringing him for the past couple of weeks and had travelled all this way just to see his museum, because I was writing a stage show supposedly about penises. Yeah, right. Maybe he thought I was the freak.

Maybe he was right.

Still very brusque and businesslike, he gave me a catalogue of the contents of the museum (every exhibit had a coloured, numbered sticker by it, for ease of identification), took my entrance fee (I'd thought I might have got in for nothing, but I was used to having to pay through the nose in this country so I didn't complain) and told me to take a look around. I'd hoped he was going to show me himself, but he stayed resolutely behind his desk.

Again I was feeling that my quest was turning into a waste of time.

Once I had acclimatised myself to the bizarre surroundings, the queasiness left me and I did begin to appreciate and even enjoy what I was looking at. Most of the specimens were in jars floating in formaldehyde (ranging from miniscule shrew cocks to more impressive bulls and dolphins and a whale penis that was taller than me), but other larger members had been dried out and were hung on plaques on the wall, like some kind of perverted moose head (disappointingly there wasn't a moose penis there – this one belonged to a narwhale).

The sheer variety in size and shape was quite breathtaking. It reaffirmed my previous findings from the survey:

I'VE NEVER SEEN A 'USUAL' PENIS.

A narwhale's penis. That'd bring tears to your eyes!

Once I had got over the somewhat disturbing idea of seeing so many penises cruelly wrenched from their rightful owners, I began to appreciate the new level of penile diversity that was being opened up to me. One cabinet contained penis bones. I hadn't realised before, but many mammals have bones in the penis, which make it much easier for them to achieve erection. I think that's just cheating!

There were also some humorous posters and novelty items, as well as a cabinet of hand-carved wooden souvenirs. It was clear that the man who had put all this together had a sense of fun, as well as a keen scientific interest. It didn't seem to match the austere man who had (barely) greeted me.

But I wondered if he was just being wary of me. He'd clearly had some experience with people who didn't understand what he was trying to do, or chose to judge him or mock him. He was well within his rights to be defensive.

I proceeded with my interview. He seemed a little nervous to start with. Occasionally some other visitors interrupted our chat, perhaps two or three every 15 minutes, but we would pick up where we left off.

The first question was obvious, but had to be asked, 'How did this all begin?'

'Well, it's a long story,' replied Mr Hjartarson, clearly not for the first time.

'You may have noticed the bull's penis on the wall on the other side.' (I hadn't.) 'That was my first item.'

He led me across to show me a decorated strip of leather which was hard to imagine had ever been a cock. He explained, 'When I was a kid, in the fifties, if a bull was slaughtered on a farm, the penis was never thrown away. No, that would be *wasteful*. Every part of the animal had to be used, even the bones for making toys or winding wool. So the bull's penis was hung up and dried and then used as a whip!'

I couldn't hide my surprise: 'A whip?!' Looking again at the item hanging on the wall I could see that was exactly what it was. Although I was immediately struck with the irony of using such an object to drive cattle, as well as considering somewhat more perverted connotations, I decided it was too soon to share such a joke with a man who apparently took all of this very seriously.

Four pizzles in a variety of sizes, catering for all bull-penis whip tastes.

'It's called a pizzle,' he told me. Apparently Shakespeare mentions one in *Henry IV*, so maybe this wasn't some kind of elaborate joke at my expense, after all.

Sig continued, 'Then I was a headmaster in a small town in the country in the seventies. This was before the International Whaling Ban of '87, and some of the teachers worked in the whaling station in vacations and they started bringing me the penises from the whales.'

I was tempted to ask why they brought them to him. What made them think he would want them? But I was keen not to offend him. I imagine he'd been showing them his pizzle and they thought, 'Maybe he'd like these too' or maybe it's some Icelandic equivalent of an apple for the teacher.

In any case Sigurdur was well into his stride by now; there was no stopping him. 'Then the idea developed,' he said, 'that it might be interesting in collecting this organ from the most possible species of Icelandic mammals.'

COCKFACT

The pig has a corkscrew penis and every time it comes it produces about a pint of semen. A pint!?
That's very nearly an armful.

Politeness be damned, this time I couldn't let that go, 'Why just Icelandic mammals?'

His eyes rolled, 'Oh, to collect the penises of all the animals in the world would be impossible. Only a lunatic would attempt it!'

Was that a twinkle in his eyes? Should I laugh? I chuckled a little and he smiled back at me. We were warming to one another.

'Now I've got a specimen from 42 different Icelandic species. So it's almost complete. I'm still waiting for one species of narwhale. Whales are more difficult now, because of the whaling ban. But if a whale dies of natural causes and is washed up on a beach somewhere, they will save the penis for me and give me a ring and I will go and pick it up in the boot of my car.' I laughed. He gave me a stern look. He was serious.

'No animal has been killed just for me. I only take the penises of animals who have died naturally or from slaughterhouses. This is very important.'

What I had mistaken for coldness I saw now was pride. He didn't want to be misrepresented. And as a recovering vegetarian I appreciated his humanity. I pressed on, 'So what gave you the idea of putting all your penises in a museum?'

'Well I just had it all in my home, but people were all telling me to open it up.[4] But that was difficult, I am still a full-time teacher. But in 1997 we were offered this site. To begin with we were sharing it with a small knitting business. I started with 63 items. Now I've got 148. The number has increased rapidly.'

I felt confident enough now to be cheekier to him. 'This is the only penis museum in the world,' I said. 'Why do you think there are no others?'

He bristled with mock outrage, 'Well I don't know! I met an Englishman

---

4. *I suspect his wife was probably finding it annoying:* 'You can't move in this house without tripping over a penis!'

once and he collected just the bones. You know, quite a lot of species have bones in the penis.'

I nodded as if I'd known this all my life, rather than just for the last ten minutes. 'He had a collection of bones, but only bones.'

He laughed with a mixture of pity, dismay and incredulity. 'Only bones!'

I shook my head too and laughed along. I was now no longer nervous of this ridiculous and wonderful man. He was opening up too, performing for me, enjoying my delight. 'No! I don't know why someone didn't do this a long time ago. You must have some hobby, you know. Some people might think I'm not completely normal, but someone has to do this!'

I didn't challenge this bold assertion. Because I agreed with him.

He was almost pontificating now, 'Not everyone can be collecting coins and stamps! To some people it's a taboo. But I like playing on the edge, on the fringes of being taken seriously as a collector – which really I am. Making some fun, making fun of people or something like that. So not everyone knows how to react. Quite a lot of people think I'm crazy or a pervert or something.'

He paused with masterful comic timing, before smiling and jokingly confiding, 'I *like* that!' I laughed along, but he was clearly worried that he might have pushed things too far, no doubt mindful of those who have misunderstood his humour in the past, and he added, 'But I'm extremely normal and conventional. I have been married to the same woman for more than 40 years. We've got four children and seven grandchildren. This has nothing to do with pornography or erotica. It is just an interesting collection. You have a penis. It is nothing to do with pornography …'

'Well not most of the time!' I quipped, sort of wishing I hadn't as he was truly on a roll.

He ignored me. 'But if you go close and look at them and compare them, you see that every penis has its own variety, its own special shape. So that perception should be interesting for people.'

He didn't have to worry that I might misconstrue his motivation. It was now quite clear to me why he did this and it wasn't because he was some animal equivalent of Hannibal Lecter. He was challenging conventional thinking. This was one in the eye for the killjoys and the puritans who see this wonderful bodily part as something unclean or evil. He was also truly celebrating the wonder and diversity of this much-misunderstood organ. Yet he still enjoyed the consternation and confusion that such a project caused.

We were on the same wavelength and he was the perfect modern-day ambassador for my own efforts to venerate the giggle-stick.

I decided to put this to him, in a question that I guessed he might not have been asked before: 'Would you like to see a day where Reykjavik is made into the world penis capital?'

He considered this, quite seriously for a second, and replied, 'It would make me proud ... but I don't know how the mayor would react. The city council has given me a small grant, but it's very little. I have never paid myself a salary, but I break even now. I am not losing money any more. Recently I got an interview with the Minister of Tourism. We had gone to the same school, he was a year or two ahead of me and knew me. I had an interview at 9.30 in the morning and he must have had a hangover or something, he was in a very bad mood. He pointed to me that I should sit and I said I was there to ask about some grants for my penis museum and he stood up, walked to the door and showed me out. So the interview lasted for 15 seconds. It was the shortest ministerial interview ever ... very, very funny.'

How could I not like this man? He was not interested in financial reward, and yet had correctly realised that Iceland could attract more tourists if it publicised his marvellous attraction (and if it halved its beer prices). If you live in Iceland, please lobby your parliament to have Mr Hjartarson's work for your country officially recognised. Maybe some kind of statue could be (literally) erected in your town centre.

COCKFACT

The elephant has the biggest penis of any land mammal: it's about six feet long. So maybe there is some correlation between the size of the nose and the size of the penis after all.

The blue whale beats that into a cocked hat. Its penis is about ten feet long. You can make up your own Moby Dick joke. By this stage in the book I am too fatigued to do so.

Sigurdur and the disappointingly healthy penis-donor Pall Arason.

We had been talking cock for over an hour, but I couldn't leave though, without asking about Pall Arason, the man who had promised the museum its first human exhibit.

Sigurdur showed me a picture of the two men together. Arason was a short, grey-haired man. He looked like someone's grandad (which he probably was) rather than a pioneer in phallological display.

'This is Arason,' said Sigurdur, 'he's 87. He's a famous guy here in Iceland. He's a famous womaniser, one of the most famous in the century. He's a boaster, a bragger. He's very far from being modest. He's ultra-right wing in politics. He boasts of being a Nazi!'

I looked shocked, but Sigurdur just nudged me and laughed, 'He's a very funny guy! He wants to be in the limelight. I think this is part of all that.'

He showed me an official-looking certificate on the wall of the museum. It was the contract by which the two unlikely friends had made their arrangement. A very specific organ donor card. It was even witnessed by two other people.

'They are the doctors responsible for bringing me this organ in the fullness of time,' he explained. 'And we all agree, the doctors, Mr Arason and myself,

195

COCKFACT

The gorilla's penis is about two inches when erect. According to our old friend Dr Terri Hamilton this is because 'They live with stable harems, impress their rivals with their large body size and never felt the evolutionary need to develop large organs.' Whether this is true of the blokes who look like gorillas who work as bouncers at clubs isn't an issue that I ever intend to bring up with them directly.

that the penis must be taken warm! So if they take it warm they can bleed it out and then inject it and raise it again. Because it is very, very important for Mr Arason to be kept with some dignity.'

I almost laughed at the apparent incongruity, but again this was a moment of intense seriousness for Sigurdur. 'No, if it cools down, the blood clots in the veins and you can do nothing. It'll be like this, you know.' He demonstrated with his bent little finger.

His eyes seemed to glaze over with excitement as he told me the final details. 'So these doctors will rip off the penis and bring it to me and I will take it and build a beautiful case around it. It will be my prize exhibit.'[5]

Now Jeffrey Dahmer, the Milwaukee Cannibal, had a similar plan to create a shrine to the human penis, but the mistake he made was not to get a signed and witnessed contract from his donors. Indeed, since Mr Arason had signed up for the ultimate sacrifice, three or four other men had also taken the plunge. One of them, I noticed, lived in Balham, the same part of South London as me. I was not prepared to see this coincidence as a sign that me and my little chap should be divorced from one another at death.

'Would you be happy to have your penis put in the museum after you have died?' I asked Sig.

---

5. *I emailed Mr Hjartarson as the book was going to press to enquire about Mr Arason's health, secretly hoping that he might have passed away in the intervening months, but Sigurdur responded that 'Mr Arason seems to be in excellent health'. I'd hate to wish death on anyone, but if Pall had died it would have made a great conclusion to this chapter. But, no, he wants to carry on living. Some people have no humanity.*

'I will give mine here, of course,' he replied. 'My wife knows that. And I just hope she will do as I ask her. My last will. My last wish.'

That's dedication for you. Though I have a feeling that once Sigurdur is gone, his wife might accidentally put his entire collection in a giant furnace which she will dance around, laughing. I may be wrong. I'm only guessing.

On the way out Mr Hjartarson showed me some of the souvenirs he had made for sale at the museum. Many included penises carved from wood, like barbecue skewers and skipping ropes with penis-shaped handles. There were also light-shades made out of the stretched skin from a ram's testicles. Sigurdur had carved a penis-shaped handle for the door of the museum (a bona fide door-knob), his phone was the same shape, and he even had a cock clock. With a degree of pride and a wicked smile, he revealed that he had used his own penis as an artist's model for his creations, so he was already very much a part of his museum even before his death.

As I left I thought of one more question that really needed to be answered. I stopped and turned to him and said, 'How does having this museum make you feel about your own penis?'

Sigurdur stopped and considered for a second and he looked me in the eye and said, 'I am rather more proud of it, I think.'

He smiled and shook my hand. I left the museum, and walked through the vagina-like arch into the streets of Reykjavik, which no longer seemed so claustrophobic or threatening.

I had been reborn and rejuvenated after my audience with the modern-day Enki. I felt like my mind had bathed in one of the hot springs of Iceland and had come out refreshed. I was chomping at the bit to get back to my research. It was as if Mr Hjartarson had seen I was flagging on my approach to the finish line and had jumped on to my back and whipped me from behind with a bull's todger. Only metaphorically, despite my earlier concerns.

Let now Mr Hjartarson's penises be praised.

All of them!

I asked men:

HAVE YOU HAD ANY SEXUALLY TRANSMITTED DISEASES?

Yes: 804 (16.34%)   No: 4,117 (83.66%)   Total: 4,921

A surprisingly low 16 per cent of men admit to having had a sexually transmitted infection of some kind. The sobering fact is that many of the others might have one and not even know about it.

Many STIs have unpleasant symptoms involving burning pains, pus, spots or boils, but it is possible to have many of these conditions and know nothing about it at all. Chlamydia, for example, is particularly prevalent at the moment and is often without symptom (50 per cent of men infected will not experience any indication that they've got it, while 70 per cent of infected women are also without symptom). If left untreated it can lead to ectopic pregnancy, miscarriage and infertility in women.

I find it slightly bizarre that even in this day and age, there is still a great social stigma over VD. These men's reaction is typical:

- **I got gonorrhoea. It made me feel rather dirty, and tainted.**

- **Crabs. Made me feel dirty and common.**

Typically some men chose to pass the blame on to the person they got it from:

- **Herpes. I felt pissed off that I slept with a dirty slapper!**

- **Crabs. I was fucked off with the person who gave them to me.**

Getting an STD doesn't make you dirty, and there is certainly nothing to differentiate between you and the person you got it from (unless they passed it on deliberately).

If you've ever had sex with anyone whose ever had sex with anyone else there's a chance you could get one. Using a condom can seriously minimise the risks, but even then you're not immune.

Let's face it though, many men have had sex without using a condom. If the woman involved isn't bothered, we may think we've hit the jackpot, but you may end up with a bonus prize that you weren't after:

● **I got an NSU (non-specific urethritis), contracted in the mid-80s, during my first serious sexual encounter, from a woman who told me we didn't need a condom because I could 'trust her'. These days, I don't believe anything a woman tells me about her sexual condition or contraception.**

So whether we've gone on to catch something is more down to luck than judgement for most of us. It only makes you dirty if you think that having sex is dirty. Which is why some men can see the positive in it:

● **It was a bit embarrassing and well, 'itchy' – but I felt almost proud in a way – 'I had an STD!' It was like a badge of maturity.**

● **Crabs – I felt quite proud 'cos it was only this year: 39 years with nowt, and then along came my very own portable zoo!! Whoo-hoo!**

The thing to remember is that most STIs are easily treatable with ointment or antibiotics or in the case of genital warts by the rather sci-fi means of being frozen off. So don't try to treat yourself like this bloke:

● **I got genital warts. I was so ashamed – too ashamed to go to the clinic, so went to the chemist and got some over the counter wart remover. I blatantly ignored the 'do not use on genital warts' warning and ended up in the clinic with a very sore penis.**

Going to the clinic can be embarrassing and tedious (and with current NHS under-funding extremely time-consuming). I know, because a few years back, during a time when I was enjoying being single, I had a strange sensation in my genitals. I tried to ignore it for a while and couldn't face the shame of going to the clinic, but eventually I realised that I had to. Being the unparanoid man that I am, I was fairly sure that I had testicular cancer, but as it turned out it was Chlamydia. Yet the tests they administered were relatively painless (they didn't, as I had been warned by a friend, insert an umbrella-like device into your Jap's (Herring's) eye and then open it, though they did use plastic swabs to take some cells from inside my Gulliver's Hose, which wasn't altogether pleasant) and the treatment was a couple of weeks of taking antibiotics which did the trick.

Ringing up my recent sexual partners was less amusing, though to be honest they were mostly grateful that I had been responsible enough to tell them, aware of what the disease can do if left untreated. Anyone who is mature and sensible will also realise that there is no point in apportioning blame. You both did what you did and either of you could have been the source of the infection.

Again it's one of those issues that would be much less problematic if we were all open about it.

It was a weight off my mind to know for sure. I really would advise anyone who is single and sexually active, or has been in the past, or has anything that is worrying them, to go along and get checked out. You really are better off knowing the truth whatever it may be.

Because, of course, not all STIs are treatable.

Herpes, although not dangerous, can cause extreme discomfort and it can't be eliminated from the body once contracted (though the same is also true of the virus that causes chicken pox). There are anti-viral medicines that can cut down the length and discomfort of herpes outbreaks. It usually recurs throughout your life and can thus lead to all sorts of anxiety and embarrassment. Some statistics suggest that up to one in five people have the herpes virus and that only 50 per cent of people will have significant enough symptoms to realise that they have got it. It does not kill anyone and it is certainly possible to live a normal life with it once you understand the truth about the virus. Here's some comments about how contracting herpes made men feel:

- **Shock-denial-anger-acceptance.**

- **Angry ... Since I've only had two partners, it was very upsetting to learn almost a year after I'd slept with one that I'd gotten herpes from her. I showed no symptoms, but passed it on to my girlfriend. That made me feel horrible.**

- **The most innocuous virus in a way – same as the cold sore – but once you've got it, it's there forever, and if you're unlucky, you can get recurrent attacks every few weeks for years. It's – forgive the expression – a cunt.**

- **Disappointed in myself, ashamed, scared of giving it to someone else. Worried about finding the way to tell a new partner. Worried that no one would want to go out with me or marry me or have children with me. Horrible experience. I am more informed now and realise that it actually isn't that big a deal and my life hasn't been affected by it.**

Stick a blob on your knob, fellas.

Of course, HIV, the virus which leads to AIDS, also has no cure as yet. HIV infects the cells of the immune system. It can be dormant for many years after initial infection. Eventually it starts to destroy the cells and so destroys a person's natural defence mechanism. As immunity falls, the body is susceptible to infections and diseases it would normally shrug off. The appearance of these infections and diseases classify someone as moving from the HIV-positive stage of the illness to the stage known as AIDS. I will let the men below speak for themselves. They are all HIV-positive.

- **Made me feel 'cheated'. Despite my high number of sexual partners, I have NEVER had unsafe sex. I contracted the virus through oral sex. I have now accepted it as part of me but am highly confident that a cure will be found soon.**

- Initially I used to think about it all the time, but I've never had any adverse effects from it so it tends to stay way at the back of my mind. Sometimes I think I'm probably living with a time-bomb, but I always conclude that worrying about the future doesn't do any good.

- I know I have had it for the past six months but may have had it longer. Sometimes I feel a bit abused, a bit angry, a bit sad. But that is the price to pay for bare backing in a male sex club. I thought 'It won't happen to me!' But it did. Now I just get on with life and am careful when I have sex with others. I have only told a handful of people my status. In the club I do not tell others but make sure I use condoms.

If you have any worries or want to know more about any STIs then I would recommend the excellent website www.afraidtoask.com. There are also some very unpleasant photos which are some of the best advertisements for condoms that I have ever seen.

And on a lighter note you can always use the phantom of the STI as an excellent revenge on an ex-partner, as happened to this fella:

- A disgruntled ex told me she had herpes so I went through the whole spatula up the jap's eye treatment etc. I had to go for annual checkups for three years until I got the all clear. I was a very worried 24 year old; did a lot of horrified reading up. I later found out she didn't have herpes and had just said so out of spite. Wish I'd thought of it.

No, don't do that. It's not nice.

PRICKMYPRICK:DOESITNOTBLEED?

Those of a nervous disposition may like to skip this chapter.

Seriously, I mean it. When I told one of the stories that follow at a gig in Brighton a young man fainted. What you are about to read has the power to fell an otherwise healthy male in his mid-twenties. Are you brave enough to venture onwards ...?

Good.

One of the ultimate ironies of the penis is that although it represents strength, power and masculinity, it is itself incredibly vulnerable, fragile and easy to break.

I asked men:

HAVE YOU EVER HAD ANY PENILE INJURIES?
Yes: 932 (18.92%)   No: 3,994 (81.08%)   Total: 4,926

All kinds of calamities have befallen these unfortunate one in five.

Some have been bitten by inexpert cock-suckers (and possibly beagles, we don't know).

● **I bled after getting blow job from girl with prominent front teeth.**

A fairly common occurrence if my survey is anything to go by.

- One of my close friends had his bitten into when his girlfriend was performing oral sex on him. It bled like a bitch! It got infected (apparently a human bite is worse than an animal's for infection) and he had to have his foreskin surgically removed after his knob swelled up to the size of a peach. He asked for the foreskin to be placed in a jam jar so that he could give it to his girlfriend, which he did while he told her he didn't want to see her any more.

What a wonderful memento. Giving a girl your heart is easy, but to actually give her a piece of your dick shows her she was something special!

Masturbation, as you might guess, leads to almost as many mishaps:

- Blood blister or two from skanky south London girl who rubbed me off a little too violently while wearing rings on every finger.

- I think I have a high libido, which was even higher in my adolescence. I often masturbated so much that I wore the skin away.

It seems that for some guys wanking genuinely is self-abuse.

Sexual intercourse itself can be a dangerous occupation. I think most men will have been pranged in a similar (though possibly not as extreme) fashion to this:

- During intercourse my partner straddled my penis (she was on top), she squatted down but we were not properly aligned. My penis kind of snapped in the middle. A terribly painful experience.

You have to be careful where you have sex too.

- Chaffing due to fucking with a johnny that had sand in it (I was on a beach, not in a sandpit).

- I trapped my penis in the rickety old mattress of my ex-girlfriend's bed. It got stuck between two pieces of mangled metal. There was a little blood and my girlfriend almost fainted. She had to call the fire brigade because we could not detach my penis from the mattress. The fire brigade arrived ten minutes later, to free my member from its prison. They laughed a lot. One of them said they get this kind of call all the time, and are used to seeing people with trapped willies. I told them that I wasn't used to my penis being rescued by loads of blokes in uniform. My girlfriend started laughing. Bitch!

Over 18 per cent of the men who had been injured had caught their cock in their zip fasteners (an experience that the comedian Dave Gorman rather neatly refers to as 'The Penis Fly Trap').

- Family bathroom, Saturday, June, 1969, 3pm 'zipper incident'.

- Caught my foreskin in a zip when I was a kid, I had to go to the hospital with the skin poking out of my trousers, the nurse and Dad had a jolly good laugh about it as if I wasn't there – thus adding insult to injury.

Your exposed penis is doubly vulnerable if you're a smoker:

- Got a fag burn from taking a pee while a bit pissed.

While deliberately putting an inappropriate substance on your penis, or dipping it into something you shouldn't, can also have catastrophic side effects:

- I put Immac[1] on it, to get rid of the pubic hair round my balls and knob – I left it on too long and ended up with horrific burns.

- Drunk and naked at party, I had whisky poured into eye of cock. Nice at first, hurt most of the night, and the following day.

---

1. *This is not called Veet. It is a hair-removal preparation, usually used by ladies to remove other bodily hair. It is not intended for use on the genitals.*

- A mild 'injury' when my partner at the time smeared Vick deconges-
  tant salve (in the distinctive blue bottle) all over my penis. I have never
  repeated the experience.

- My ex-girlfriend (now my ex-wife – yes, I still married the bitch!)
  decided she wanted to shave my cock and balls. She managed to nick
  my scrote in a few places, which stung a bit, so I asked her to rub in
  some post shave balm ... This was bliss, so as she was doing this I had
  my head tilted back and my eyes closed, which meant that I didn't see
  what was coming next ... Imagine my surprise when she splashed
  concentrated Paco Rabanne on my balls! The pain was absolutely
  horrendous!! I had to stand with my bollocks under cold water for
  about 20 minutes. Childbirth ... pah!

Yes, of course, because after childbirth women only have to stand under cold
water for 20 minutes and the pain is forgotten. Hands up all the ladies who
think this man deserved everything he got!

Showing we have balls can often lead to mayhem for our cocks:

- I was riding the back of a shopping cart down a hill when I hit a bump
  and was thrown into the air. I landed on the handle of the cart and hurt
  my meat puppet. The next day when I woke up IT WAS TOTALLY
  BLACK-PURPLE ALL OVER and I freaked out. AAAARGH!!! I was
  sure it was going to fall off, but the doc assured me I had merely broken
  a blood vessel and the color would go away in about a month (it did)
  with no loss of function (no loss occurred).

- I was sledging as a kid and as I came down to the bottom of the slope,
  I hit a brick-lined path under the snow. The sled stopped dead. I did
  not. I was lying face down and bounced along the surface of the ground
  like a stone being skimmed across a lake. Of course my friend thought
  this was very funny. So did I, until I went to the toilet and the salty flow
  of urine got into the wound. By God, I knew about it for the next week.
  To this day, I have a little bit of scar tissue around the end of my cock.

On that subject, quite a few men made a comment similar to this one:

● **Don't know what happened but I have a scar along the underside, most of the length. It possibly happened as a baby because I've always had it and you'd think I'd remember any injury.**

In fact what is being referred to here is a normal feature of all penises. The dark line (which stretches all along the underside of the penis and scrotum) is in fact formed in the womb when our sex is determined and our penis is fused together.

However, I think my favourite answer for this question is this one:

● **I was stung by a wasp in nudist camp.**

If you look hubris up in a dictionary there is a picture of that incident.

However, about a third of the men who admitted to having had a penile injury had experienced the same horrendous event. According to the *Guardian* newspaper it has happened to around 5 per cent of uncircumcised males. It is something that doctors call 'frenulum breve'. You might know it better as 'snapping the banjo string':

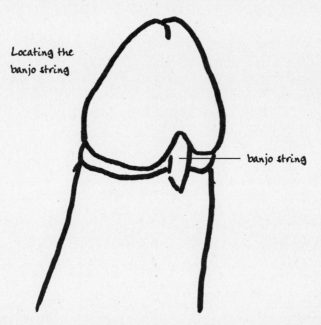

Locating the banjo string

banjo string

It is the little strip of skin at the top of the underside of the penis that connects the bullet (glans) to the shaft. A lot of men probably don't even notice it's there, which is why I advise any blokes reading this to look at the other side of their cock occasionally. It's really different. It's like the moon in that respect.

The frenulum is one of the most sensitive parts of the human body, so, girls, if you lick it during oral sex it's one of the most pleasurable things you can do to a man. If you bite it during oral sex ... that's not so good. It can be incredibly painful.

I could share many horrific stories from men who've experienced this,[2] but here are just a few of the more distressing ones:

- **I'd acquired a new girlfriend of high libido and was round at her place, having sex for the third of fourth time that night,[3] when I became aware of a remote snapping sensation, followed by spreading wetness. She was rather horrified about the amount of blood coming out of her and began to accuse me of damaging her internally ... The look of relief that crossed her face, when she saw the blood still pumping out of my 'little general', did not bode well for the relationship.**

This next story slightly smacks of an old urban myth that I remember from school. Though I would say even if this is made up, it is something that must have happened in reality many, many times:

- **It was on Valentine's Day when I was 17. I had just started seeing this girl that very day and we decided to go to a club out of town. The plan was to stay at her friend's house with a group of her pals as the girl's parents were away. So, we got pissed, danced and inevitably got horny so we made an early exit. When we got back to the house, we fell on to the futon and started getting it on. Soon I was naked,**

---

2. *For example, I know a relatively well-known comedian who had it happen to him when he was dry humping his girlfriend when he was a teenager. His jeans ended up covered in blood. Don't worry, Stew, your secret is safe with me.*

3. *Incidentally, I've noticed how blokes will often include unnecessary bragging details, even in a story like this one. It's not strictly relevant.*

lying on my back getting my dick sucked. Everything was cool. Then I felt a sharp pain. I voiced my discomfort with a mandatory, 'Ow!' to which she pulled her head up quick to say 'What?' But my 'ow' had become an 'AAAAAAAAAH'. She jumped up and turned the light on. I was shocked to see her mouth covered in blood. Her eyes were wide in horror staring at my crotch. I looked down to see blood, all over my old boy, and my stomach and legs, dripping on to the white futon. I couldn't help laughing. She started crying. What had happened was the bit of flesh that connected my foreskin to my japs eye had been pierced by the hook on her brace. When I said 'ow', she instinctively pulled back, tearing it apart. And all I could do was lie there, giggling nervously as I looked at the fine bloody spray coming from my wound.

A similar lengthy story ends with the respondent having a plume of blood shooting out of his still-erect penis and his girlfriend commenting, 'Christ, get into the bathroom, you arsehole. You're ruining my sheets!'

Nice to see how sympathetic women can be, isn't it fellas? Also good to see that the bloke in the second example was able to even find it amusing at the time!

Although the experience is painful and embarrassing, it should not really lead to any long-term problems, provided that you consult a doctor if it doesn't heal naturally. An easy solution that some doctors will take is simply to circumcise you under anaesthetic and this is occasionally the only option available. If you are attached to your foreskin (albeit a little less securely than you were before) you might prefer to have something called frenuloplasty. It is all fairly painless, apart from the brief sting of the needle which will apply anaesthetic to the tip of your penis (possibly something you might want to look away for). Then a vertical incision is made into the banjo string, creating two little flaps which are then stitched together to restore you to your former glory.

You might have to stop having sex for a while to allow it to heal, but then if you've just had blood spurting from your cock like water from a broken drain, you might never want to have sex again.

According to Freud (and simple common sense) the greatest fear most men have about their man-flap is that they might lose it altogether. The prospect of living life without it is not something that most of us want to contemplate.

I asked men:

WOULD YOU RATHER LOSE YOUR PENIS OR ONE OF YOUR LEGS?

Penis: 1,212 (24.66%)   Leg: 3,703 (75.34%)   Total: 4,915

WOULD YOU RATHER LOSE YOUR PENIS OR BOTH YOUR EYES?

Penis: 3,484 (70.99%)   Eyes: 1,424 (29.01%)   Total: 4,908

IF YOU HAD THE CHOICE BETWEEN CASTRATION AND DEATH WHICH WOULD YOU TAKE?

Castration: 3,655 (74.71%)   Death: 1,237 (25.29%)   Total: 4,892

IF YOU LOST YOUR PENIS IN AN ACCIDENT WOULD YOU KILL YOURSELF?

Yes: 584 (11.86%)   No: 4,341 (88.14%)   Total: 4,925

Though it is unlikely (one would hope) that we would ever have to make such choices, you can see the reasoning. It would be possible to get a prosthetic leg, not so easy or enjoyable to have a prosthetic penis, which is why two-thirds would ditch a limb. Eyes are equally irreplaceable and arguably more useful to us than our cocks, so only a quarter of men would give up visual before sexual pleasure. Similarly the survival instinct is stronger than the sexual one, and though it would diminish our lives to live without sex, most of us conclude that it would more diminish our lives to be dead. I think if men were genuinely presented with this choice they would instinctively opt for life. It is still interesting that over ten per cent of men value their penis so highly they believe they would commit suicide if they ever lost it.

Of course there are men who actively want to lose their penis. Most obviously are the people who feel that they are a woman born in a man's body, who will opt for a sex change. This procedure is much more than a dismemberment, the penis is adapted into a vagina. The penis is cleft in twain and the testicles (bollocks) are removed from the scrotum (jizz-bag). Only the skin and the bullet-head of the penis are retained, as this contains the nerve endings. The skin is pushed back into the abdomen and the nerves from the tip are formed into a clitoris. The skin of the scrotum is used to form labia.

Historically, castration has been willingly adopted by quite a few religious cults. In ancient Rome, initiates into the cult of Cybele would dance wildly until they reached a peak of religious ecstasy and then cut off their bollocks. These were the eunuchs who have provided so much fodder for the *Carry On* team over the years (which I am sure made their sacrifice worthwhile). Usually the penis was not cut off (which meant these peculiar lady-men could still get

Still from the little-known film, 'Abbott and Costello Meet Some Eunuchs'. Eunuchs are usually mild-mannered and peaceful, but the knockabout humour of the annoying double act has made the eunuchs quite angry. Even more angry than they were when they found out they'd had their genitals cut off.

erections and have sex, obviously without fear of impregnating anyone), but for some eunuchs it was an all-inclusive deal, giving them that smooth-groined look of the Action Man (though clearly they saw very little action).

The Christian Church also sanctioned castration in the interests of choral singing. To prevent young choirboys losing their sweet high voices at puberty they had their balls squished or removed and they were able to keep singing the high notes for their entire lives (I bet Aled Jones is pleased that this practice died out in the nineteenth century).

Other pseudo-Christian cults such as the Skoptsy in eighteenth-century Russia, or more recently the Heaven's Gate cult in America, also practised removal of the penis and/or testicles. The former believed that you could only get to Heaven if you were pure and chaste (they obviously missed the bit in the Bible about men with damaged genitalia not being allowed in); the latter believed that they were going to be picked up by a flying saucer, but had to be dead and have no genitalia for that to happen.

For most men that would be taking religious faith a bit far.

In modern times when we talk about dismemberment, most of us will think of the same name – John Wayne Bobbitt.

On the night of 23 June 1993, this thoroughly unpleasant man got drunk, allegedly forced his wife Lorena to have sex with him and then fell asleep. Lorena took a spectacular revenge by cutting off her husband's penis with an eight-inch carving knife, driving off with it in her car and then throwing it out of the window of the moving vehicle.

Luckily for John, the penis was found on the kerb and reattached by Dr David Berman using microsurgery. Berman never got paid as Bobbitt wasn't insured and was declared bankrupt, but as the doctor quips on his website, 'I guess you could call it *pro bono* work!'[4] (He needn't have worried, the resulting publicity has seen his plastic surgery practice boom. People tend to figure that if he can reattach a penis, then their breasts will be in safe hands.)

---

4. *This is quite some way from being an amusing joke.*

COCKQUOTE

For any of you unlucky enough to become detached from your penis either by accident or design, I include this excellent advice given by Dorothy Baldwin in her book, *Understanding Male Sexual Health*:

'If the penis is accidentally amputated, stay alert. Wrap it in a bag to prevent freezer burn and place it in the fridge. Total replant surgery is possible by highly skilled microsurgeons ... the time lapse between injury and re-attachment should be less than six hours.'

The reaction to the story was incredible. Few people seemed genuinely appalled by the allegations of sexual assault or the rather brutal revenge (both Bobbitts were acquitted for their misdemeanours – Lorena by reason of insanity, though some might argue she finally acted with supreme clarity after years of mistreatment); mostly it was treated as a comedic event.

Nor was it an entirely negative experience for either of them. Lorena became a hero to many women; the castration of her husband served as a symbolical dismemberment of all the men who had abused (or even annoyed) women. John, bizarrely, became a celebrity. Everyone wanted to see his reattached penis and to find out if it still functioned. Something he was able to demonstrate in porn films such as 'John Wayne Bobbitt – Uncut!' (Ha ha, do you get it?) His self-styled Franken-penis was a celebrity, and because you couldn't have the penis without John (however hard Lorena had tried to prove otherwise), he became a celebrity too.

More recently (and possibly predictably) Bobbitt was imprisoned for beating up his second wife. Does this man never learn? Doesn't he remember what happened last time he did that?

Lorena's only real mistake is that she threw the penis out of her car in a place where it would easily be found (conveniently beside a 7–11 convenience store). She should have taken a leaf out of the book of the wife of Lin Yuk-Sang, who when she found out her husband had been cheating on her, cut off his penis with a pair of scissors and (this is the genius part) flushed it down the toilet.

John Wayne Bobbitt hears his thousandth Bobbitt joke of the day.

Lorena Bobbitt in court, looking at the judge as if to say, 'Convict me and I'll do the same to you.'

There's no way the police were going to bother to search for that one. Imagine them wading up to their waists in sewage in the dark: 'I've found it! ... Oh no, another false alarm. Well, it was shaped like a penis.'

So why are stories of sexual catastrophe so amusing to us? In Bobbitt's case there is a general feeling that he had done something to deserve his punishment. Yet most of us will still laugh at the men whose penises bleed during consensual sex and who have done nothing wrong. Why is that funny? A torn vagina wouldn't be a cause of merriment. What is the difference here?

I think most men laugh at these stories out of a mixture of fear and relief (that it hasn't happened to them). Such a concept makes us anxious (believe me,

COCKFACT

In January 2002 in Brazil, Ana Alves da Silva cut off her husband's manhood when he came home late from a party ... possibly a slight over-reaction on her part. But it is one way to teach a man about the value of good time-keeping.

She said she did it because she was sick and tired of her husband's drinking and affairs and his visiting prostitutes ... well, she hasn't stopped him drinking.

I have witnessed the crossed legs and cupped hands of the men in my audience when they hear these tales), but to admit to our anxiety would make us seem weak. So we laugh in the face of fear.

Yet as with so much comedy, I think the humour derives from status. Traditionally women have been the low-status characters in our society. They have been put upon by men, bossed around by men, abused by men and irritated by men and this is a moment of revenge. Women are empowered by such stories, because they challenge this masculine dominance. What better way of getting back at them than attacking the very symbol of their masculinity? To warn them what could happen to them if they aren't careful?

Subconsciously there are times when most of us would like to kill our bosses, or punch our politicians, or punish our parents. It's natural to feel this way. Humour is an important release valve in our society that allows us to voice those ideas, and get them out of our system, without having to actually commit the crime and go to prison.

Lorena Bobbitt epitomised the victim triumphing over a bully. We can celebrate that (perhaps choosing to ignore the reality of the violent way she chose to express her anger).

When I ask women in my audience why they are laughing about a man having a plume of blood shooting out of his penis, they generally conclude it is because men 'deserve' it, because they are macho and arrogant.[5]

I think it's important to ask why men are sometimes macho and arrogant. If you were made to feel that having an unusual or unerect or small penis actually makes you unmanly, maybe you would try and overcompensate in the macho stakes?

I asked men:

HAS THE SIZE OR SHAPE OF YOUR GENITALS EVER CAUSED YOU ANXIETY OR EMBARRASSMENT?

Yes: 1,463 (29.2%)   **No:** 3,548 (70.8%)   **Total:** 5,011

---

5. *Though one woman did comment that it's because women are used to blood coming out of their genitals so it's good for men to get an idea of what that's like!*

Nearly one in three men admitted that it had.

I asked women:

HAVE YOU EVER OPENLY LAUGHED AT A MAN'S GENITALS?

Yes: 630 (28.6%)   No: 1,573 (71.4%)   Total: 2,203

Twenty-nine per cent of men are mortified with embarrassment and 29 per cent of women are laughing in their embarrassed faces. To be fair many of them are laughing at them for different reasons than you might imagine:

- It was the first time I saw an uncircumcised penis and it scared me! I thought something was wrong with it!!

- Because it was REALLY SMALL. The funniest part was when he said to me, 'It'll get bigger, it'll get bigger.' It didn't. But he was the one laughing in the end because it was THE most amazing sex I've ever had.

- My current boyfriend once wrapped his penis up in its foreskin and somehow trapped it all curled up. Then he tensed and relaxed his pelvic muscles until it all popped open. He was trying to make me laugh and it worked.

- It was so huge I was really quite taken aback. I soon shut up. He put it in my mouth.

- He had drawn a silly face on it. It would have been rude not to laugh.

- Only laughed at the ginger pubes, not the manhood.

- Because he was laying on his back pretending to drive a car – using it as his gearstick – he thought I was asleep. It was when he started making the 'Brrrmmmmm …' noises that I couldn't help but piss myself laughing.

Even so, a fair proportion of women have laughed at a man because his penis differs from the 'norm'.

I make this point not to criticise women, because I think male and female are both equally indoctrinated into believing in the uniformity of the penis. I am only trying to acknowledge that although men might appear to be unfeeling, emotionless automatons, there is a lot of confusion and pain beneath the surface.

Men are just as affected by body fascism as women, and yet we are unable to discuss many of our worries in the open.

It seems to be the length of the flesh canoe that causes the most hilarity, or concern, pretty much depending which end of it you're at. So is it the size of your boat, or the motion of the ocean that's important?

Or is it more to do with the amount of seamen on the poop deck?

Although most men go to great pains to avoid ever having pieces of sharp metal thrust through their genitalia, there are a minority for whom such a thing is highly desirable.

I asked men:

DO YOU HAVE ANY GENITAL PIERCINGS OR OTHER ADDITIONS TO YOUR PENIS?

Yes: 181 (3.69%)   **No:** 4,728 (96.31%)   **Total:** 4,909

I also asked those who had, what had possessed them to do it:

- Frenum bar, 2000; Prince Albert, 2001 – the pain exorcises troubling memories.
- Prince Albert. Drunk.
- Prince Albert – always wondered what it would be like. I was fucking around too much, so I thought the 6 week recovery period would be a good break.
- Snake Tattoo.
- Tattoo of smiley face on bell end.
- A Prince Albert. I'd heard it was a pleasure for everyone involved. And yes, it is.
- My rabbi advised it. He said that the Jewish God preferred them studded.
- I have an 8 gauge apadravya, which is a piercing passing top to bottom through the glans vertically. I started getting a few piercings which looked good but really didn't have any function, then I got my tongue done. I then realised how much fun the more practical piercings are so I bit the bullet and got the apadravya a while after.
- Used to have an ampallang. Thought it was worth a try, because I'd heard it made sex nicer, makes you come faster, etc. As it happens,

the bastard of a tattooist put the thing too far forwards, so it was just bloody uncomfortable. And I paid forty quid to have it done too. (Grumble, whine)

● **The sun was out so I added a key ring.**

The Prince Albert was the clear favourite in my survey. This involves inserting a ring through Herring's eye which comes out at the base of the glans (bullet), so half the ring is inside you and half is out. It is generally believed that this device was named after Queen Victoria's husband. According to Charlotte Ward in *The Illustrated Book of the Phallus*, the Prince Albert was in fact named after Victoria's son, Albert, Duke of Clarence (one of the prime suspects for fanciful loonies in the Jack the Ripper case), who was blessed with such a big cock, he attempted to make the job of his royal dressers a bit easier, by lashing the beast to his leg.

The Frenum is a ring that pierces your oh-so-fragile banjo-string and goes round the shaft, rather like a ring on a finger.

The Ampallang is a bar which passes right through the head of the penis and comes highly recommended by the *Kama Sutra*.

The Apradravya is a bar which goes vertically through the shaft or the head of the penis.

The Dydoe – poor old Dido, not only does her name sound like 'dildo', it is also a pun for a stud placed through the upper and lower edge of the bottom part of the glans. This is probably the one recommended by the rabbi above as it is popular among the Jewish community because it is supposed to give more sensation to a circumcised penis.

It is not recommended that you try to create any of these effects on your own. Please seek professional help if you decide you want to join this brave cock élite!

However big you think you are, there's always someone bigger.

10
IDON'TUSEITASARULE

The medieval Indian sex manual the *Ananga Ranga* had some comforting words for the less well-endowed:

> *The man whose lingam is very long, will be wretchedly poor*
> *The man whose lingam is thin, will ever be very lucky.*
> *And the man whose lingam is short, will be a Rajah.*

The cynical small-cocked man (who has yet to be invited to rule India) might argue this is just an attempt at consolation, matched today by the much-repeated mantra of 'It's not how big it is, it's what you do with it that counts.'

Although like the Ancient Greeks, the Hindus saw a small penis as an indication of manliness and fertility, in the modern Western world big is beautiful and if you've got a long lingam, far from being wretchedly poor, you can make a killing in the porn industry.

How much difference does it really make though? And what constitutes a big pocket rocket anyway?

In my survey erect penis size ranged from:

Min: 3.3 inches[1]

---

1. *Although in all other matters I am a great fan of the metric system it seems to me the penis should always be measured in inches. For those of you who are not imperially minded 1 inch = 2.54 centimetres. You do the maths.*

to

    Max: 14 inches

with an average of 6.73 inches.

Now, don't worry too much about that, fellas. That average is about half an inch to an inch longer than any other survey I've ever seen on this subject.

Which could mean one of two things: either big-cocked blokes particularly enjoy filling in questionnaires or, more likely, when the men came to measure their penises, they really dug the ruler in ... as far as it would go. They were breaking skin and hammering the ruler through so it came out the other side, then triumphantly proclaiming, 'See, I told you it was seven inches! Justice! Now get me to a hospital!'

The problem with any attempt to measure the erect penis is that it is generally a self-administered test. So wishful thinking and downright lies tend to warp the results. It also makes a difference which side you measure (most surveys measure the top – well it's nearer. It also avoids the tricky 'Do I include the testicles?' issue) and you should also remember that your erection can vary in size dependent on just how turned on you are.

Something that one survey I was sent (I get sent a lot of this kind of stuff now) was not going to take any chances with. Juliet Richters, John Gerofi and Basil Donovan from Sydney wished to determine whether condoms were the

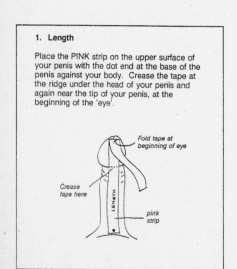

1. Length

Place the PINK strip on the upper surface of your penis with the dot end at the base of the penis against your body. Crease the tape at the ridge under the head of your penis and again near the tip of your penis, at the beginning of the 'eye'.

Fold tape at beginning of eye

Crease tape here

LENGTH

pink strip

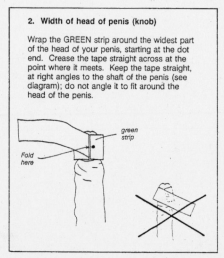

2. Width of head of penis (knob)

Wrap the GREEN strip around the widest part of the head of your penis, starting at the dot end. Crease the tape straight across at the point where it meets. Keep the tape straight, at right angles to the shaft of the penis (see diagram); do not angle it to fit around the head of the penis.

green strip

Fold here

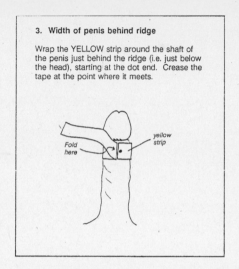

3. **Width of penis behind ridge**

Wrap the YELLOW strip around the shaft of the penis just behind the ridge (i.e. just below the head), starting at the dot end. Crease the tape at the point where it meets.

Fold here — yellow strip

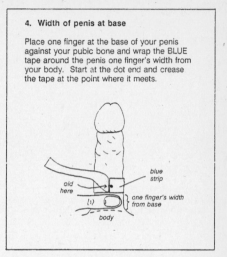

4. **Width of penis at base**

Place one finger at the base of your penis against your pubic bone and wrap the BLUE tape around the penis one finger's width from your body. Start at the dot end and crease the tape at the point where it meets.

old here — blue strip — one finger's width from base — body

Detailed instructions on penis measurement from the Sydney based survey.

right size for everyone. They persuaded men to take part by offering them a free lottery scratch card (as if Australians need any incentive to get their cocks out) then gave them a self-measurement kit that came complete with various paper tape measures and these very specific instructions.

Of their sample of 156 men the mean penis length was 16.0 cm (6.29 in) with an average base circumference of 13.5 cm (5.31 in). The range of lengths was 11.7–22.5 cm (4.6–8.86 in) and circumference at base ranged between 10.5 and 17.5 cm (4.13–6.89 in).[2] They did, however, survey a fairly small sample of men.

Other surveys I've seen (usually based on self-measurement, but with more participants) provide length averages of between 5½ and just over 6 inches and an average circumference of between 4½ and 5½ inches.

Although three-quarters of men fall into the average range of 4½–6 inches erect, the extremes of cock length once again show the variety of penises that are out there. A few men are born with so-called micro-penises that can be under an inch in length even when erect, while the upper limit is clouded with myth and exaggeration. According to the gorgeous Dr Terri Hamilton, the

2. *They concluded that condoms should be manufactured and marketed in a wider range of lengths and widths.*

largest natural penis ever recorded was 13.5 inches long (so if the bloke who said he was 14 inches in my survey is reading and was telling the truth, I'd advise you to get in touch with Norris MacWhirter, mate. You're a record-breaker!)

Unfortunately, ladies, there genuinely is no way to judge how big a man's member will be without actually checking it out for yourself. Although people may claim that the size of other body parts are a factor, there is absolutely no correlation. A girlfriend of a friend of mine was convinced that she had discovered that the length of a man's erect penis was equal to the lengths of his thumb and first finger combined. She said it was true of every man she'd been with. I can confirm that this theory definitely isn't universal from personal testimony (which is lucky for me, as I have very short fingers!)

The assumption that a big nose equals a big hose can prove to be fatal. The fourteenth-century Queen of Naples, Johanna, particularly liked well-hung men and believed in the size correlation between schnoz and schlong when she chose the big-hootered Prince Andrew of Hungary as her husband. Her wedding night was not all she had hoped. 'Oh nose,' she reportedly lamented, 'how horribly you have deceived me!' The whole experience was even more disappointing for Andrew. She had him strangled for his husbandly shortcomings.

Although not all less-blessed men will suffer such a terrible fate, the psychological scars of having what you yourself consider to be a small penis can be devastating.

I asked men:

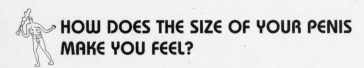

HOW DOES THE SIZE OF YOUR PENIS MAKE YOU FEEL?

Here are some of the very sad answers from men who think they have small penises:

- I wish that it was bigger.

- Embarrassed.

- Pitiful, suicidal, depressed, alone, unloved and unwanted.

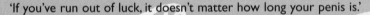

COCKQUOTE

'If you've run out of luck, it doesn't matter how long your penis is.'

Juvenal

- Totally fucking inadequate – I know my wife is a liar about the level of satisfaction with me.

- Awkward ... Is it big enough to do the job?

- Afraid to go with girl because I'm afraid it's small.

- At school I was always embarrassed about the size of my penis in typical changing room situations. Compared to other boys I felt almost like a woman, or some hermaphrodite. Not like a man anyway. At the time I just felt ashamed, though later in the day I would get angry about it.

- Sometimes I feel a bit like I have a serious problem, but I have been with my partner for nearly two years now and whenever its mentioned she just says I'm a twat.

Most blokes should listen to that woman. Out of interest I went back to look at the sizes of those guys' penises ...

- I wish that it was bigger ... 6 inches.

- Embarrassed ... 6 inches.

Both these men are on the large side of average.

- Pitiful, suicidal, depressed, alone, unloved and unwanted ... 4 inches.

COCKFACT

The best way to determine the length of a man's penis is to get him to show it to you and then measure it with a ruler.

Four inches is smaller than average, but it's not *that* small. It's perfectly adequate and definitely not worth killing yourself over.

- **Totally fucking inadequate – I know my wife is a liar about the level of satisfaction with me … 5 inches.**

- **Awkward … Is it big enough to do the job? … 7.5 inches.**

Seven and a half inches?! Yeah, I think it is big enough to do the job. What job were you planning on doing with it? Digging irrigation ditches? Maybe not.

- **Afraid to go with girl because I'm afraid it's small … 5.2 inches.**

- **At school I was always embarrassed, etc. … 4 inches.**

- **Sometimes I feel a bit like I have a serious problem, etc. … 7 inches.**

The bloke whose girlfriend says he's a twat has a seven-inch penis. You know what mate, she's right. Grow up!

Not one of these unhappy men is significantly smaller than average and most of them are actually bigger. Yet some of them are clearly so convinced that they don't measure up that they have given up on the idea of ever having sex with anyone. Isn't that truly tragic?

Of course most straight men will never see another man's erect penis outside of a porn film. If you judge your own erection by those of some of the freaks they employ in those skin flicks then you are bound to feel inadequate.

The only other chance men have to compare themselves is through glimpses caught in toilets or changing rooms, but there are a couple of important things to consider here.

First, the size of the flaccid penis is no indication of how big the penis will be when erect. Some start small and expand beyond all imaginings; (it's a grower, not a show-er) others may look big on the soft, but barely alter once the blood has pumped in; others start big and then inflate to the size of a bouncy castle. You can't tell that from glancing at them. Let's face it, the size of a flaccid penis can vary significantly dependent on temperature, nerves or sexual excitement. Maybe the fella next to you in the toilet has got a semi. Maybe he's noticed you looking and he likes it.

Secondly, and this is something that isn't quite so obvious, the other fella's pecker might look more impressive due to your perspective. If you look at a penis from the side (as you tend to when you're looking at someone else's) it looks bigger than it would do from above (as you tend to when you're looking at your own). If you looked at it from underneath it would seem even bigger, which explains some of the unusual camera angles that are employed in porno-graphic movies.

For any younger readers who are concerned, your penis will not reach full adult proportions, on average, until just before your fifteenth birthday. I'm afraid for any older fellas that you've reached your final size by the age of 17 and there's no further growth.

Unless, of course, you're prepared to give Mother Nature a helping hand.

I asked men:

 ## HAVE YOU EVER TRIED TO MAKE YOUR PENIS BIGGER?
Yes: 1,087 (27.55%)   **No:** 2,858 (72.45%)   **Total:** 3,945

Amazingly over a quarter of men have tried to increase the size of their cocks.

So what did they try and did it work?

The majority of men who answered yes to this question had tried a vacuum pump (similar to the Swedish one that Austin Powers denies owning, despite substantial evidence, in his first movie). Here are some testimonials:

- It made it all swollen and a bit uncomfortable, and it was messy and fiddly and I couldn't be bothered with it, so it went in the bin.

- Used a Vac-u-pump – it only worked while the pump was on it.

That seems to be the response from most of the men who've tried it. The next response was quite unique:

- When I was about 16 I found one of those vacuum pump things in the street, took it home, washed it!!, and then used it for a few nights. Made the erection very strong (like I needed help then!) but made no difference to size. After about a week I actually said out loud to myself, 'What the hell are you doing?'

There can be little in this world less appealing than a secondhand penis vacuum pump. That's why you don't often see them advertised in the local paper. These things should only be used in a practical joke setting, where for example you leave one on your boss's desk before an important meeting with clients!

Other men tried making home-made suction devices with Hoovers and one thought he might improve things if he got his boyfriend to suck it really hard

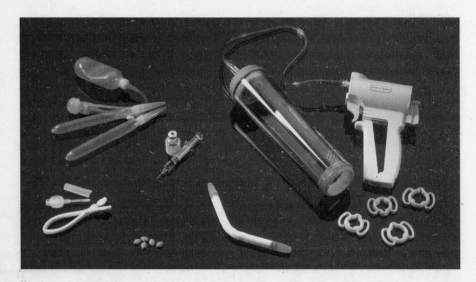

What the song "Pump up the Volume" was really about.

(that's his story). He reckons it added a tenth of an inch, but the medical facts are that any gain from the vacuum method is temporary or due to wishful thinking. Having said that, I love this home-made version:

- **I used to suck mine through a half-filled bubble bath bottle while thinking of Chrissie from Grange Hill!**

If that didn't work then surely nothing could.

Any method reliant on increasing or trapping blood in the penis is doomed to long-term failure:

- **I tied elastic bands around it, as an experiment. Subjectively became bigger, and extremely painful. Then struggled hard to remove elastic bands. Horrible sweaty handed moment as I thought, I've really fucked it up now.**

Another popular method is to hang things on your cock in the hope that it will stretch:

- **Hung weights on it, and stuck it in a door and pulled. It looked longer and thinner, but not for long.**

- **A yogi exercise: Hanging weights with a string around the dickhead every day for a long time. Did not have the patience to see if it really worked.**

I don't remember seeing Yogi Bear doing that. But it highlights the problem with most of these methods. They involve so much effort that most people will eventually become bored and give up. Almost as if the people selling this particular brand of snake oil had planned it that way. Only one man claimed success:

- **Tied a brick to it. Some African tribes do it, and it works!**

If you want a long thin cock which quite possibly might not work any more, then I advise you to try the same thing.

Others hang things from their prick in the hope of making it stronger:

- **I tried getting it erect and then draping a towel over it and flexing/ relaxing to lift the towel. It didn't work.**

Nor did the wet sock that someone else plumped for. Manual stretching is also a popular choice, which seems equally doomed to failure:

- **Read somewhere that regular stretching would increase length. What a con that was, and ended up with a sore dick to boot.**

- **I used an exercise called the 'jelq' for adding girth and I did a stretching exercise for adding length. I did not gain any length except temporary gain, because I did the stretching wrong and injured the ligaments at the base of my cock. I know people who have gained length when they have done the stretches correctly. I did gain girth from the jelqing exercise and most of that gain is permanent.**

Yes, it was because he did it wrong that it didn't work. Of course! And injured ligaments are a small price to pay for a (possibly imaginary) gain!

Jelqing wasn't something I had previously heard of, so I looked it up on the Internet to be greeted with the rather dubious claim that

> *The Jelq technique was reportedly first used by Arab tribesmen centuries ago as part of the passage from puberty to manhood ... By using this method 5 times a week for 10 to 30 minutes a day, some men have attained sizes over 18 to 20 inches in length and nearly 8 inches in circumference.*

So it can give you a penis that is six inches longer than the recorded maximum, and that is so wide it will presumably be impossible to have sex with anything but a female elephant. The technique claims to thicken and lengthen the penis by forcing more blood into the *corposa cavernosa* (lungs of desire). Supposedly, by continually milking the penis the reservoirs inside will grow bigger and be able to accommodate more blood, so your erection will be bigger. It promises

Some women will try anything to stop you leaving the house.

a two-inch growth within the first year for an investment of thirty minutes a day (though you mustn't get more than a semi-erection through doing this or you can damage yourself internally).

The whole idea seems ludicrous, time-consuming and bogus to me, and the elasticity of the penis is not something you want to fuck around with.

If you want to make your penis bigger your only real non-surgical option is what this fella tried as a teenager:

● **Prayer and excessive wanking.**

The effects of the pills and the lotions that you are constantly offered in small ads and spam emails are perfectly summed up by this next man:

● **'Amazing herbal tablets.' Did they work? Did they bollocks?**

How about this for a cheaper, safer, less time-consuming option:

● **Shaving my shaft and balls – certainly makes it look bigger.**

In fact according to Dr Terri Hamilton (I grow to love this woman more and more – I hope one day we will be married and can talk about cocks together all day) if you simply remove some of the pubic hair around the base of your penis, the shaft will be less obscured and your cock will miraculously appear to be bigger. She says 'Shave directly straight up the penile shaft about an inch onto the pubis (not too high for a natural look) … and bingo! An instantly longer penis.' Bingo?

The next suggestion is even more effective and less dangerous (unless you were to stand in direct sunlight):

● **Put a magnifying glass over it.**

It might be tricky to achieve that effect constantly. Though a bloke currently sitting near me in the British Library has managed to attach a magnifying glass to his spectacles. Maybe I could get him to adapt it to fit over his balls. Hold on, I'll ask him.

He said no.

A couple of the men from the survey did turn to surgery in order to increase cock size, one unsuccessfully:

● **Circumcision on NHS in mistaken belief that it increased (apparent) size.**

Cutting pieces off something generally makes it smaller. Unless you have a penis like a Hydra, in which case you don't have much to worry about, unless it starts biting you.

The other man who opted for surgery was more successful:

● **Had enlargement surgery. Yes it did work on girth.**

In America in 2002, 15,000 men opted to have penile enhancement surgery, which cost them each between $3,000 and $5,000 dollars. Although this is something to be considered for men with extremely small penises (the *Journal of Urology* advises that such operations should only be conducted on men with erect penises that were less than 2.9 inches long), the majority of men who seek out such an operation have penises that are average or above average in length.

This is even more astonishing when you realise what such an operation involves and what can go wrong. Why are men with perfectly 'normal' penises putting them in the hands of a stranger with a scalpel?

There are two main kinds of surgery:

Ligament transaction

This will slightly increase the length of your penis. This surgery utilises the fact that there is a small part of your penis (around about an inch, occasionally a little more) submerged inside your body. It's kind of like an iceberg in reverse. The bit of dick inside you acts as an anchor and if you look back at the diagram in Chapter 1 (that you are *supposed* to know off by heart) you will see it is attached to the pubic bone (cock rock) by suspensory ligaments (guy ropes). The surgeon will thus cut the main ligaments, allowing the skin to be

COCKFACT

If you're overweight you can easily add length to your penis simply by losing weight. The bigger you are, the bigger the pad of fat which surrounds the base of your cock will be. This will have the effect of making your penis appear smaller. If you lose 35 pounds (nearly 16 kilos) you can add an inch (2.54 cms) to your little soldier. Given that being overweight increases your chances of experiencing erectile dysfunction, you might seriously want to go on a diet after reading this book.

The fact that I have lost two stone in the last year and a half is just something I'll throw into the mix, ladies.

pushed back and the submerged few centimetres appear outside of the body. The Scottish journalist Kate Copstick flew to New York to witness a Dr Douglas Whitehead[3] perform this surgery and wrote that the surgeon goes in, up to his knuckles with a pair of secateurs.[4] The tendons holding the penis in place are cut. To marvellous comic effect, as he cuts, he calls 'pull' and his assistant yanks the dick, pulling it so it hangs lower down.

On the positive side, the operation might add an extra inch or two to your flaccid penis (it makes no real noticeable difference to your erection). On the negative, you have cut the guy ropes that kept your tent of love standing up securely. Your erection will be extremely wobbly and probably point directly at the floor. You will also end up having to wear weights on your penis to stop it retreating back into your body.

---

3. *Interestingly the overwhelming percentage of his work involves repairing the damage done by other surgeons' attempts at enlarging the penis. You can visit his website at www.drwhitehead.com*

4. *Presumably not literally.*

Is this what was in the suitcase in Repo Man?

Girth enhancement

This is a bit more complicated. Skin and fat are taken from another part of your body and placed under the skin of the penis. Alternatively you can have liposuction taking fat out of your thigh or abdomen which is then injected into your penis. The danger with this is that the fat can coagulate into lumps rather than spread out in an even fashion. There are cases where the fat for the graft has been taken complete with hair follicles, which means hair grows under the skin of your new penis.[5]

Things can go even more badly than that though. As I write, the papers are reporting the story of a man (Mr A) who is suing a surgeon for a botched operation. According to the London *Evening Standard*, Mr A said that after the operation 'I went home to bed. I was in severe pain. When I first looked at my penis I virtually passed out with shock. It was deformed.' Not only that, his previously average-sized penis had ended up shorter than before.

The American Urological Association considers 'subcutaneous fat injection for increasing penile girth and division of the suspensory ligament of the penis for increasing penile length, to be procedures which have not been shown to be safe or efficacious'.

To put it more succinctly:

DON'T DICK WITH YOUR DICK!

So what makes men risk damaging such an important body part, even when they are above average in size? Why do men all seem to want to have a big cock?

Does it genuinely make them better in bed?

I asked women:

 IS SIZE IMPORTANT IN LOVE MAKING?
   Yes: 1,408 (63.28%)   No: 817 (36.72%)   Total: 2,225

---

5. *Dr Whitehead has a different technique called 'allographic dermal matrix graft' which uses tissue harvested from dead bodies, sterilised, denuded of its DNA and cut into little oblongs reminiscent of pork fat. The doctor arranges it in layers and stitches it into an implant to make the penis as thick as the patient desires.*

I asked gay men the same question:

Yes: 1,125 (60.98%)   **No:** 720 (39.02%)   **Total:** 1,845

Obviously it's quite important to two-thirds of people on the receiving end. Here's some of the comments from women:

- Despite the polite noises women make, a larger penis is both more satisfying and more visually erotic.

- It's not the size of the boat but the motion of the ocean!

- My clitoris should be satisfied for which size does not matter.

- If you're hungry and you eat a chipolata, let's face it, you'll still be hungry.

- I once said 'I'm not really a finger person ... I'd rather you just put your cock in there!' It turned out, yes you guessed it, that WAS his penis!

- If it's too small then I feel embarrassed for him.

- It's the man on the end of the cock that makes it a fulfilling experience. Find him sexy and the size isn't such an issue.

- Obviously! The larger the better. A large penis feels wonderful, looks wonderful and is a major turn-on.

- Being ultimately stretched feels WONDERFUL. Plus, a large cock goes DEEPER and fills the vagina more. OH MY GOSH, I think I need to go play.

All right, calm down. What is it with you people?

- If it's too small it's like whisking a toothpick around in a bucket!

You're the one who called it a bucket, darling. That's not our problem, is it guys? Because I'm telling you now, no one's got a cock as big as a bucket. A hundred tooth picks Sellotaped together wouldn't touch the sides.

How much difference does it really make? When it really comes down to it, is size really as important as the survey answers suggest?

I asked women:

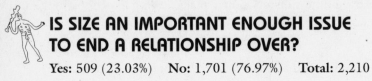

IS SIZE AN IMPORTANT ENOUGH ISSUE TO END A RELATIONSHIP OVER?

Yes: 509 (23.03%)　**No:** 1,701 (76.97%)　**Total:** 2,210

Amazingly, approaching a quarter of women would finish a relationship over the size of their partner's dick, which I think proves that women can be just as shallow as men ... well, maybe not. Maybe if they were shallow, this wouldn't be such a problem.

Here are some specific answers to that question:

- **No, love, friendship and compatibility are much more important. There are always more interesting ways of getting the same effect.**

- **Yes. Although I suppose a man could make up for it by being loving, dextrous, imaginative, adventurous and incredibly sexy ... I haven't met one yet.**

- **Sort of, if he's got a small dick AND can't fuck for shit AND doesn't take constructive criticism, then he's gone.**

- **It would have to be a seriously small and unpleasuring penis but I would indeed end a relationship if it were, if it meant that I was sexually unfulfilled. But if I were sexually unfulfilled by a man with an absolutely huge penis I would end the relationship too. So it's the fulfilment aspect rather than the size per se.**

- Maybe – if you want your pussy stuffed by a man, that's it. Go for broke. But you can have your man's little dick up your ass, a vibrator in your cunt and him sucking your nipples. Better? Yes!

What a fantastic woman she is. It's at times like this that I wish this hadn't been an *anonymous* questionnaire.

At first sight this seems like a dispiriting statistic – essentially one in four women would finish with a man over the size of his penis. If we're honest, though, I think we've all got physical expectations of a potential partner. What they might be can vary significantly from person to person, but each of us (men and women) have something we require to be present in a lover for them to be sexually attractive to us.

I think that one in four women probably wouldn't go out with me because I'm only five foot seven; one in four women might turn down a fat guy; one in four women might not like bald blokes; one in four might turn their nose up at men with hairy backs.

Which means if you're a short, fat, bald bloke with a hairy back and a small penis then five out of four women won't go out with you.

Statistics don't lie.

My point is we've all got physical imperfections – most of them are more obvious than our genitals and so possibly we learn to live with them more easily (though at least by the time someone sees your genitals they have usually made a fair degree of commitment) – but we're all insecure about something about our appearance. Women are especially guilty of this sensitivity. Women are constantly worrying that tits are too small or their bum's too big. I don't know why you bother girls, we've already established that men will have sex with a toilet roll full of jelly. I wouldn't worry too much about your arse if I was you!

Provided it's been spooned in.

We have some standards.

No one is going to be attractive to everyone (and where would be the fun if we were?) For some women a big dick is the most important thing, just as for some men big tits are the most important thing. God help anyone who chooses a life partner based on those qualities alone (unless she's got *really* big tits).

I think the way to look at the statistic is that three out of four women wouldn't finish with you over the size of your penis. That way round it seems a lot more positive. Some of them might prefer it if you had a bigger one, but to be honest they'd probably prefer it if you were Brad Pitt. You can't have everything.

Your partner can still love you if you've got a small one, fellas. Just as you can still love a small-titted, big-arsed woman with a bucket fanny. These things aren't important ... when you're in love. It's love that's important.

The fact is that the average penis is six inches long, the average vagina is also six inches long. It's a match. Most women don't actually enjoy being poked in the cervix during sex. Psychologically some women might like to be filled, but they don't have nerve endings more than three inches inside their vaginas because it would make childbirth too painful (rather than the walk in the park it is at the moment).

That is according to the findings of a study carried out by a Brazilian doctor called Paulo Palma. He concluded that size isn't important, but width may be. According to him, because of a woman only having nerve endings three inches inside her fanny, a man only needs a 2.7-inch penis to satisfy her. His survey found the average Brazilian cock to be 5.7 inches long ... but no one thought to ask him how long his penis was. My guess is that it's 2.7 inches long, but quite wide.

However, the women on my survey certainly seemed to confirm the importance of thickness over length:

- It's more girth than length, but it's technique more than anything that matters.

- Size not really, though GIRTH (a great word) is a bit more important. Pencil Dicks aren't very satisfying.

- Length isn't necessarily important but girth is. If a man's penis isn't thick enough to fill my vagina, I'm not going to feel anything and therefore, I won't get off.

- Girth means mirth.

COCKSTAT

I asked men:

 WHAT IS YOUR GIRTH WHEN ERECT?

Pepparami sausage:	!87 (4.4%)
Cocktail sausage:	176 (4.14%)
Regular sausage:	1,807 (42.53%)
Jumbo sausage:	1,884 (44.34%)
Delicatessen salami:	195 (4.59%)
Total:	4249

Which might seem like good news for the short and stubby, but bad tidings for the long and thin.

However, this is to deny the fact that vaginas also come in all shapes and sizes. It is interesting that if there's a mismatch it is the cock that gets the blame. One woman said:

● I detest the way it is acceptable for women (or anyone) to make loads of crummy gags about dick size. It misses the point. It's so reductive, so hung up, so ENGLISH. It isn't really acceptable to make jokes about large vaginas (a problem a lot women face after childbirth), so why dick size? Sorry to be humourless.

As Tom Arnold said when his ex-wife Roseanne Barr was disparaging about his size, 'Even a 747 looks small landing in the Grand Canyon.'

It shouldn't be insulting to point out the truth, that some vaginas are bigger than others (and this is regardless of having given birth, though clearly that will help loosen things up). One woman wasn't ashamed to admit the reason she liked big cocks:

- It corresponds with my size – I am a big lass – and my vagina is correspondingly so – thus a pencil-slim penis doesn't touch the sides or the depths – but a larger chap – say 6 to 8 inches is a snug-fit. If I was a smaller lass, then I would want a smaller penis. Hence I reckon everyone has a corresponding size that suits their dimensions.

This observation was made as long ago as the fourth century in the *Kama Sutra*. It acknowledged that men and women came in three different genital sizes (the hare, the bull and the horse). In an ideal world a hare would mate with a hare, rather than a horse (imagine the bizarre off spring such a union would produce).

We are all little Cinderella-fellas and out there is the slipper (or boot) that will be our perfect fit! Of course, we don't go to Clarks shoe-shop to find ourselves a partner (though I've just conjured up a wonderful image of the measuring machine they would have in such a boutique) and sometimes a hare ends up with a horse.

It still isn't anything to worry about. Being a great lover isn't about how big your cock is and most women of experience realise this and the ones that don't will move on and you'll be better off anyway. I had a lot of responses from women like these:

- I once had an amazing one night stand with a guy who had THE smallest penis – and the sex was amazing … The key was to excite my brain, and by doing so he gave me loads of pleasure even though his penis was tiny!

- Men with small cocks put more effort into pleasuring women in other ways (which women enjoy just as much cos they lead to orgasm). Also, the frequency of sex/foreplay, etc. are much more important.

- Of the men I've been with, a couple have been quite small, and one was strikingly large (at first almost daunting). But, in the end, the size of his penis was not the defining point in the pleasure of the experience. The man with the smallest penis is still one of the best lovers I ever had.

Other women argued that men with big penises can be complacent, they think that's enough on its own and they don't know what they're doing:

- I have slept with someone who was particularly well endowed, and he was my worst shag ever!

- Men with large members can have tendency to sit back and not try as hard.

- I have had big and small penises that were both very satisfying. As long as the guy knows how to make up for the smallness by moving the right way.

Let's face it, lesbians claim to have the best sex lives of any of us, as this lady testifies:

- Heterosexual sex is way too focused on the penis – in lesbian relation-ships I had lots of really lovely sex without a penis or penis substitute being involved – I enjoy penetration (with men) but it's not the be all and end all and it's certainly not the most effective way to orgasm.

However small your penis is, it's not as small as a lesbian's penis.

Being a good lover is about caring about the person you're with, trusting them, being sensitive to their needs, loving them if possible. While acknowl-edging that, at least to some people, size can make a difference, I genuinely believe that it is what you do with it (or with your tongue or your fingers) that ultimately counts.

Yet even if all men accepted this, I think they would still say they wanted a big one.

So why is that?

Why are men prepared to pay thousands of pounds to go under the knife, in an operation that will make no difference to the erect size of their penis? Who are they trying to impress with their larger flaccid knob?

There is a very convincing argument that men have evolved larger penises (proportionately) than the other primates, not to attract women but to intimidate other men. Most men who have penile augmentation say they are doing it for self-image. The most common client for the plastic surgeon is a businessman who wants to impress his competitors in the locker room. For all our insistence on our heterosexuality, we want a bigger cock to impress the boys. The only people who genuinely suffer from penis envy are, of course, men.

One of the things that surprised me most from the survey – and I'm guessing it's something that 90 per cent of men have never considered – is that there is an enormous downside to having an enormous chunk of topside. Consider for a second that you are a horse making love to a hare or an ugly sister's foot in Cinderella's slipper. One word sums it up – Ouch!

Of those one in four women who said they'd finish with a man over the size of his penis, almost a third were talking about men with big cocks (to be honest, many of them mentioned both):

- If it's too small it doesn't feel as good, but if it's far too big it can hurt.

- Not necessarily 'bigger is better'. I have a friend who is very small and large penises cause her pain; she prefers small men.

- Too small is ineffectual – too big is scary.

- You don't want something that feels like you are giving birth back-wards.

In fact I didn't quote you the complete comment of the toothpick in the bucket lady. She also said:

- If it's too big, it's like trying to stick a melon in a squirrel's ear hole.

Doesn't she have an excellent turn of phrase?

Most women, like Goldilocks, conclude that somewhere in the middle is 'just right'. An average-sized penis is actually a plus for most women, but believe it or not there are fans of (and websites dedicated to) both extremes, so no one needs to feel left out.

To a male population raised on the idea that a big cock is what women want and a guarantee of happiness, the next sad story may come as something of a shock. It was receiving this email quite early on in my research that made me determined to tackle this subject from both the male and female point of view. Here's what she said:

> I've never had sex with my boyfriend of 12 years. His penis is too big to penetrate me. The joys of a big penis can be somewhat overplayed. For the first year we tried constantly, but even an inch of penetration was agony for me. After a year we stopped trying, just concentrated on other methods of fulfilment. But then even foreplay got too much for me. What was the point when we couldn't take it any further? Any sexual contact was a reminder of the problem. I went on a binge of one night stands to prove to myself that I wasn't a freak, I could fuck like anyone else. I'll regret that for the rest of my life. But it did prove a point. After all, none of them had a large penis. Last year I went to the GP. Apparently I have a perfectly normal vagina. A little bit dainty, perhaps, but nothing untoward. She asked me, 'Does your boyfriend have a big willy?' Not a question I had expected to be asked by a small, middle-aged Indian lady. She offered me surgery. Apparently my vagina can be cut and widened to accommodate him. Other doctors have told me that the surgery never works and women have waited years for reversal operations. What price the chance to have sex with my partner?

This size thing, it does seem to be an issue that almost defines masculinity – but only because we let it. And we all do it. Throughout this book I've made jokes about the size of my penis either to aggrandise or demean myself. The fact is I actually have a pretty average-sized penis …

245

There I've said it in print. Does it matter?

To paraphrase Sid the Sexist, 'It's not much, but it'd fill a pram.' It's a flap of skin. Having one at all, that makes me a man. The size of it thereafter doesn't actually affect that issue. I think most of us know the jokes and comments are just jokes, but men are still suffering in silence over something that really doesn't matter.

Being a man isn't about the size of your organ. And if you have to have a big organ, then a big heart and a big brain are going to get you a lot further, believe me ...

To be honest even a big bladder is a more useful gauge of manhood.

'Blimey, he can drink six pints before he needs the toilet ... What a top bloke!'

" NORMALLY, I DON'T LIKE GUYS WITH SMALL PECKERS, BUT YOU'RE DIFFERENT!"

POPSHOTS8

When Richard Jobson, the English explorer, returned from West Africa in 1623, he claimed that the men in the Mandingo tribe had penises so big that they were 'burdensome to them'.

Four hundred years later the stereotype still persists. It provides the punch-line to a thousand jokes ('So the Queen says, "Is it a black man's cock!"'), it's the subject of a hundred chat-up lines ('So, is it true what they say about black men?' [wink suggestively] – make sure you only say this to a black man) and black athletes are judged as much for their lunchboxes as their performance on the track. It is one of those topics that exists somewhere between myth and reality and it's possibly not in black men's interest to confirm or deny it. I have heard more than one black male stand-up make some crack along the lines of, 'That's one stereotype I don't have a problem with.'

So what's the truth about the enigma of variation? Do black men truly have such burdensome Beaver Cleavers?

I asked women:

IN YOUR EXPERIENCE DOES ANY RACE OR NATIONALITY HAVE LARGER PENISES THAN THE OTHERS?

Over half the women who responded said they had not had a chance to compare. The ones who thought they had had enough experience of all the cocks of the world to make a judgement concluded:

Yes:	400 (43.38%)
No:	522 (56.62%)

Of the 400 women who said yes, over 300 of them said that it was black men who were bigger in their experience. Is this a significant statistic?

Almost certainly not. First, the women are making judgements based on memory and it is unlikely that any of them thought to take along any calibration equipment. We also don't know the size of their cock sample. Are they making this decision based on having seen one black penis and one white one, or one white one and ten black ones? Most women are not going to have seen enough men's penises to be able to make any kind of useful assessment. We might conclude that with so much anecdotal evidence we are at least spotting a trend, but it is possible that these women's opinions are swayed by preconception and belief in the cliché. Statistically women are safer drivers than men, yet many men (armed with the stereotypical notion that the reverse is true) will manage only to observe the times when their prejudice is confirmed (and ignore all the terrible male drivers that clutter up our highways). Is something similar happening with the women here?

I think this anecdote which comes from a man is very telling:

● **In Jan 1980 I arrived in Antigua after sailing across the Atlantic and went for a shower in the municipal showers. About 30 people in open lines, 15 white, 15 black, ideal to compare. Looked and all were similar, about same size. Suddenly door opened and in walked a 5' 5" rasta – his dong dangled down to his knees! TRUE!**

The implication here is that this story proves the myth. In fact it does almost exactly the opposite. The vast majority of the men he saw had cocks of the same size. Given that there is a range in sizes between all men, it is not significant that one of the 16 black men had a large penis. Statistically one would expect something like this range in either black or white men.

You also have to ask yourself, if it had been a white man with a massive cock who had walked in, would the story even have been recounted? Was it merely because in this instance the stereotype was seemingly confirmed that makes it worthy of telling?

Similarly it is more significant that the majority of women who felt qualified to make a comparison reported no noticeable difference. If black men's penises were significantly bigger than white men's then you wouldn't expect quite so many women not to have noticed.

There have been some attempts to find out 'scientifically'. According to a follow-up to the Kinsey Report made in 1979 based on self-administered tests involving 10,000 white men and 400 black men, the average erect penis was 6.15 inches for the former and 6.44 inches for the latter (the average circumference was also 0.13 inches bigger in the black correspondents). In the flaccid state black men were 4.34 inches long and 3.78 inches in circumference, while white men were only 3.86 inches and 3.16 inches.

We should remember that self-measurement tests cannot be relied on for accuracy and it is also worth noting that the sample of black men is much smaller than that of white, so it would only take a few self-aggrandising participants to skew the figure. In any case the difference is only a third of an inch, which hardly suggests the monstrous proportions that the stereotype would have us believe.

Richard Edwards has set up a website called www.sizesurvey.com which attempts to answer many questions about size based on results sent in (again self-measured) by readers of the site. He concedes that the samples for black and Hispanic men are still small and says therefore, 'the results reported below concerning the aforementioned groups must be considered tentative, pending a larger number of responses'. His findings report these average erect lengths:

Caucasian:	6.5 in
Black:	6.1 in
Hispanic:	5.9 in
East Asian:	5.5 in

Interestingly the average flaccid lengths were 3.7 inches for black men and only 3.4 inches for Caucasians. Edwards tentatively suggests that this fact may be responsible for the perception that black men are bigger, though again I would point out that the difference is very small. Edwards also asked men about their perceptions about their own size. He concludes, 'It is also interesting to note that the vast majority of Black subjects stated that they tended to be well endowed; an opinion which was not borne out by the results of this study.'

Although a really conclusive scientific study of this subject is never likely to be carried out, I would say that the evidence we have suggests that East Asian penises are generally a little smaller than those of European and African races, and that the photo finish in the race between black and white lunchboxes is too close to call.

So where did this pervasive notion of all black cocks being bigger than breadboxes originate? The truth of the matter is much less amusing than those of us who tell such jokes might imagine. Ironically far from being complimentary, the stereotype began as a means of dehumanising and demonising the African peoples.

Reports from early explorers and scientists suggest that at least in one respect, Africa was the land of the giants. Nineteenth-century British explorer Sir Richard Burton wrote, 'Debauched women prefer Negroes on account of the size of their parts. I measured one man in Somali-land who, when quiescent, numbered nearly six inches. This is a characteristic of the Negro race and of African animals; eg, the horse.'

His contemporary Jacobus Sutor, a French surgeon, went one better when he wrote 'It was among the Sudanese that I found the most developed phallus ... Being nearly 12 inches in length by a diameter of 2½ inches. This was a terrific machine, and except for a slight difference in length, was more like the penis of a donkey than that of a man.'

It is telling that in so many of these descriptions white explorers were at pains to make black men appear as animalistic as possible. Scientists such as Charles White argued that Africans' penises were similar to those of gorillas, in appearance and in their prodigious size. This discovery ignores the fact that gorillas (and all apes) actually have smaller penises than men.

It was, of course, convenient for the Europeans to equate African men as being no more than beasts, as then they would have no qualms at using these people as slaves. To emphasise the size of their members and their wild lusts would also make them a threat to civilisation and to white women, which would further justify their mistreatment and enslavement.

Throughout the period of slavery and its aftermath in the USA, stereotyping black men as savages with uncontrollable lusts and huge penises would justify many of the atrocities of the Ku Klux Klan. The feelings were so strong that even consenting couples were punished.

In her book, *White Women, Black Men*, Martha Hodes recounts this truly horrendous story:

> When a black man and a white woman were accused of cohabitation in Georgia, a doctor recalled that 'the colored man was taken out into the woods, a hole dug in the ground and a block buried in it, and his penis taken out, and a nail driven through it into the block; that a large butcher or cheese knife, as they call it, very sharp, was laid down by him, and light-wood piled around him and set on fire; the knife was put there so that he could cut it off and get away, or stay there and burn up.' The man chose to escape.

The effects of this false preconception are still being felt by black men today. We probably all laughed along at the plight of 'Horse' in the film, *The Full Monty*. He felt that he didn't live up to his nickname and was frantically trying to increase his length in time for the full-frontal strip show that he was about to participate in. Yet this is a genuine pressure. One black man that I spoke to explained that it puts him under incredible stress when he first sleeps with a white woman. They have high expectations of size and performance and often vocalise them in advance, excitedly saying things like, 'Oooh I've never had a black man before'. He said some black men do everything they can to live up to the hype and admitted that his brother uses a spray to numb his penis so he can keep going longer.

Despite its seemingly flattering connotations, once you understand the reasons for the stereotype, the jokes suddenly don't seem as funny any more.

I would have to conclude that in a world of amazing penile variation there are some things which are the same. Whether your penis is black, white or yellow, it makes no tangible difference. Though if it is yellow you should probably think about seeing a doctor.

Proof that even a man without a body thinks with his dick.

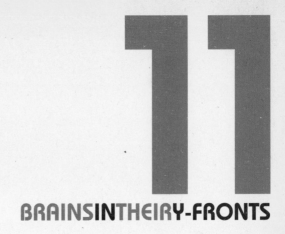

11

BRAINSINTHEIR-FRONTS

The stereotype of men is that they'll shag anything with a pulse ... We've already proven that's not true.

A folding metal chair has no pulse.[1]

So, who's in control, the man or his Cyclops sausage dog?

I asked women:

DO MEN THINK WITH THEIR DICKS?
Yes: 1,699 (78.33%)   **No:** 470 (21.67%)   **Total:** 2,169

Here's some of the comments from those eight in ten who think that they do:

- Well, if that's what they come up with when thinking with their brains, then that'd be quite scary.

- Because I'm influenced by my vagina, so it figures that men are influenced by their dicks.

- I'm afraid I am of the opinion that all men are the same. There may be one decent one in a million! Men are born to cheat.

---

1. *Not unless you connect some electrodes to it.*

- I think they are wired differently than women, through no fault of their own. They're 'wired' to spread their seed as far as possible. We're 'wired' to have one man around to help us have a stable life for the kids.

- My boyfriend is a great example. Whenever he is aroused, he seems to turn most of his brain off, and his main intent is sexual satisfaction. It's almost animalistic.

- Given obvious visual stimulation, then yes, they do think with their dicks. But I'd like to think they had a brain to think about other things as well (like remembering birthdays and stuff ...)

I think she might have taken the question a bit literally (though we can at least write birthdays on our penis to help us remember).

- Those that aren't actually thinking with it are usually thinking about it. Take women in skimpy clothing. No bloke's first thought is 'I wonder what her IQ is', is it? Even in relationships, and this is my current experience – I can be talking about my day, my friends whatever and I know he isn't listening, but throw something in there about another girl's breasts or quietly whisper 'fancy a blow-job' and his trousers are down in seconds. It is a fully operational antennae on stand-by at all times. And probably the only part of a bloke that ever really listens to us!

- I heard someone say that any man would leave his wife and children drowning in a whirlpool for the fuck of a lifetime. I think there's an element of truth in that.

That's cold.

- Men would cover up for each other if adultery happened. They almost think with each other's cocks!

- **They will do the most amazingly stupid things for sex. My boyfriend actually tried to extort me into having sex with him (for the second time of the day) this weekend by coming into my computer room and farting horribly smelly farts until I agreed to have sex with him. Didn't he have something better to do?**

If she agreed after that then she's only got herself to blame. You can't bargain with terrorists.

The most common response was something along the lines of:

- **Hormones rule the poor dears!**

Because, of course, hormones have no effect on women at all, do they?

Yet despite the offensiveness of many of these remarks, this is an argument that you will also hear from men. Ever since Adam ate that apple and tried to blame it on his snake, men caught with their pants down have defended themselves by claiming, 'I wasn't thinking straight. My mind went blank. It was a moment of madness.' Has sexual lust really driven these men into temporary insanity? Or is it actually as this woman suspects?

- **They don't think with their dicks, but isn't it clever of them to have people believe they do? It's a very handy excuse.**

How much part do our hormones really play in this? No one would deny they have an influence. One gay man said:

- **I get into a mindset where my dick takes over. Like my brain has somehow clicked on to auto-pilot. I'm like a dog with a bone ... sometimes literally.**

So are we all 'poor dears' who would watch our wife and children be sucked off by a whirlpool if it meant we could be sucked off by Natalie Imbruglia? Are men merely slaves to the whim of their testosterone?

In *The Book of the Penis*, Maggie Paley includes an interview with 'Jack', a woman who was living as a man, while waiting for body-modifying surgery. At this point she/he had been taking testosterone for two years and comments:

> *I got a feminist education and I didn't really want to believe that men think differently than women. But especially when I started taking hormones, I couldn't stop thinking about sex, it was just constant. I was like a fifteen-year-old boy. Before, I used to see a woman on the subway and I would have a thought process – she's attractive, I would like to get to know her – and it would be sort of narrative. With the testosterone the narrative is gone – it's just flashes of these sexual, aggressive images. For the first six months or so I found myself leering at women. I used to think, 'You don't have to leer. Couldn't you be less obvious about it?' But you just want to look.*

This is pretty compelling evidence for the power of our hormones. But what strikes me about Jack's statement is the comparison with a fifteen-year-old boy. For men, surely the onset of puberty and the first burst of testosterone is the hardest of times (in both senses). We suddenly have to cope with a new range of desires which we are not psychologically or emotionally equipped for. Like Jack discovered, women are little more to male teenagers than visual stimuli, that we can't help staring at, that we would do anything to be with. And because of that attitude we usually totally fail in our objective!

As we get older we learn to live with our hormones, to control them at least a little, to learn about responsibility and the value of relationships, to stare less obviously at women's breasts (though admittedly not much less obviously). So I have a theory that all the times when men do stupid things, we have regressed to adolescence (though now we are suddenly capable of sleeping with the women we could only dream about as teenagers). Just as old hippies have acid flashbacks, perhaps the uncontrollable madness is like some kind of testosterone flashback.

What do you think? Good theory, hey? Sounds vaguely plausible in a totally unscientific way. But if I am honest with myself I know that this 'theory' is just another 'moment of madness'-style excuse. It is indeed convenient for men to allow the 'hormone' argument to justify their selfish Priapic activities.

COCKQUOTE

'He's got his root in my soul, has that gentleman! An' sometimes I don't know what ter do wi' him. Ay, he's got a will of his own, an' it's hard to suit him. Yet I wouldn't have him killed.'

D.H. Lawrence, Lady Chatterley's Lover, *Mellors discusses his relationship with his friend John Thomas*

The truth is that there have been many occasions in my life where I have been tempted to do the 'wrong' thing in a sexual scenario. Maybe I've had the chance to cheat on a partner, or to have a liaison with a friend's girlfriend or been offered no-strings sex with someone I should not get involved (or re-involved) with. It hasn't happened that much unfortunately, but there have been occasions. In the majority of those cases (or maybe a large minority) my head has stayed in control. My head has said, 'No, think of the consequences. This is wrong.' And I've listened. I have done the right thing. Not without regret, but at least with some degree of control. But in those minority (or small majority) of cases where I have given in to temptation I genuinely do not believe that my brain has been over-ruled. Yes, for certain, there are strong forces at play, but in every case my head has said, 'Think of the consequences,' and I've thought, 'There won't be any consequences ... if no one finds out.' But you know I have thought about it much harder before I've cheated. To quote another woman from the survey:

● **I think that there is a constant competition and collaboration between men's intellect and their dick.**

If we are honest about it fellas, we know we have desires, they can be strong desires, they can be difficult to control, but we can control them if we want to. I asked men:

WHO'S THE CAPTAIN OF YOUR SHIP, YOU OR YOUR PENIS?

Me: 3,491 (71.27%) **Penis:** 1,407 (28.73%) **Total:** 4,898

COCKQUOTE

'Real knowledge comes out of the whole corpus of consciousness; out of your belly and your penis as much as out of your brain and mind. The mind can only analyse and rationalise.'

D.H. Lawrence

Admittedly some sailors may have been confused by the analogy, but even accounting for that, most of us know the chain of command. There's certainly conflict, but our brains are in our head. We're not being driven around by lots of little men inside our heads, as the popular comic strip 'The Numskulls' would have us believe[2] (though it never showed the bloke whose job it was to crank up the penis, which was a missed opportunity).

That's not to downplay the effect of our hormones. Our dicks might not make the decisions, but they are certainly a very trusted and somewhat persistent adviser to the king. Our penis is a kind of Peter Mandelson figure. We listen to it a bit too much and when his advice screws things up for us, we ignore him for a while, but he never shuts up and eventually we start listening again despite ourselves (unless we finally decide to cut him off completely).

So, it is instinctive for men to check out the bodies of all women we see to ascertain if they are good breeding material (and women check out men too, though with a slightly different emphasis and a bit more subtly). Yet if we're with our girlfriends or wives our brain allows us (usually) to override that command. You shouldn't be chastising your man for absent-mindedly glancing at the occasional woman, girls, you should be applauding him for the hundred that he pretends not to notice. He's doing it because he loves you.[3]

It's our hormones that make us feel horny as hell and fantasise about making

2. *Were each of those little men in turn operated by little men, and so on to infinity? A philosophical question that the creator of the strip failed to address.*

3. *And don't have a go at us when we stare at your breasts, girls. We're trying not to. It's difficult. Anyway you should be much more insulted if we don't stare at them.*

love to every woman we see. Yet we manage to control those feral desires. How many times a day do we override our natural propensity to at least shout our lust from the rooftops?[4]

If women could be men for a day, I think they would end up admiring our restraint (as the comments of Jack above possibly show). We exercise a lot more control than a non-man might imagine.

The point is that we can and we do control it.

I think if we're young or if we haven't had sex for a long time (just as if we haven't eaten for a long time) we might be more easily influenced by our bodily needs and less capable of a totally rational intellectual decision. Also, if we get to a certain point in the proceedings it can certainly be more difficult and annoying to turn back, but there was a point where we made a decision with our heads to go down that route. If we are drunk that might also affect things, but how many of us (women and men) get pissed on a Friday night just so we have a valid excuse to explain away our naughty behaviour.

Before I started writing this book I blindly accepted the stereotype that all men are promiscuous, unfeeling and selfish, out-of-control sex addicts. It would be a brave or foolish person who would deny that sex is an important thing to most men (especially if that person had devoted a chapter of his book to the bizarre lengths men will go to for sexual satisfaction and especially also if that person was having difficulty concentrating on writing this chapter because of the rather cute girl sitting opposite him in the British Library[5]).

When I stopped to think about it I realised that that stereotype isn't fair on the vast majority of men I know. Just because we don't like the film *Sliding Doors* doesn't mean we don't have feelings. It means we have excellent taste.

Most men will go through a period of chasing after women: how long this lasts for varies massively from man to man. Some men end up spending their

---

4. *Builders don't do so well on this one. But as they're already on the rooftops it makes the temptation so much harder to resist.*
5. *Who seems to be experiencing no such difficulty at getting on with her work, however much I wave at her.*

whole adult lives with one woman, some end up still acting like teenagers long into old age. I admit that I, personally, tend to fall more into the second category, and I'm not making any judgement about which lifestyle choice is right or wrong. People are different and have varying needs. I'm merely challenging this perceived notion that this is how all men are.

I actually think most men ultimately realise that there is more to life than having sex with a string of nameless, faceless strangers (not that the idea ever totally loses its appeal), that there are more pleasures and rewards to be had out of commitment (however frightening it is and however much our hormones protest). Yet increasingly we have tended to ignore the majority of men who love the women they are with and who are dutiful fathers, in favour of this lad-mag image of the adolescent man behaving badly.[6]

There are plenty of good men out there. Here's what the woman who sent me the email about her and her boyfriend being unable to have sex because of the size of his penis had to say on the subject:

- **To the charge that men think with their dicks – he has been unerringly reasonable throughout the last 12 years. Yes, he has bad days when I can see the frustration seeping through but he's never used it against me. No angry words have ever been thrown at me regarding the lack of sex. He forgave me my affairs, even though they ripped his heart to shreds. To my knowledge he has never been unfaithful. We still hold hands, kiss and hug like newlyweds. He accepts the situation, much as he'd like it otherwise. So no, men don't all think with their dicks.**

How about this commonly held belief that men are selfish lovers: is that fair either?

I asked men:

---

6. *Though, even as I write, the newspapers are reporting a new trend of 'dad mags', periodicals aimed at the 'new' breed of doting fathers (with David Beckham being held up as the prime example of this cultural shift). Which probably just shows what manufactured bullshit all these cultural trends actually are. Because it's not like there were any doting fathers in the 1990s were there?*

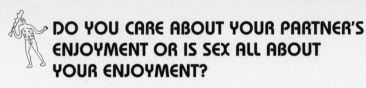 # DO YOU CARE ABOUT YOUR PARTNER'S ENJOYMENT OR IS SEX ALL ABOUT YOUR ENJOYMENT?

A massive 94.65 per cent of men (3,608 in total) said they cared about their partner's enjoyment. Only 204 men out of 3,812 admitted to the ultimate self-ishness (and only 47 of those men were over 30).

Of course men want to make their partners happy. If we want to think just of ourselves then there are plenty of toilet rolls and bowls of jelly out there to satisfy us. Even if you were to look at this on a purely selfish level, it is obvious that sex is much more exciting and better if you are both enjoying it. There is nothing more arousing than making your partner scream with delight, and little more disappointing than making love to someone who is getting nothing out of it. Our masculine pride demands that we be perceived as the greatest lover in the world (which is possibly why so many men feel under pressure to perform). When we are young we perhaps feel that quantity of partners is what makes us real men; as we get older we realise that quality is more important (but if we can achieve quality and quantity then that's even better!)

Although there certainly are men who seem to think only of themselves in bed (though how much of this is down to incompetence, rather than design is questionable), most grown-up men want to please their partner because they love them and care for them and want to demonstrate that affection. What makes sex with someone else so great is the reciprocal nature of the act. Men understand this just as much as women. Sorry to state the obvious, but I think it needs to be stated, because we seem to have forgotten it.

So do men really deserve this reputation of being more promiscuous than women?

I asked men:

 # HOW MANY SEXUAL PARTNERS HAVE YOU HAD IN YOUR LIFETIME?

These are the figures for straight men:

0–10:	70.44% (2,351)
11–50:	25.41% (913)
51+:	4.15% (149)

Seven in ten men on this survey have slept with ten or less women, which is hardly promiscuous. In fact 26.11 per cent have had one or less sexual partners. Now I know this survey took place on the Internet, so might not be representative of men who've actually met any women (and we must also take into account that some of the men are still young and so presumably their tally will go up in the future), but even so, that's a remarkable statistic.[7]

Only around 4 per cent of straight men have slept with over 50 women (which I would call properly promiscuous). Why are we all judged by that 4 per cent? Even if you include all the men who've slept with over ten women, less than 30 per cent of men are 'promiscuous'. We don't judge all women as being insensitive even though 28 per cent have laughed openly at a man's genitals. Why do we judge men by the minority?

To be honest this widely held belief that heterosexual men are more promiscuous than heterosexual women doesn't make any kind of sense. Heterosexual men and heterosexual women must be having exactly the same amount of sex on average. There's always one of each of us at every coupling. Either we're having the same amount of sex, on average, or there is one superslag woman servicing the entire male population.[8]

That's not what's happening. The figures for the number of sexual partners for straight women on my survey are interesting.

---

7. *Also according to my survey, men had had an average of 1.18 partners in the last four weeks, which implies most men tend towards monogamy or (possibly enforced) abstinence.*
8. *Steve Jones argues that this is the case, claiming that the average number of sexual partners for men is higher than that of women, because men use prostitutes, who make up such a small proportion of the population that they generally get missed out of such surveys. Even if this is true (which I'm not convinced about) that would still mean that there are a minority of women who are the most promiscuous of all. If we judge women (like we seem to with men) by the minority, this would make women more promiscuous than men.*

0–10:   66.51% (1,241)
11–50:   31.08% (580)
51+:   2.41% (45)

Those percentages work out pretty similar to the ones for men. Although slightly fewer women have had sex with over 50 men, there are also fewer with under 10 partners (and only 18.6 per cent of women have had one or less sexual partner). So my results at least suggest that things average out overall because there are more women than men who fall into the middle group, somewhere between monogamy and promiscuity. In layman's terms there are some men getting a lot, but loads getting none, while most women seem to get a bit.

For all men's talk of sexual conquest and notches on the bedpost I think the truth is that women control sexual access in all normal situations. A woman can pretty much have sex whenever she wants and so they set the level of sexual activity.

It's likely that men would like to be more promiscuous than women, which we might be able to prove by looking at the number of sexual partners of gay men.

It's a generalisation but I think it's fair to say that it is easier for gay men to have as much sex as they want. Which makes them, in a sense, men in their default setting, giving us an idea of how much sex all men would have if women weren't involved.

Here are the number of sexual partner figures for gay men:

0–10:   51.12% (479)
11–50:   24.55% (230)
51+:   24.33% (228)

That does seem to confirm that men tend towards promiscuity. Almost a quarter of gay men have had more than 50 sexual partners as opposed to the 4 per cent of straight men. However, what I find interesting about these figures is that over half of gay men have had under 10 sexual partners and 28.5 per cent have had one or less.

Now I'm not claiming that these figures are totally scientifically accurate and one might argue that gay men's promiscuity has been checked somewhat because of fears over AIDS.

Yet, by looking at all these statistics, as well as observing the relationships of the people I know, I would say that some *people* are promiscuous, some *people* are monogamous. To be honest, most of us are a mixture of both those things throughout our lives.[9] But men and women aren't that different. Some men cheat and so do some women; some men lie – you know what, I've been with some women who do that too; some men go around shagging recklessly and not giving a shit if they get anyone pregnant; some women go around shagging recklessly and not giving a shit about who ends up being the father.

Most of us want to be in a relationship, most of us want to be loved and in love, most of us want to have kids (that's why the human race still keeps going). To repeat my refrain, men and women aren't as different as we like to pretend. Are men so anxious to distance themselves from all things feminine because they are aware of just how 'feminine' (actually 'human') they are? Is it the same deal as with the gay thing? Is the gay and feminine thing all part of the same deal?

Although women clearly have a healthy cynicism about men's sexual motives, the survey showed that in another sense they have some kind of faith in us.

I asked women:

DO YOU THINK MEN CAN BE MONOGAMOUS?
Yes: 1,721 (79.35%)   **No:** 448 (20.65%)   **Total:** 2,169

So although 1,699 women said that men think with their dicks, 1,721 believe men are at least capable of control.

Maybe they don't think we're all bad after all, lads! Perhaps there's some hope.

---

9. *Just because you've had over 50 partners, doesn't mean you won't eventually end up with just one. Ask Michael Douglas.*

POPSHOTS9

I asked men:

 HAVE YOU EVER HAD THREE IN A BED OR GROUP SEX?
Yes: 1,576 (33.63%) **No:** 3,110 (66.37%) **Total:** 4,686

Over one in three have.[10] The bastards.

Clearly that scenario has never happened for me, not for want of trying. I did try and persuade one girlfriend to give it a go. We were going through a bit of a sexual malaise and looking for ways to spice up our love life. So I suggested that she bring her best friend to bed with us. I said to her, 'Imagine it. Three in a bed! Ménage à trois! You two lezzing up! It'd be great.'

She said, 'You have enough trouble satisfying *one* woman at a time, what makes you think you could cope with two?!'

She thought she'd got me there. She thought she'd been clever, but she was wrong. I said 'That's the whole beauty of the system. When I'm done, you two can finish each other off for me ... while I sleep. A woman knows what a woman wants ... and has the patience to see it through to its tedious conclusion.'

She finished with me shortly after that conversation. So now I'm reduced to having one in a bed sex. Ménage à un. Which has worked out great, because the thing about me is that I really like to have sex with someone that I pity.

It's the only way I can get off.

---

10. *Although only 23.86 per cent of straight men have done this, a whopping 64.37 per cent of gay men from my survey have been to bed with multiple partners.*

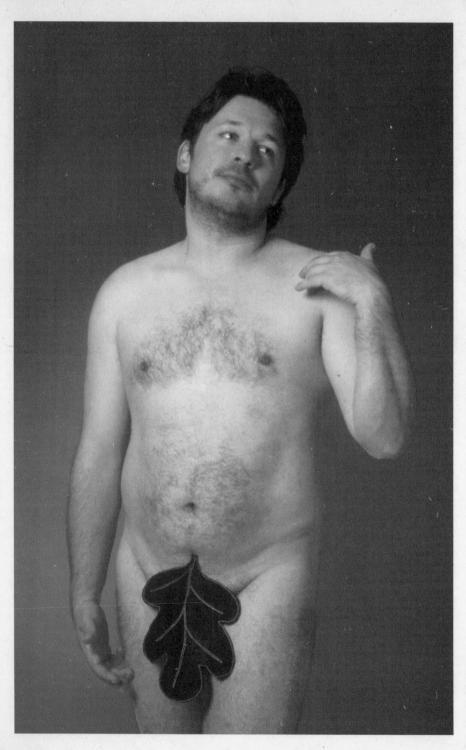

12

FILLINGTHEUNFORGIVINGMINUTE

I can't tell you how pleased I am to be nearly at the end of this journey (I hope you aren't feeling the same way). I can't pretend that a year of eating cocks, breathing cocks and sleeping cocks hasn't got to me. I have cock fatigue. I am about to finish the project, so I'm going to put my cock to bed and it feels good, though part of me worries about what I will become without the cock that I have become so reliant upon for sustenance. I am also slightly concerned that I might not have told the whole story. Being a man involves so many contradictions, so can I really come to any useful conclusions?

I do genuinely believe in all the things I have told you. I don't think we are defined as men by our penises, I don't think size is as important as we are led to believe, I think there is much more to being a man than being obsessed with sex to the exclusion of all else. I believe we need to stop putting ourselves down and allowing others to put us down too and acknowledge all the great things men have done.

Despite all this, last night, with the book swimming around in my head, I had me a dream.

I had decided to have a penis enlargement operation, because I thought it would impress a woman that I was seeing (who had been holding things back on the sexual front). The process involved me having my penis removed, and then sent away to be worked on by surgeons who would reattach it the next day.

Consequently I had 24 hours (though the dream didn't run to scale) of having no penis (or testicles, they'd taken them too) at all. I remember being quite upset about this. I was fearful that the operation might go wrong or that my penis might

267

get lost in the post. I also wondered whether my penis would be recognisable. Would I still be ME? What if I ended up with someone else's penis by mistake? That would be a tragedy. Would it all have been worth it for the sake of a couple of inches of length?

Then, by magic, my new cock was there, swaddled in bandages and inside my trousers. I didn't want to get it out and I was worried about how it might look. I also wondered if it would burst if I got an erection.

Inevitably, I got a hard-on and I could see from the bulge that my knob was substantially bigger. So could a group of women who were passing by, who started taking an interest in me. One of them kissed me. My apparently gargantuan penis naturally made me attractive to all women.

Then the girl who I'd had the op done for turned up and shooed off the girls (though she was understanding that they couldn't help themselves). Together we undid my trousers and unwrapped the bandage and there it was.

It was enormous.

It was slightly bent at the bottom, presumably where the extra inches had been added, but it was still beautiful. Much thicker, much longer and so very hard and virile. I felt fantastic and much more manly than I had before. The girl I was with cooed and touched it and wondered if it was ready to use.

I thought that it might be a bit risky, but within moments I had decided that I just didn't care. That I would use my wonderful new manhood to make love to this beautiful woman and prove what a man I had become.

Then my alarm went off and it was time to get up and finish this sodding book about cocks. So, I had to endure all that stupid transparently symbolic rubbish, without even getting to dream about having great sex.

I can't believe that I genuinely had that dream, but it is sadly true. In spite of all my claims that being a good man was about your heart or your self-respect and that you should learn to love your penis however it looks, my huge new penis had, for my subconscious at least, made me a better person. It had made me a *man*.

Worse still, what disappointed me on waking wasn't the fact that I had just betrayed everything I have spent the last twelve months writing about (nor that I had confirmed what you already know, that I am obsessed with male genitalia). No, it was that I hadn't got to have sex with the girl in question. So much for men being more than their cocks!

I don't think you have to own an amazing Technicolor dreamcoat to realise that my night-time vision shows how deep are our preconceptions about what a penis is supposed to look like and what it stands for (yes, in both senses).

It probably shows that I should have a couple of months when I don't think about male genitalia even once.

It also reveals the turmoil and confusion within all men: how much of this is due to nature and how much to nurture is impossible to decide. I am not alone in this bewilderment.

I asked men:

 ## WHAT DO YOU THINK A MAN IS?

The vast majority believe the definition is simply down to ownership of a cock:

- **A man is a human with a cock instead of a fanny. Issues of masculinity are bullshit.**

- **Someone with a penis. Doesn't matter what they're like personality-wise – it's just a physical thing.**

A few think that we are nothing more than our penis:

- **A huge walking erection.**

- **A fucking machine.**

- **A poor sap forever driven by the search for sexual gratification.**

Quite a few see men purely in terms of genetics:

- **1 X and 1 Y chromosome usually does it.**

- Half of human DNA's cunningly clever survival program. By making men and women as different yet complementary as possible, human DNA has the maximum survival possibility.

Others feel we haven't really evolved all that much:

- A talking ape.

- A chimp with less hair.

- A caveman. Hunter/gatherer.

Some men see their sex as noble:

- Courageous, sensitive, caring, daring, humorous, witty and just.

- A man is someone who is in touch with himself, and with others. Who understands himself. Who is not afraid to show his true feelings.

- Someone who can put emotions aside when necessary to carry out what needs to be done. A good man does this for moral reasons. A strong man serves the common good, rather than merely personal lusts. A man is unable to bear a child alone, thus devotes his life to others.

- A responsible person able to make decisions for himself and take care of anyone who depends on him.

While many are dismissive:

- An idiot.

- For the most part, I think men are misogynistic, narcissistic fuckwits who do not take responsibility/accountability for the choices they make in their lives regarding sexuality, fidelity and commitment.

Quite a few men were happy to reinforce the accepted stereotype:

- Someone who likes beer, breasts, football.

- Someone who is not prone to crying, who is sceptical of women.

- Ideally a tough guy – generally provider/protector.

A minority argued for our ascendancy over women:

- A superior being.

- The dominant species, I mean, hey, man invented the computer that allows us to fill in this questionnaire, for starters.

A few more saw us as the underdogs:

- A servant of women.

- A woman's doormat.

- The sorriest bugger on the planet. We have to be kind and sensitive, rough and tough, do the dishes and change the tyres. Our 'new deal' really sucks.

Plenty of men recognised the duality in us all:

- To me, being a man means being self-reliant, undemonstrative, reliable, faithful, capable of great love, yet also able, when necessary, to be hard. Men are responsible for almost all the discovery and advances of our species, yet this noble behaviour is balanced by a destructive streak which is almost completely unrivalled in female behaviour. Men are responsible for all the wars in history.

- Loyal, witty, sarcastic, idiotic, easily persuaded, dangerous, despite appearances less competitive than women, lousy at PR.

Several recognised that they themselves do not conform to the usual generalisations:

- As a gay man, that question becomes very loaded. What the concept 'man' signifies for a straight guy would probably be different for what it signifies to me. But I think a man is someone who has a particular type of strength both emotionally and physically.

As always a few correspondents are living on their own little planet:

- Someone who buys full sugar Polos instead of the sugar-free ones – even though the latter taste better.

I think my favourite answer, or at least the one that is closest to the truth, is this one:

- An amalgam of flesh, and after that whatever he decides.

There isn't too much consensus among men about what defines us, possibly because it is as ridiculous to attempt to define a group of people by what's between their legs as it is to judge them by the colour of their skin or to judge what's between their legs by the colour of their skin.

Yet while it is correctly seen as inappropriate to generalise about women or other races any more, it does still seem to be open season on treating men as a clump of beings, bound together by their own testosterone. Ironically this is probably because we are the only group with no actual cohesion or common aim, so we don't do anything to stop it. Some might argue that it is quite the opposite, that the competition between all men means we can never unite.

According to most commentators the writing seems to be on the wall for the male sex. In the last 40 years we have seen an enormous cultural shift, as the feminist movement has challenged perceived gender roles. Men have chosen to respond to this either by burying their heads in the sand and pretending it isn't happening or by becoming reactionary and heading into the woods to beat drums and find their inner caveman. There were a few, who claimed to be 'New Men', who wanted to help the women in their struggle, but most men simply sat back and complained that they now felt more oppressed than women.

Men also had to contend with a pervasive image of all being potential rapists and women-beaters. Andrea Dworkin was one of the most outspoken advocates of this idea. She claimed (among many other things) that the penis 'distinguishes the male conqueror from the female conquered' and added that 'the use of the penis to conquer is its normal use. In the male system, rape is a matter of degree.' The light-hearted battle of the sexes looked like becoming a war and no male psyche could fail to be influenced by such provocative and widely reported ideas. It seemed that women hated us and that we were being made to feel guilty for being born with this deformity between our legs.

Feminist polemic is certainly softening, with authors such as Susan Faludi arguing that men have been 'stiffed' by the changes in the Western world since the 1950s, but the future for men still seems bleak. The façade that males were ever supreme is starting to crumble.

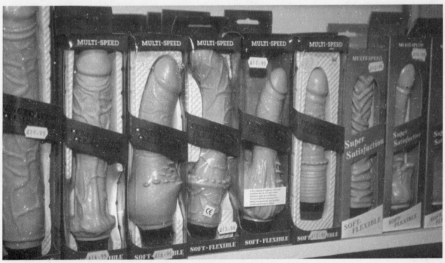

Eight reasons why women don't need men anymore.

Germaine Greer claims that men's uselessness was implicit even before the advent of feminism, saying:

> *Men are redundant not because of women or anything that women might do to them or without them, but because of biology. With every second the world's men produce 200,000,000,000,000 sperm, while in that same space of time the world's women produce only 400 eggs; intensify that imbalance by considering that a woman becomes a mother only after nine months, and a man can be a father as many times as his billions of spermatozoa meet a viable egg, and you can see that the human race could continue on earth if 99.9 per cent of human males were wiped out by some sex-linked disorder.*

In *Y. The Descent of Man* Steve Jones concludes that, 'The chromosome unique to men is a microscopic metaphor of those who bear it, for it is the most decayed, redundant and parasitic of the lot.'

What do ordinary men make of all this? Are things as low for them as they seem?

I asked men:

 ## HOW DO YOU FEEL AS A MAN?

The vast majority of men said something along the lines of simply 'OK' or 'fine'. Many others went as far as 'wonderful' (in fact 84 per cent of men claim to be proud to be a man, yet I can't deny many of their more specific answers were reactionary or defensive).

Here are a few of the comments from men about how they feel, presented in no particular order and without comment. I have not tried to keep them balanced or in proportion (though looking through them I wouldn't say it is far off). I have merely chosen the ones that I think are the most interesting:

● **I feel more secure and confident as I grow older. Maybe I'm just slightly less stupid than I was when I was younger.**

Germaine Greer looking a bit coquettish and sexy in this pic don't you think? I wouldn't say no.

- Great. I am happy with my lot. I now have a wife and son. We are all pretty good together and work well as a team. We now live very 'normal' lives – me working, him drooling and crawling and herself minding us both ;-)

- Under attack.

- Stereotyped and sometimes shamed by my fellow men for their fuck-wit behaviour.

- Pretty okay most of the time. Sometimes I wonder how it would be to be a girl, but don't we all?

- I feel powerful. And horny a lot.

- When I'm getting regular sex ... in control. When I'm not getting regular sex ... like a drunk driver crashing through his established female friendships.

- I feel OK as a man. Mind you I've never been a woman, so that might be better. I'd like to be a cockteaser.

- Worried. I mean, men aren't even needed for reproductive purposes any more. I think we'll be extinct within fifty years, and women will inherit the Earth. They can't really make a worse job of it.

- I feel good, I enjoy being male and have no qualms about admitting it. I do get pissed off about feminist movements when they impinge on or forget about men's rights.

- Alright, I s'pose. I do sometimes wish I was gay.

- It's more difficult to be a man today as there are very few male role-models left. On TV men are portrayed in two ways, either as weak, stupid, no match for the female (adverts are the worst for this) or as a violent, oppressive person that the woman will overcome by the end of the series. On the one hand women say they want equality, love, romance and passion, on the other hand they end up going out with complete bastards that treat them like shit. I think the answer is that I feel confused as to my requirements as a man in today's society.

- I am 33 and still feel like I am a boy. I am sort of ready for kids but can't believe I am going to be responsible for anything that amazing.

- Fine on the whole, but I'd love lots more guilt-free casual sex with other women. I'm married though and I'd hate to hurt my wife.

- Disappointed that attractive young women (or even older ones) don't find me sexually attractive any more.

- Like a dog – inventive but thick as shit, loyal but foul-tempered.

- Guilty and anxious. Also increasingly annoyed at the way we allow ourselves to be mocked in ways women wouldn't stand for.

- I am glad I have girl children as I simply do not know what I would say to boys about how to live their lives these days.

- Happy to be a man and content that I like sex with other men but it has taken a long time to reach this state. Initially I was ashamed and embarrassed but once I got over that I really enjoyed it. I have met some wonderful men in my time and some have been very influential.

- As a born-again virgin I am happy to exclude myself from the shallowing of the human gene pool. But a blow job might be nice.

- Like a 12 year old with more money and the ability to get into 18 films.

- Pretty good but I WANT A BIGGER DICK!!!

- Reading Andrea Dworkin made me feel like the Yorkshire Ripper. I was very young.

- Happy. Powerful yet vulnerable. Trusted – and that means a lot to me. Ashamed – for what I've done and what other men have done. Yet mostly content.

- Huge amounts of guilt for being male, white and educated/middle-class (even though my parents are working class). Sometimes feel people (well, mainly women) don't understand that even though I am part of the demograph that's responsible for all the bad things in the world I'm not the stereotypical chauvinistic, racist, capitalist scumbag they take me to be. But, if they can't see past the pale skin, IT job and dick hanging between my legs, then that's their problem.

In April 2003, I was in the birthplace of 'Puppetry of the Penis', Melbourne in Australia, doing my own cock-based show at the annual Comedy Festival[2] and writing this book despite the distractions of plentiful booze, wonderful weather and beautiful women.

For some reason, I didn't get that much written and the little I did was indecipherable babble, which had got covered in vomit and was thus exorcised from this final version by my over-fussy editor who believed that the public didn't want to see vomit-covered babble. I said we could wipe the vomit off, but he said that he'd rather I wrote something else that babbled less and that didn't have vomit on it. I thought he was being very conservative. He was paying me and consequently won the argument (but I left in this paragraph of babble to prove him wrong, though you really need the vomit on it to get the full effect).

I was battling with all these notions of masculinity, trying to make sense of it all. I needed a break and so on my night off I went to see a stage show called 'Defending the Caveman'. It's written by Rob Becker, but like *The Vagina Monologues* is being performed all over the world by various indigenous actors.

---

2. Not so much bringing coals to Newcastle, as bringing cocks to Melbourne, then.

Essentially the show argues that men are like they are because of traits we evolved as lone hunters in caveman times, while women sociably gathered berries and looked after the kids. Consequently men can only concentrate on one thing at a time and communicate differently and it's also why we won't ask for directions and leave our pants on the floor. It's like men and women are from separate tribes, which explains their communication problems. If you had spent your whole life communicating with people from the men's tribe, then you'd get into trouble when communicating with people from the women's one and might appear rude.

Weirdly for a show that was supposedly about what it is like to be a man, I felt just as excluded as I had when I went to see *The Vagina Monologues*. I didn't recognise myself as being like the man on stage at all. To be honest I felt the simplistic stereotypes in the show were patronising and offensive to men as well as women, which I suppose is some kind of achievement as most people only manage to do one at a time. It was an hour and a half of the 'aren't men and women different?' schtick that you can see in any stand-up club, any night of the week, done quicker and better.

This whole 'man is just a caveman' argument seems somewhat bogus to me, and worst of all, merely another excuse to justify men behaving like arseholes.

The truth is that we have no idea what the gender roles were in caveman society and I am very suspicious of arguments that claim that the attitudes of that time are hard-wired into us in any case. While there may be some very general observations we can make about the sexes, the reason I didn't recognise myself as being like the man on stage is because we are all different. Although I am a man I am not a great fan of competitive sports, I am able to concentrate on two things at once, am reasonably adept at discussing my feelings, though pretty clueless when it comes to reading maps, making shelves, killing bison or reverse parking my car. I also very much enjoy having bubble baths, my particular favourites are the ones you can get in Lush and that smell of flowers. If that makes me sound like some kind of girl, I should add that I do like drinking beer, sleeping with women, driving my ear quickly and howling at the moon in despair. Once I got angry with a drunk man who was pestering me and I almost had a fight with him.

See how I attempt to justify myself to you? Do you notice that my admission

Is this all a man really is?
Or is this just the prehistoric Max Wall?

of supposedly female traits and lack of supposedly male ones makes me feel self-conscious, that I'm worried you might think I'm a 'girl'?

Is it not more likely that men behave as they do because (a) they don't want to be perceived as feminine and so disguise or lie about the 'girly' aspects of their personality and (b) because they can get away with it (largely by arguing, 'Yes, I'm a lazy slob, because that's what cavemen are like'.)

Out of all the answers about manhood that I got on the survey there is a predominant theme, which manifests itself either as a man despairing how macho, violent and stupid the rest of his sex are (though rarely him), or as a man claiming that he is unusually feminine. This one's fairly representative:

- **I don't feel like a typical man, whatever that is, and a lot of characteristics that are accepted as masculine seem pretty unpleasant to me. I have a lot of what people have called feminine or girly traits, but I don't mind hearing that. I like not being a stereotype.**

It seems possible that men are just as taken in as women are by the swaggering macho behaviour of other men. Men behave like dickheads when they are overcompensating for something that is (or that they think is) lacking in their lives. How much of male behaviour is inherited and how much is down to men doing what they believe is expected of men?

Whatever the effects of testosterone and the Y chromosome, I think we should remember that men and women are built to the same template and that genetics is complicated. Men aren't amoebas that separate from their fathers, any more than women are clones of their mothers. When the DNA is mixed up in our mother's cauldron and stirred around by our father's knobbly Gandalf staff, a magical splicing of their genes creates us. So we inherit qualities from both our mother and our father, feminine and masculine. We are raised by men and women, we go to school with boys and girls and are taught by male and female teachers. If you don't learn how to communicate with the opposite sex by the time you are an adult, then you haven't been paying attention. Pretend it's because we're from different tribes or planets if you want, but we come from Earth, and we all shoot from our father's cock into our mother's womb. Our genitals and our hormones will prioritise different goals for us all, but what it means to be a man or a woman is as individual as the man or the woman you are looking at.

Men aren't from Mars. Women aren't from Venus.

That's a pathetic, childish, patronising, simplistic, stupid idea.

In fact men are from Britain and women are from mainland Europe.

I shall explain. This is quite a complicated and convoluted metaphor, so I am going to help you through it a little bit, but unlike the bloke who wrote the Mars and Venus crap I am going to do it over the course of a couple of pages, rather than spinning it out into a complete book which essentially just repeats the same two ideas over and over again.[3]

OK, here we go! Like the British Empire, men have had to get used to the idea that our position and influence in the world has totally changed in the last 50 years. Some of us refuse to accept it and still think we're 'Great', some are angry that we are blamed for the mistakes made by people 100 years ago. Many of us are now ashamed to be British. None of us know who we really are any more.

Apart from gay men. That's because gay men are from Ireland.

I'm not saying all Irish men are gay. It's an extremely clever metaphor.[4]

After years of oppression the 'Irish' have won back most of their freedom and are now loved round the world for their vibrant culture. These blokes love the craic, that's for sure.

The rest of the British (men, remember) don't trust the Europeans. Let's face it, most of us have had a couple of really destructive relationships with metaphorical 'Germans', if you catch my drift (usually between the ages of 14 and 18 and 39 and 45, funnily enough). Despite that, it's important to remember that all 'Europeans' (women) aren't 'Germans' (whores).

For the last 30 years, the Europeans have worked together, towards a common cause, despite their differences, to form a union based on equality. But the British are reluctant to get involved in that, aren't they? Why is that, do you think?

It's because secretly, in our hearts, we still think we are superior (despite all evidence to the contrary). We're nostalgic for a past that was, quite frankly, pretty shit for the vast majority of us. (Think of the lives our grandfathers led: the manual labour, the wars, the lack of freedom to be who or what you wanted.)

We've got a chance to move forward, forget about the past, not blame ourselves for the sins of previous generations and redefine what it means to be 'British' in a new world, based on equality. We don't want a men's movement,

---

3. *Well, not unless someone is prepared to pay me the money he got for doing that.*
4. *I know Graham Norton is ... and Brian from Big Brother ... oh, and the bloke from Boyzone. Maybe this works on both a metaphorical and genuine level.*

any more than we want a British movement. We need to do this together. Men and women. Britons and Europeans.

No one's saying we have to give up the things that make us British. No one's saying we have to become European (as that would involve surgery), but wouldn't it be better if we had a common currency?

If you want to look at the world in an evolutionary sense then don't look at men as cavemen. It's bogus and unhelpful and patronising. The truth is that human beings exist on this earth because of our forefathers' knack for adaptation. Your ancestors were amoebas that begat fish that begat lizards that begat little ratlike things that climbed some trees and begat monkeys that came down from the trees and begat apes, who were told to stand up straight by their mums and then begat you. Each begetting took some time, but came about because those that didn't adapt would simply die in a world that had changed.

When the fish started getting eaten by bigger fish they didn't say, 'This isn't working out, let's go back to being amoebas'; they said,[5] 'Hey, let's grow some legs and go and live on the land. Nothing's going to eat us up there!' Of course they got that wrong, which is how they ended up in the trees.[6]

The world has changed and men need to adapt or die. Germaine Greer has got it right, men aren't all necessary, women could carry on without most of us (or with the aphid dungeon arrangement I mentioned in an earlier chapter). Men have to prove to women that we're worth keeping around, because I'm not sure we can just rely on the fact that they find us a bit cute, though infuriating, forever.

What feminism and the gay and civil rights movements have been trying to achieve is to create a world where people are treated as equally as possible

---

5. *All right they didn't say it, or even think it, they didn't even do it. It just happened. If you want accuracy then read Stephen Jay Gould or Dawkins. If you want laughs then read me. Or Stephen Jay Gould. Probably more efficient to just read Stephen Jay Gould then. But it's too late, you've nearly read me now. You might as well finish and see what else I've got to say. Then read Stephen Jay Gould.*
6. *The big fish stayed in the sea, thinking they were it, but after a few million years the offspring of the little fish got their revenge on the big fish when they invented trawlers and nets and intensive fishing practices.*

regardless of their gender, sexuality or race. They are saying that everyone has the right to be proud of who they are. Men are people. We're part of this. We shouldn't fight against these crusades, we should be fighting alongside them. As Susan Faludi concludes in her book, *Stiffed*, the dream of feminism was

> *To create a freer, more humane world. Feminists have pursued it, particularly in the last two centuries, with great determination and passion. In the end, though, it will remain a dream without the strength and courage of men who are today faced with an historic opportunity; to learn to wage a battle against no enemy, to own a frontier of human liberty, to act in the service of a brotherhood that includes us all.*

I think a lot of men feel that women hate us and our cocks for the bad things that we undoubtedly do, which is possibly not surprising when you read Andrea Dworkin. I don't think her views are representative of many women (or indeed right about men or the sexual act).

I asked women:

 ## IS THE PENIS A FRIEND OR AN ENEMY TO YOU?
Friend: 1,977 (94.91%)   **Enemy**: 106 (5.09%)   **Total**: 2,083

Ninety-five per cent of women say the penis is a friend – 95 per cent! They don't hate us guys.

Here are some of the specific answers:

- It responds well to love – if you love it, it loves you back.

- It has given me three wonderful children ... and it feels so damned good during sex.

- It's ridiculous. How can anything ridiculous be an enemy?

- It's a frienemy. If it's attached to someone you love who is treating you right it's great but if it's on the front of some lying bastard then it just contributes to the general fucked-upness of your life.

● It fills me up, it calms me down, it gives me warmth and moisture, and it gives me something to play with. Bit like a Kinder egg, but better.

Hey, there's no way a cock is as good as a Kinder egg.

● Because of all the pleasure they've given me over the years, I think some cocks are beautiful, but even the little slightly weird ones are interesting. And on the occasions when I've been approached by an aggressive or nasty cock, I tend to blame the owner.

● It's yummy, a delicious lollipop.

● I think penises are kinda cute like those troll dolls people used to collect.

When I started this project I thought that I would conclude that women's increasingly high sexual expectations were a problem for men's self esteem. There might be some truth in that. However, the vast majority of responses from women and men are wonderfully positive. It's easy to forget that most people are in happy relationships with people that they love, which for most people is an enjoyable way to share this love or just to have fun with someone that you (hopefully) like a bit. If you stop and think about it for a second, women knowing what they want from sex is a fantastic turn of events for us all.

Would you rather live in the world of your grandfathers where women lay back and dreamt of a united Europe? Or in a world with the woman who said this:

● You can have your man's little dick up your ass, a vibrator in your cunt and him sucking your nipples. Better? Yes!?

Because I don't have to think about it for a second. I love the twenty-first century.

Fellas, we've a chance to redefine what it means to be a man, without having to conform to all this penis-waving macho bullshit. We have the opportunity to be an amalgam of flesh and, after that, whatever we decide. So perhaps we should be striving to stop trying to create a template that describes half the population of the world.

If we needed a code of behaviour, I suppose that I would say that being a man is about taking responsibility for yourself and those that you care about, using your physical strength to protect those who are weaker than you, using your mental strength to accept assistance from those that are stronger than you and to learn from your many mistakes. That's pretty much what being a woman should be too. It's about being a grown-up more than anything.

Be what you want, but try to be it well. Don't underestimate the power of honesty and communication. Whether you want to be a monogamous father, or a promiscuous lover, or if you just want to take baths using shampoos and bubble baths that would usually be associated with women.

Incidentally, on a slight tangent, I also think men should all just agree that we will put the toilet seat back down after we've had a wee. I know women are being stupid about it and we could equally well argue that they should be the ones to do it, as it bothers them so much, and they're the ones who have to put it back down again. But let's all just do it and see whether that makes them happy or if they find something else to complain about.[7]

I realise I am being idealistic and I am not saying the journey is going to be easy. I hope this book will pave a very small way to helping women realise that men are not as idiotic as they might appear (or at least explain some of the reasons for our idiocy). I am deeply aware of my own flaws as a man, more so than I ever was, but I think realising that and having the desire to change is probably the first step on the journey.

And the second and biggest step on this road to equality is for us to accept all the varying penises in our lives and to let them be praised.

---

7. *Also statistically it makes sense as men also need to sit for maybe one in five of their toilet visits, so the seat is in the down position more often than the up.*

This week I want you all to set some time aside, alone or with a friend, or for 33 per cent of you and two or more friends (you bastards), and celebrate the penises in your life. Let them be praised.

Guys, I want you to say out loud to yourself:

I love my cock!

Ladies, next time you are with the man that you adore, please say to him:

I love your cock!

Gay men and bi-sexual men, next time you are with the man that you adore, I'd like you to say:

I love my cock and your cock!

And lesbians, I haven't forgotten about you (let's face it, if nothing else, this book clearly demonstrates that you're constantly on my mind). Stop the next man you see in the street and say to him:

Although I have no real feelings or interest in your ridiculous penis, I do at least grudgingly respect the penis's part in giving me life … and the fact that it is the template for dildos.

Don't become obsessed (Heaven forbid). Don't let your love for those penises be arrogant or narcissistic or all-consuming. Simply love the cock in your life as you would love a childhood toy (not necessarily as literally as the 'various teddy bears' bloke did in Chapter 6). Appreciate them for the good things they can do, look after them, protect them, talk about them, try not to think about the mechanics of how they work as you're actually using them, for Christ's sake keep them clean and enjoy them! But don't let it go to their heads.

Guys, you aren't your penis and your penis isn't you. Your penis works for you and for whoever (or whatever) you choose to share it with. He's your bitch.

The penis isn't a battering ram.

It's a drawbridge that brings us together.

Though it can be a battering ram if you want it to be, girls.

As for me, my Cock has taken me all over the world, it has paid my wages and put food on the table. It's been seen by thousands of people from London's West End to down-town Melbourne and has made them all gasp, groan and laugh. It increased in length by over a third between August and September

2002. It's been placed in small and sweaty, tightly packed fleapits, and huge, gaping auditoria. I have kept it up constantly for over a year.[8]

I come away from all this as a better person. Any worries I have had in the past have been proven to be practically universal and without foundation. My understanding of the psychological causes of erectile dysfunction has helped me overcome any problems I may or may not have been experiencing in that area. Despite telling over 150 audiences (probably around 30,000 people) about my failure to have three in a bed sex, nobody had offered to rectify that problem. I like myself more than I used to and also appreciate the many great things that my penis can do for me, the great things I can do for my penis (though, alas, I can't put it in my own anus). Like Sigurdur Hjartarson, I am rather more proud of it, I think.

I hope my Cock has touched you in similar ways and that when you hold it in your hands for the last time, you will think, 'Here Lives Happiness.'

LET NOW MY PENIS BE PRAISED!

My cock-quest is over.

Coming soon – 'Talking Massive Tits'.

---

8. *On re-reading this paragraph I realise that it might be taken to be referring to my actual penis, rather than the Talking Cock project as a whole. I apologise if anyone has mistakenly read it this way as this was never my intention.*

APPENDIX

Copy of the email I sent to Nestlé

Dear Sir or Madam,

I am a writer and am currently working on a textbook about the anatomy of the penis for the good people at Ebury Press. I know this might not seem in any way relevant to your good selves at Nestlé, but please bear with me and I'll think you'll see that it is.

This textbook aims to revolutionise the study of biology in schools and I am working along with examination boards to totally redefine the dull terminology which is currently employed in biology textbooks. I am sure you remember from school how confusing and off-putting all those Latin terms for body parts could be. We have realised that if children are going to learn about and more importantly understand how their bodies work we have to re-invent the language of biology, to make it hip and 'down with the kids' so to speak.

Still don't see how this would involve Nestlé? Stick with me, I'm getting to that!

You must also be aware that education is currently in financial crisis. We are constantly searching for ways to pay for all the books and equipment that schools need. Sponsorship is obviously a great thing for both the schools and the companies who give them money. The kids are your target market for so many of your products, so obviously if they see your brand-names in their lessons, they are more likely to buy your wares. Surely that kind of publicity (as well as the good publicity of helping the cause of education - and I don't need to tell you that Nestlé could do with being seen as the good guy at the moment) is almost priceless to you.

So, how can we make this come about? Simple. One of the essential components of the penis is a body known as the CORPUS SPONGIOSUM. I know, dull, dull, confusing name. But it strikes me that what this body most resembles is a tube of spongy Polo mints. My idea is to rename this structure 'The tube of spongy Polos', and I think kids will respond to the power of the imagery, as well as the humour. We will be bringing science and the penis to life for them. Of course, I wouldn't want to give such advertising away for free.

Clearly if Nestlé were to sponsor this book and the new terminology, then we could tie in some promotional idea. Perhaps the guys at Polo could even bring out a special edition pack of spongy polos as a new line! Think about it. The opportunities are endless.

I'm hoping we can come to some arrangement and I am in negotiations with other firms about other possible tie-ins so would appreciate a swift response.

I hope we can work something out on this one, for the good of education and of Nestlé.

Yours faithfully

Richard Herring

Unbelievably Nestlé chose not to respond. I feel they have missed an important opportunity to publicise their products and as a protest I think we should all boycott Polo mints, until these people see sense.

BIBLIOGRAPHY

Banner, Lois (1992) 'The fashionable sex', *History Today*, April.

Burton, Sir Richard (trans) (1886) *The Perfumed Garden of the Shakyh Nefwazi*. Kama Shastra Society of London and Benares.

Castledon, Rodney (1996) *The Cerne Giant*. Wincanton. DPC.

Darvill, Timothy (1999) *The Cerne Giant – An Antiquity on Trial*. Oxbow.

Dening, Sarah (1996) *The Mythology of Sex*. Macmillan.

Ensler, Eve (1998) *The Vagina Monologues*. Villard Books.

Evans, Christine M. and Kell, Philip (2000) *Erectile Dysfunction, Clinical Drawings for Your Patients*. Health Press.

Faludi, Susan (1999) *Stiffed*. Chatto & Windus.

Faulkner, Raymond O. (trans) (1985) *The Ancient Egyptian Book of the Dead*. British Museum Press.

Friedman, David M. (2001) *A Mind of its Own*. The Free Press.

Giles, Fiona (ed.) (1998) *Dick for a Day*. Indigo.

Gollaher, David (2000) *Circumcision*. Basic Books.

Gore, Margaret (1997) *The Penis Book*. Allen & Unwin.

Gould, Stephen Jay (1995) *Adam's Navel*. Penguin.

Grange, Dr Felix (1981) *The Male Genital Organs – and Their Improvement*. Roberts.

Green, Jonathon (1999) *The Big Book of Filth*. Cassell.

Hamilton, Dr Terri (2002) *Skin Flutes and Velvet Gloves*. St Martin's Press.

Hodes, Martha (1997) *Black Women, White Men*. Yale University Press.

Holy Bible.

Johnson, M.H. and Everitt, B.J. (2000) *Essential Reproduction*. Blackwell Science.

Jones, Steve (2002) *Y The Descent of Men*. Little Brown.

Kramer, Samuel Noah and Maier, John (1989) *Myths of Enki, the Crafty God*. Oxford University Press.

Laqueur, Thomas W. (2003) *Solitary Sex: A Cultural History of Masturbation*. Zone Books.

Legg, Rodney (1986) *Cerne's Giant and Village Guide*. Sherborne, Dorset.

Leick, Gwendolyn (1994) *Sex and Eroticism in Mesopotamian Literature*. Routledge.

Manniche, Lisa (1997) *Sexual Life in Ancient Egypt*. Kegan Paul International.

Mellie, Roger (2002) *Roger's Profanisaurus*. Boxtree.

O'Connor, Dan (2003) *Between Their Legs and in Their Heads: The Place of the Penis in Transsexual Identities*

Paley, Maggie (1999) *The Book of the Penis*. Grove Press.

Parsons, Alexandra (1989) *Facts and Phalluses*. St Martin's Press.

Pinto-Correia, Clara (1997) *The Ovary of Eve*. University of Chicago Press.

Richards, Dick (1993) *The Penis*. BabyShoe.

Schwartz, Kit (1985) *The Male Member*. St Martin's Press.

Spence, Lewis (1990) *Egyptian Myths and Legends*. Dover.

Strage, Mark (1980) *The Durable Fig Leaf*. Morrow Quill.

Taylor, Timothy (1996) *The Pre History of Sex*. Fourth Estate.

Vicary, Grace C. (1989) 'Visual art as social data: the Renaissance codpiece', *Cultural Anthropology* 4.

Ward, Charlotte (1999) *The Illustrated Book of Phalluses*. Erotic Print Society.

Wedeck, H.E. (1994) *Dictionary of Aphrodisiacs*. Bracken Books.

Weeks, Gerald R. and Gambescia, Nancy (2000) *Erectile Dysfunction*. W.W. Norton.

Zacks, Richard (1994) *History Laid Bare*. HarperPerennial.

WEBSITES

www.afraidtoask.com – a good source of facts about the penis for anyone who is concerned or interested in finding out more.

www.cicumstitions.com – source of many of the quotes on circumcision.

www.cnn.com and www.ananova.com – very helpful in finding out about the various awful things that have happened to penises over the years.

www.cynthiaplastercaster.com – has all the info on the eponymous heroine.

www.embarrassingproblems.co.uk – lots of problems about all kinds of things, clearly explained.

www.fannybatter.co.uk – this unpleasantly named site has a large stock of novelty penis-related items and Andy, the man who runs it, was kind enough to send me a box for free. Suspiciously, the penis enlarger that I specifically requested has made no appearance either in the book or the stage-show. He also does great 'mould-a-willy' kits which allow you to make a vibrator in the exact shape of your cock. Why not make one of your boyfriend's, girls, and then see how he likes it stuffed up his arse.

www.nocirc.org – anti-circumcision movement's homepage. The full article, 'Circumcision: What I Wish I Had Known', by Marilyn Milos, can be found at this address.

www.norm-uk.org – foreskin restoration site.

www.philliphodson.com – Phillip was kind enough to chat to me about erectile dysfunction and he was once agony uncle on *Going Live*, so please buy all his books from this site!

www.restrooms.org – the place to go if you want to find out more about female (or any other) urinals.

www.sizesurvey.com – the excellent site with all kinds of stats on penis size.

www.snopes.com – a brilliant urban myth site which has some astounding stories about cocks and tells you if they're true or not.

www.terrihamilton.com – find out more about the wonderful Dr Terri.

www.thecoffeeplace.com – where I got my Bobbitt jokes.

www.the-penis-website.com – another site to visit if your hunger for penis-based info has not yet been sated.

www.richardherring.com – this is my personal website and it contains a diary called 'Warming Up' which has a fair bit about the process of writing this book, if you're interested in that kind of thing. The site also contains enough information about me to satisfy the most inquisitive stalker and will save you the trouble of having to follow me around everywhere.

The Penis Museum

www.mh.is/vefir/phallus – the site for the Icelandic Phallological Museum. Please do go and visit the museum and petition the Icelandic government until they declare Reykjavík the penis capital of the world.

http://dir.salon.com/sex/feature/2001/03/27/iceland/index.html – the place to see Josh Schonwald's account of the penis museum.

www.lionessden.com/archives/reviews/darvamammals.html – the address for the other, negative, review of the museum.

www.time.com – has a good article about the penis museum.

Please let me know what you think of the book. My email address is richardherring@richardherring.com or you can write to me care of Avalon, 4a Exmoor St, London, W10 6BD. Please don't bother sending me any more of your cock tales though. I've seen enough for one lifetime!

ACKNOWLEDGEMENTS

First and foremost I would like to thank the 7,500 people who completed my questionnaire, especially those whose answers I have used. Your opinions and anecdotes about cocks have now appeared in a book. Imagine how proud your parents will be when you show them.

Imagine how proud my parents are.

Massive thanks also to the man who created both the Talking Cock website (www.talkingcock.co.uk), Rob Sedgebeer. He is the Hobbit lord of the Internet.

There are dozens of other people who lubricated the passage of my Cock: Jeremy Herrin, who directed the stage-show and provided much useful information and quite a few gags; Simon Streeting, my tour manager, Stewart Lee and Dave Gorman who were both kind enough to let me use a couple of their jokes, Chris Durant, Sigurdur Hjartarson, the gorgeous Dr Terri Hamilton who shall one day be my bride, Marilyn Milos, Denise Decker, Dr Catherine Hood, Petra Boynton, Phillip Hodson, Stephanie Merritt, Kate Copstick, Pint of Mild, Maggie Durand, Emma Calverley, Paul Putner, Bill Noble, Deborah Bruce, Juliet Richters, Al Murray, Tim Richardson and all the staff at the British Library, apart from the woman who took my membership number down because she said I was using my mobile phone, even though I wasn't (well, not really!)

Many thanks to my patient editor Jake Lingwood and his improbably named assistant Ken Barlow; also to Stina Smemo, Claire Kingston and everyone else at Ebury Press. Thanks for publishing my book about cocks.

I am also very grateful to all the staff at the theatres that have put on my stage show, particularly Christopher Richardson at the Pleasance in Edinburgh, everyone at the Soho Theatre in London, and Tony and all the guys at the Capitol Theatre in Melbourne.

The unenviable task of finding the pictures for this book fell to Laura Murby, Alison Robert and especially Sandie Huskinson-Rolfe, who had to look at some truly disgusting images.

Also I am very grateful to Jon Thoday, Richard Allen-Turner, James Taylor, Rob Aslett, Anna Lusser and everyone at Avalon.

If there is anyone else I have forgotten, then please forgive me.

I would be hypocritical if I did not thank my mother and father for using their godlike abilities to create me, then having the humanity to hang around and nurture their creation until I could practically fend for myself. A lot of gods (and people) don't bother with that bit. Apologies that I have rewarded you for your patience with such a crude work. Next time I will try and write a book that you can show off about at the golf club.